A FAILURE OF PROPORTION

This book explores non-consensual adoption – an area of law which has sparked considerable debate amongst academics, practitioners and the judiciary nationally and internationally. The emphasis of this book is on the circumstances in which non-consensual adoption may be regarded as a proportionate measure and when less severe forms of intervention, such as long-term foster care or kinship care, may also meet children's needs while providing protection to children's rights under the European Convention on Human Rights. The book builds on existing literature on adoption law but takes the discussion in new directions, placing an emphasis on the need to closely scrutinise children's and parents' rights at all stages of the adoption process, not simply when parents appeal against the making of an adoption order. A unique feature of this book is its emphasis on routinely incorporating key provisions from the United Nations Convention on the Rights of the Child into analysis when determining whether an adoption order is a proportionate measure.

A Failure of Proportion

Non-Consensual Adoption in England and Wales

Samantha M Davey

•HART•

OXFORD • LONDON • NEW YORK • NEW DELHI • SYDNEY

HART PUBLISHING
Bloomsbury Publishing Plc
Kemp House, Chawley Park, Cumnor Hill, Oxford, OX2 9PH, UK
1385 Broadway, New York, NY 10018, USA

HART PUBLISHING, the Hart/Stag logo, BLOOMSBURY and the Diana logo are trademarks of Bloomsbury Publishing Plc

First published in Great Britain 2020

A catalogue record for this book is available from the British Library.

Library of Congress Cataloging-in-Publication data

Names: Davey, Samantha M, author.

Title: A failure of proportion : non-consensual adoption in England and Wales / Samantha M Davey.

Description: Oxford ; New York : Hart, 2020. | Based on author's thesis (doctoral - University of Essex, School of Law, 2016) issued under title: The proportionality of non-consensual adoption in England and Wales under S52(1)(B) of the Adoption and Children Act 2002. | Includes bibliographical references and index.

Identifiers: LCCN 2020002832 (print) | LCCN 2020002833 (ebook) | ISBN 9781509929139 (hardback) | ISBN 9781509929146 (Epub)

Subjects: LCSH: Adoption—Law and legislation—England. | Birthparents—Legal status, laws, etc.—England. | Custody of children—England. | International and municipal law—Great Britain.

Classification: LCC KD777 . D38 2020 (print) | LCC KD777 (ebook) | DDC 346.4201/78—dc23

LC record available at https://lccn.loc.gov/2020002832

LC ebook record available at https://lccn.loc.gov/2020002833

ISBN: HB: 978-1-50992-913-9
ePDF: 978-1-50992-915-3
ePub: 978-1-50992-914-6

Typeset by Compuscript Ltd, Shannon

This book is dedicated to my late grandmother,
Barbara Maureen Davey (1940–2018).
You are forever in my heart and in my memories.

PREFACE

This work provides a conceptual analysis of the proportionality of non-consensual adoptions in England and Wales. It does so by examining the English legislation and case law on adoption and the jurisprudence of the European Court of Human Rights (ECtHR). This book considers and applies rights from the European Convention on Human Rights (ECHR) and the United Nations Convention on the Rights of the Child (UNCRC) to determine when non-consensual adoption may be regarded as a necessary and proportionate interference with children's and parents' rights.

The proportionality principle requires the domestic courts and the ECtHR to strike a balance between the various rights and interests of children and parents, while taking into account children's welfare. The final strand of the proportionality principle identifies whether the state measure is the least restrictive measure available to satisfy the state's objective. This strand is not applied in all non-consensual adoption cases heard by the domestic courts or the ECtHR. However, it is argued that it is essential to identify whether less restrictive alternatives exist, as these measures may prove equally effective in protecting children's welfare when compared with adoption and may also protect children's and parents' rights.

This research makes a conceptual contribution to the academic scholarship on non-consensual adoption law by identifying how the UNCRC, the ECHR, the best interests principle and ECtHR jurisprudence can be applied so as to provide optimal protection for children's and parents' rights in adoption cases. This book concludes that judicial reasoning in the courts should routinely consider UNCRC rights and the effectiveness of less restrictive alternatives. Furthermore, it argues that there is a positive obligation under Article 8 ECHR to provide state assistance in circumstances where children can safely be raised by their parents, which is not yet recognised in English case law.

ACKNOWLEDGEMENTS

I would like to thank my colleagues here at the University of Essex. In particular, I would like to thank Sabine Michalowski, Karen Hulme, Theodore Konstadinides and Lorna Woods for being important mentors who have helped me grow in many ways. I would also like to thank Maurice Sunkin, Laure Sauvé and Aoife Daly, who have provided me with valuable feedback over the years, which has served to improve the quality of my work. Additionally, I would like to acknowledge the meticulous copy-editing work undertaken by Catherine Minahan.

I am very appreciative of Kate Standley, David Sykes and Nick Joll for their feedback and their encouragement. I would also like to thank my friends Bart, Sharon, Ray and Julia for being incredibly supportive during the evolution of the book.

I would like to thank my family for their encouragement in the difficult moments and for their help in caring for my lovely daughter Meredith, which enabled me to work on my book. I am very grateful, as I could not have completed the book without their assistance.

Last but not least, I would like to acknowledge the importance of the love and support of my late grandmother Barbara Davey. During her lifetime she acted as my proof-reader, sounding board and friend. She encouraged me to write from a very young age and would have been delighted to see this book become a reality.

Thank you to everyone who has been a part of my journey.

CONTENTS

1

Introduction

I. Non-Consensual Adoption: The Legal Issue and Social Climate

A picture is worth a thousand words. In a well-publicised YouTube video,[1] which later gave rise to the case of *Re J (A Child)*,[2] a social worker can be seen forcibly removing a baby from a crying mother's arms. The video is highly emotive and disturbing, and yet the parents' situation is just one example of many troubling stories alleging that the making of a care order and a subsequent non-consensual adoption have been disproportionate measures. Stories emphasising the lack of transparency in adoption proceedings and the perception that parents' and children's rights receive insufficient protection in non-consensual adoption cases can be discovered on divergent sources online, including the BBC,[3] *The Telegraph*,[4] *The Guardian*,[5] *The Daily Mail*[6] and various blogs.[7] Television documentaries,[8] online petitions[9] and freedom of information requests[10] have been made. Non-consensual

[1] 'Harrowing. Six-hour-old baby taken away by Social Services' at https://www.youtube.com/watch?v=XOZPsSuINco.

[2] *Re J (A Child)* [2013] EWHC 2694 (Fam).

[3] 'MP claims 1,000 children "wrongfully" adopted every year' (13 December 2011) at http://www.bbc.co.uk/news/uk-politics-16157124; 'Rape victims children face "barbaric" adoption' (27 March 2014) at http://www.bbc.co.uk/news/uk-26768256; 'Families flee UK to avoid forced adoption' (6 October 2001) at http://www.bbc.co.uk/news/uk-29502832; 'Adoption: Thousands of children forcibly taken into care' (2 February 2015) at http://www.bbc.co.uk/news/uk-31089412.

[4] Christopher Booker, 'Forced adoption is a truly dreadful scandal' *The Telegraph* (3 July 2010) at http://www.telegraph.co.uk/comment/columnists/christopherbooker/7870342/Forced-adoption-is-a-truly-dreadful-scandal.html.

[5] Owen Bowcott, 'Latvia complains to UK parliament over forced adoptions' *The Guardian* (9 March 2015) at http://www.theguardian.com/uk-news/2015/mar/09/latvia-complains-to-uk-parliament-over-forced-adoptions. See, for example, a case that attracted media attention: *CB (A Child)* [2015] EWCA Civ 888.

[6] Frances Hardy, 'Blood chilling scandal: of the thousands of children stolen by the State: Denise Robertson writes about her lengthy investigation' *Daily Mail* (27 May 2015) at http://www.dailymail.co.uk/news/article-3098468/Blood-chilling-scandal-thousands-babies-stolen-State-TV-agony-aunt-Denise-Robertson-s-spent-years-investigating-says-s-monstrous-injustice-age.html. Denise Robertson has written a work of fiction, *Don't Cry Aloud*, which she states is based on real-life situations she encountered, where parents had their children removed by the state.

[7] 'Punishment without Crime' at https://punishmentwithoutcrime.wordpress.com/; 'Suespiciousminds' at http://suesspiciousminds.com/tag/forced-adoption/.

[8] For example, the ITV series, *Don't Take My Child*, and *Panorama*, 'The Truth About Adoption'.

[9] At https://www.change.org/p/eu-parliament-abolish-adoptions-without-parental-consent.

[10] At https://foi.brighton-hove.gov.uk/requests/3233 19 May 2014; http://www.lincolnshireecho.co.uk/Courts-act-protect-133-risk-youngsters/story-11225063-detail/story.html.

adoption is controversial and has, in recent years, been scrutinised closely in the UK superior courts.[11]

At present, the Adoption and Children Act 2002 (ACA 2002) allows non-consensual adoption[12] in England and Wales even though it interferes with parents' and children's human rights under the European Convention on Human Rights (ECHR).[13] This author expresses concern about the application of the proportionality principle in English law in non-consensual adoption cases. It is not disputed that adoption orders can, in some circumstances, be the best measure available to protect children's rights and welfare once children have been removed into care. There may be cases where children will not be safe in the care of their parents, and where ongoing contact between children and parents may not be in the children's best interests due to severe and even life-threatening neglect or abuse. In other circumstances, children themselves do not wish to live with or maintain relationships with their parents due to the severe neglect[14] and/or physical[15] or emotional[16] abuse they have experienced.[17] In these situations, it will not be in their best interests to be reunited with their parents. In the absence of other suitable alternatives, children's rights may be best protected via adoption orders.

However, adoption orders are sometimes made in circumstances where less intrusive and equally effective measures are available to protect children from harm. These measures include court orders (eg supervision orders, care orders and special guardianship orders) and alternatives such as kinship care and the provision of practical and financial assistance to families vis-à-vis the state. Furthermore, in circumstances where parents are unfit, it may still be possible for children to have safe and beneficial contact with their birth parents via open adoption.[18] The question is then whether adoption should be the first choice to ensure stability and permanence for children, or the last resort when other options have been exhausted?

This book tackles the aforementioned issue by exploring the relationship between non-consensual adoption and the proportionality principle. This principle is significant because it is taken into consideration by the superior courts

[11] See, eg, *Re P (A Child)* [2014] EWHC 1146 (Fam); *B-S (Children)* [2013] EWCA Civ 1146 (CA); and *ANS and another v ML (AP) (Scotland)* [2012] UKSC 30.

[12] This term will be used interchangeably with 'adoption without *parental* consent'.

[13] European Convention for the Protection of Human Rights and Fundamental Freedoms, as amended by Protocols nos 11 and 14, 4 November 1950 (European Convention on Human Rights (ECHR)), ETS 5, available at https://www.refworld.org/docid/3ae6b3b04.html.

[14] This refers to the failure to meet a child's basic needs. A child might be unfed, dirty or lack proper clothing, supervision or medical care. See at https://www.nspcc.org.uk.

[15] Deliberate injury to a child that results in bruises, broken bones, burns or cuts. See at https://www.nspcc.org.uk.

[16] This is more difficult to define when compared to other types of abuse, but it may include humiliation, isolation or failing to promote the child's social development. See at http://www.nspcc.org.uk.

[17] Department for Education, *Foster Care in England: A Review for the Department for Education* (London, Department for Education, 2018) 82–83.

[18] An adoption order where children continue to have contact with their birth parents or other birth relatives.

in England and Wales – as well as by the European Court of Human of Rights (ECtHR) – when parents choose to appeal against adoption orders that have been approved by the courts. The proportionality principle is a set of legal criteria that establishes whether or not a measure taken in the furtherance of a state objective is commensurate to that objective.[19] This book is thus concerned with the circumstances in which a non-consensual adoption will and will not be regarded as a measure commensurate to the state's objective of protecting children's welfare.

Proportionality can potentially be applied by the courts when making an adoption order and is an important principle that ought to be considered by the domestic courts, but it is not routinely considered by the inferior courts. The proportionality principle is applicable once adoption orders have been made and challenged by parents. It is argued that proportionality ought to play a more important role in determining whether an adoption order should be made in the first place, with reference to the United Nations Convention on the Rights of the Child 1989 (UNCRC)[20] as an important tool of interpretation. A shift in approach has important consequences for legal decision-making, and is likely to improve the protection of children's and parents' rights from the outset of the adoption process. Throughout this book, it is emphasised that children must be protected from harm but that legal and practical protection from harm must be proportionate.

The book will navigate the relationship between children's welfare and the human rights of children and their parents under Article 8 ECHR (which concerns the right to respect for a private and family life). In principle, non-consensual adoption constitutes an interference with children's and parents' rights, which may be justified under Article 8(2) to protect children from harm. There are instances, therefore, where parents' rights under Article 8 ECHR to relationships with their children may clash with their children's rights under Article 2 ECHR (the right to life) and Article 3 ECHR (the right to protection from torture or from inhuman or degrading treatment or punishment) to be protected from the risk of significant harm. There may also be a clash between children's own rights under Article 8 ECHR to relationships with their parents on the one hand and their rights under Articles 2 and 3 of the ECHR on the other to be protected from the risk of significant harm. The principal focus here is on the relationship rights of children and their parents, but this book will also consider children's relationships with other members of their birth family, particularly grandparents and siblings.

II. Background to Non-Consensual Adoption: A Controversial Solution

Understanding the legal landscape of adoption requires an explanation of the government policy objectives that led to the increased usage of non-consensual

[19] N Forman, *Constitutional Change in the United Kingdom* (London, Routledge, 2002) 263.

[20] United Nations Convention on the Rights of the Child, 20 November 1989, 1577 UNTS 3, available at https://www.refworld.org/docid/3ae6b38f0.html.

adoption. In 2000, the Waterhouse Inquiry[21] raised concerns about the poor social, emotional and educational long-term outcomes for children in care.[22] While parental neglect or abuse may predispose children to poor long-term outcomes,[23] remaining in state care is, nonetheless, seen as detrimental to children's well-being.[24] Statistically, figures suggest that children in care are more likely to suffer from mental illness, to perform poorly at or fail their GCSEs[25] and are more likely to go to prison than children outside of the care system.[26] The high numbers of and poor outcomes for children in care considered in the Waterhouse Report sparked discussion on how law and policy reform could best tackle this social problem. Based on the positive social, emotional and educational outcomes for adopted children,[27] adoption was seen by the (then) Labour Government as the best option for removing children from care and for improving their long-term outcomes in life.[28] This led to the enactment of the ACA 2002, which sought to increase the number of adoptions and speed up the adoption process to avoid undue delay and uncertainty for children and prospective adopters.

This policy led to a significant increase in the number of non-consensual adoptions,[29] which made these adoptions more controversial. The numbers of adoptions steadily increased until 2015. However, there has been a shift in this trend. In the year ending March 2017, 2,520 children in care were placed for adoption, which accounted for 3 per cent of all children in care.[30] This was a decline

[21] *Lost in Care – Report of the Tribunal of Inquiry into the Abuse of Children in Care in the Former County Council Areas of Gwynedd and Clwyd since 1974* (2000). See also The Special Standing Committee on the Adoption and Children Bill, 29 November 2001 (afternoon).

[22] It should be noted, however, that poor educational outcomes may be associated with pre-care experiences or pre-existing special educational needs rather than being in care, even though while in care children's problems may persist. See A O'Higgins, J Sebba and N Luke, *What is the relationship between being in care and the educational outcomes of children? An international systematic review* (Oxford, Oxford University Press, 2015).

[23] ibid.

[24] M Szilagyi, D Rosen, D Rubin and S Zlotnik, 'Health Care Issues for Children and Adolescents in Foster Care and Kinship Care' (2015) 136 *American Academy of Pediatrics* 1131.

[25] National examinations taken by children in England and Wales at the age of 16.

[26] This is still the case today. See, eg, R Blades, D Hart, J Lea and N Willmott, *Care – A Stepping Stone to Custody?* (London, Prison Reform Trust, 2011) 1. Government figures consistently demonstrate that more children in care commit criminal offences than children who are not in care. Children in Care in England Statistics, 13 August 2014. In the year ending March 2012, for example, 7% of looked-after children aged between 10 and 17 were subject to a conviction, final warning or reprimand compared with 2% of all children. See also Department for Education, *Foster Care in England: A Review for the Department for Education* (London, Department for Education, 2018).

[27] Department of Health and Social Care, *Adoption: A New Approach* (Cm 5017, 2000). For example, see J Castle, C Beckett and C Groothues, 'Infant Adoption in England' (2000) 24 *Adoption and Fostering* 26. See subsequent research that confirms the benefits of adoption: J Triseliotis, 'Long-term foster care or adoption? The evidence examined' (2002) 7 *Child and Family Social Work* 23; D Quinton and J Selwyn, 'Adoption: Research, Policy and Practice' (2006) 18 *Child and Family Law Quarterly* 459.

[28] *Adoption: A New Approach* (n 27).

[29] Children looked after in England (including adoption and care leavers), year ending 31 March 2015 (London, Department for Education, 2015) 9.

[30] Children looked after in England (including adoption), year ending 31 March 2017 (London, Department for Education, 2017) 9.

of 20 per cent on previous years.[31] Several factors may have led to this decline, including wider concerns from campaigners about the high numbers of adoptions that had taken place and increased superior court scrutiny of non-consensual adoptions.[32]

Section 52(1)(b) of the ACA 2002 provides for adoption orders to be made without parental consent on the basis of the child's 'welfare'.[33] Section 52(1)(a) of the Act similarly provides for parental consent to be dispensed with, but does so on the basis of parental capacity. The discussion will focus on whether or not the rights of birth parents and children to develop and maintain relationships with one another are given sufficient weight and consideration in non-consensual adoption cases. This will involve exploring the potential for conflict between parents' and children's rights under the ECHR and the UNCRC, in cases where children are at risk of significant harm, and how such conflicts may be resolved.

This analysis will inform the central issue in this book, namely whether non-consensual adoption in England and Wales under section 52(1)(b) of the ACA 2002 can be regarded as a proportionate measure and, if so, in what circumstances it may be regarded as proportionate. In deciding whether an adoption order should be made, the courts must have regard to the welfare checklist under section 1(4)(a) of the ACA 2002. In order to determine when non-consensual adoption is a proportionate measure, this enquiry will consider when non-consensual adoption strikes the appropriate balance between the best interests and rights of the child on the one hand and the rights of the birth parents on the other. In order to determine whether or not the appropriate balance has been struck, this book will explore whether there are less restrictive alternatives available (such as state assistance, kinship care, special guardianship or non-consensual adoption with direct contact), which may be equally effective measures to protect children from harm.[34]

This book explores how the courts apply the best interests test and human rights (the ECHR in particular) in adoption cases. In doing so, the analysis considers the tensions that underlie the relationship between children's best interests on the one hand and children's and parents' rights on the other.

[31] ibid.

[32] L Sprinz, 'Adoption in 2014' [2014] *Family Law* 335; A Bainham and H Markham, 'Living with *Re B-S, Re S* and its implications for parents, local authorities and the courts' [2014] *Family Law* 991.

[33] J Herring, 'Family: Revoking Adoptions' [2009] 159 *NLJ* 377; A Bainham, 'The Peculiar Finality of Adoption' [2009] 68 *CLJ* 283; Bainham and Markham (n 32); S Harris-Short, 'Making and Breaking Family Life: Adoption, the State and Human Rights' [2008] 35 *Journal of Law and Society* 28; B Sloan, '*Re C (A Child) (Adoption: Duty of Local Authority)* – Welfare and the Rights of the Birth Family in 'Fast Track' Adoption Cases' (2009) 21 *Child and Family Law Quarterly* 87; B Sloan, 'Conflicting Rights: English Adoption Law and the Implementation of the UN Convention on the Rights of the Child' (2013) 25 *Child and Family Law Quarterly* 40; S Choudhry and J Herring, *European Human Rights and Family Law* (Oxford, Hart Publishing, 2010).

[34] Donnelly has argued that there is increased emphasis on the need to consider alternatives to adoption which may be equally effective. See M Donnelly, 'The Supreme Court and the welfare ground for dispensing with parental consent to adoption: *ANS and another v ML (Scotland)*' [2014] *International Family Law Journal* 110.

Thus, the identification and discussion of the approach taken by the courts provide a platform for examining when and whether children's best interests may clash or be in alignment with their own rights and/or those of their birth parents in non-consensual adoption cases, and the best possible manner for addressing potential clashes between (i) children's own rights (ie such as balancing the right to maintain a relationship with parents versus the right to be protected from harm), (ii) children's rights and best interests, (iii) children's rights and parents' rights, and (iv) children's best interests and parents' rights. Examining human rights instruments (in particular the ECHR and the UNCRC), and how they are applied by the courts in England and Wales and by the ECtHR, will help to determine whether the legislation and court decisions on adoption in England and Wales are proportionate.

There is a considerable body of academic, governmental and judicial commentary, as well as media criticism, of the current law[35] on non-consensual adoption in England and Wales. Superior court judges such as Lady Hale,[36] non-governmental organisations[37] and high-profile figures such as John Hemming MP[38] and Dr Peter Dale, a former NSPCC adviser,[39] have voiced their concerns about how readily children may be taken into care[40] and, in some cases, placed for adoption without the consent of their parents. The British Association of Social Workers has considered that a serious rethink of the law may be needed, with adoption regarded as a 'runaway train often breaching rights of birth parents'.[41] This demonstrates

[35] C Barton, 'The Adoption Bill – The Consultative Document' [1996] *Family Law* 4; L Davis, 'Adoption and Children Act 2002: Some Concerns' [2005] *Family Law* 294; Herring (n 33); S Harris-Short, 'Adoption and Children Bill – A Fast Track to Failure?' (2001) 13 *Child and Family Law Quarterly* 405; S Harris-Short, 'Making and Breaking Family Life: Adoption, the State and Human Rights' (2008) 35 *Journal of Law and Society* 28; Sloan, 'Conflicting Rights' (n 33); Sloan, '*Re C (A Child) (Adoption: Duty of Local Authority)* (n 33); B Luckock and K Broadhurst, *Adoption cases reviewed: an indicative study of process and practice* (London, Department for Education, 2013); Donnelly (n 34); F Moss, 'Authorised abuse?' (2007) 157 *New Law Journal* 1310.

[36] *In the Matter of B (A Child)* [2013] UKSC 33 [197].

[37] At http://www.aims.org.uk/Journal/Vol21No2/childAbuse.htm; http://www.justice-for-families.org.uk/; http://www.fassit.co.uk/ian_joseph.htm. Ian Joseph has referred to this type of adoption as 'forced' adoption. This terminology is considered by Munby LJ in *N (Children) (Adoption: Jurisdiction)* [2015] EWCA Civ 1112 [8]. It has been noted in J Doughty, '"Where nothing else will do": Judicial approaches to adoption in England and Wales' (2015) 39 *Adoption and Fostering* 105, 107, that this terminology is derived from jurisdictions such as Spain and Australia, where many adoptions took place without parental consent in the past.

[38] For an overview of John Hemming's concerns see 'MP claims 1,000 children "wrongly" adopted every year' (13 December, 2011) at http://www.bbc.co.uk/news/uk-politics-16157124; *Children first: the child protection system in England*, Fourth Report of Session 2012–13, vol II, Q370–374.

[39] 'Adoption: Thousands of children forcibly taken into care' (2 February, 2015) at http://www.bbc.co.uk/news/uk-31089412; P Dale, *Contact Arrangements for Children: A Call for Views* (London, Department for Education, 2012) at http://www.peterdale.co.uk/downloads/.

[40] Sometimes, a child may be accommodated as a 'child in need' under the Children Act 1989 (CA 1989), s 20 before a care order is made under the CA 1989, s 31 and then an adoption order without parental consent under the ACA 2002, s 52(1)(b). This has been controversial. For example, see *N (Children) (Adoption: Jurisdiction)* [2015] EWCA Civ 1112 and J Stather, 'Is time running out for section 20 of the Children Act?' (2014) at http://www.familylawweek.co.uk/site.aspx?i=ed129019.

[41] B Featherstone, A Gupta and S Mills, *The role of the social worker in adoption ethics and human rights: An Enquiry* (British Association of Social Workers, 2016) 16.

the contentious nature of such adoptions and raises questions about when non-consensual adoption will be appropriate. The issue is one that has affected many children and parents in England and Wales, and indeed wider family members, since relationships with grandparents, siblings and other relatives may also dwindle or stop altogether after an adoption is final.

The issue of non-consensual adoption in England and Wales is not only controversial at national level. Current adoption practice in England and Wales has caught the attention of the Council of Europe, which has expressed concern about how existing legislation and practice on adoption in England and Wales may violate children's rights.[42] Moreover, the European Parliament has stated that in cases where non-UK nationals are placed for adoption, the UK's failure to inform consular authorities of the child's country of origin may mean a failure to comply with obligations under Article 37 of the 1963 Vienna Convention on Consular Relations.[43] Adoption of migrant children and adoption of children from other European countries (in particular, from former Soviet bloc countries)[44] add further weight to the need to re-evaluate existing law. What appears, at first glance, to be a national issue is increasingly becoming a wider cause for concern, due to the earlier Labour Government's policy objective in favour of increasing adoptions of children in care.

It is apparent, then, that there is tension between the principles of non-intervention in family life and child protection,[45] as removing a child into care and subsequently placing a child for adoption may potentially be a violation of children's and parents' rights under Article 8 ECHR. State intervention in family life and the removal of a child into care can be justified under the Children Act 1989 (CA 1989), section 31(2) on the basis of the child's welfare, where a child is at risk of suffering significant harm or has suffered significant harm as defined under the CA 1989. However, non-consensual adoption is a severe and permanent form of intrusion into family life. It is important to consider when such intrusion may be necessary to protect the child's right to life under Article 2 ECHR, the right to freedom from torture or inhuman or degrading treatment under Article 3 ECHR,[46] and the child's right to respect for private and family

[42] O Borzova, *Social services in Europe: legislation and practice of the removal of children from their families in Council of Europe member states* (Strasbourg, Council of Europe, 2015).

[43] United Nations, Vienna Convention on Consular Relations, 24 April 1963, available at https://www.refworld.org/docid/3ae6b3648.html; 'Adoption: Cross-border Legal Issues and Gaps in the European Union' at http://www.europarl.europa.eu/RegData/etudes/BRIE/2015/536480/IPOL_BRI(2015)536480_EN.pdf.

[44] J Porter, 'Families from Eastern Europe and care proceedings' [2014] *Family Law* 183; Borzova (n 42); B Yuksel and K Trimmings, 'Choice of law aspects of non-consensual adoption of European Children in England and Wales' [2017] *International Family Law Journal* 202.

[45] See, eg, *Re J (Children)* [2013] UKSC 9 and the discussion by Brian Sloan in 'Re J – Uncertain Perpetrators in Child Protection Cases' at https://www.youtube.com/watch?v=WYhaxBanCts. More generally on clashes between rights and welfare (or well-being) see E Kay and M Tisdall, 'Children's Wellbeing and Children's Rights in Tension?' (2015) 23 *International Journal of Children's Rights* 769.

[46] *In the Matter of J (Children)* [2013] UKSC 9 [1], *per* Lady Hale (in relation to Art 3).

life under Article 8 ECHR. These rights may, in some cases, be protected via non-consensual adoption, but potentially there may be less restrictive alternatives available that may be equally effective.

Clearly, parents have rights in relation to their children both in general and within the context of non-consensual adoption cases. This can be seen from domestic law, such as section 3 of the CA 1989, which refers to parental responsibility and states that parents have 'rights, duties, powers, responsibility and authority … in relation to a child and his property', and from the emphasis on the importance of the parental/child relationship in case law.[47] The existence of parental rights is also acknowledged by various provisions of the UNCRC and the jurisprudence of the ECtHR, including but not limited to its interpretation of Article 8 ECHR.

However, despite the legal authorities that emphasise the existence of such rights, there appears to have been a deliberate minimisation of parental interests and rights in the context of adoption.[48] Harris-Short has observed that many people may regard what she considers to be sacrificing the rights of parents as justified to ensure that children leave the care system more quickly.[49] She has acknowledged that the parents' behaviour and the reasons for taking their children into care and placing them for adoption may not warrant sympathy. Harris-Short nonetheless argues that the present adoption system sees parents being unnecessarily 'demonised' and 'marginalised' in the adoption process.[50] This has the potential to lead to non-consensual adoptions that may not be proportionate.

Adoption is a severe measure, and potentially the most intrusive measure a state can take in the context of family life. As such, children's and parents' rights must be provided with greater protection in adoption cases compared to other types of disputes that might arise in public or private family law proceedings. Sloan has been critical of the fact that parents' Article 8 ECHR rights are not given independent consideration by the courts despite the severity of non-consensual adoption.[51] Bainham has argued that human rights 'militate against'[52] adoption, and less drastic measures should be taken to preserve kinship links and contacts.[53] This would improve protection of parents' and children's rights. Donnelly has pointed out that there are increasing calls for adoptions not to take place unless there are no equally effective measures available that will protect a child's welfare.[54]

[47] *Re KD (a minor) (ward: termination of access)* [1988] AC 806; *Re G (Children)* [2006] UKHL 43.

[48] Harris-Short, 'Adoption and Children Bill – A Fast Track to Failure?' (n 35) 419; Harris-Short, 'Making and Breaking Family Life: Adoption, the State and Human Rights' (n 35) 32.

[49] Harris-Short, 'Adoption and Children Bill – A Fast Track to Failure?' (n 35) 424.

[50] Harris-Short, 'Making and Breaking Family Life: Adoption, the State and Human Rights' (n 35) 30.

[51] Sloan, 'Conflicting Rights' (n 33).

[52] A Bainham, 'Arguments about parentage' [2008] *CLJ* 322, 350.

[53] ibid.

[54] Donnelly (n 34).

III. Book Overview

This book will consider whether it is necessary for independent consideration to be given to parental rights in adoption cases and what this analysis might look like. The discussion throughout will also consider children's rights and how they may be protected when they clash with those of their parents, and the circumstances in which non-consensual adoption will also constitute a violation of children's rights under the ECHR and the UNCRC. The book will reflect on whether the emphasis on speeding up the process of adoption means that, in some cases, non-consensual adoption orders are being made where a less restrictive but equally effective alternative might have been available that would have protected the rights and interests of parents and children alike.

This is the only book, to date, to provide in-depth analysis of compliance of adoption law in England and Wales with the jurisprudence in the ECtHR and its international obligations under the UNCRC. It is also the only book of its kind to provide explicit consideration of whether the proportionality analysis undertaken by the courts ought to involve an assessment of the availability of less restrictive alternatives to adoption.

The research throughout provides a strong basis to argue that a proportionality analysis considering the different rights of children and parents ought to be undertaken when adoption orders are made, rather than when parents appeal adoption orders. It is argued that this is the best approach towards analysing the potentially conflicting rights of children and parents and the best interests of children, because it protects children's welfare and rights while simultaneously respecting parental rights. In general, there has been a great deal of criticism about the lack of protection afforded to parental rights in non-consensual adoption cases. However, while there has been increasing examination of children's rights in a range of different contexts,[55] there has been limited discussion of the minimal consideration of children's rights in adoption cases, including the child's right to have and continue to develop a relationship with his or her parents and the right to have a say in the adoption process. This author will argue that children's and parents' rights can be better protected by state intervention, where appropriate, rather than by non-consensual adoption. In fact, many parents who struggle to parent effectively and have their children removed into care and placed for adoption suffer from a range of social problems, such as learning difficulties, mental health problems, domestic violence, drug abuse and alcohol abuse. These social problems are not being dealt with holistically by the courts or policy-makers, despite recurrence of these issues.

This discussion considers the relevance of the UNCRC in adoption cases, and whether or not the rights under this Convention could assist in providing

[55] Note too, initiatives such as the Children's Rights Judgments: H Stalford, K Hollingworth and S Gilmore, *Rewriting Children's Rights Judgments: From Academic Vision to New Practice* (London, Bloomsbury, 2017). See at https://www.liverpool.ac.uk/law/research/european-childrens-rights-unit/childrens-rights-judgments/.

an analysis of whether a less restrictive but equally effective alternative to non-consensual adoption may be found. Inherent in this book is an acknowledgement of the apparent tension between the welfare principle and the child's and parents' rights to respect for private and family life under Article 8 ECHR. This research contributes to the existing academic literature and provides observations that extend beyond previous writings, by emphasising the importance of acknowledging children's rights in the specific context of non-consensual adoption.

This book distinguishes itself from previous academic literature by conducting an extensive examination and analysis of important adoption cases heard in the High Court and the Court of Appeal in England and Wales, the UK Supreme Court and the ECtHR. In doing so, it examines the rights and best interests at stake in adoption cases, different methodological frameworks that may be appropriate to be applied in adoption cases where children's and parents' rights (including but not limited to Article 8 ECHR) are at stake, less restrictive but (potentially) equally effective alternatives to non-consensual adoption that may be available, and analysis of the circumstances in which non-consensual adoption may (or may not) be regarded as proportionate. While there is undoubtedly a large body of research on adoption law, as evidenced by the critique already considered, there is no study that considers these different aspects of adoption and human rights in one text.

2

Children's Best Interests and Children's and Parents' Rights

I. Introduction: The Interrelationship between Rights and Best Interests

When determining the proportionality of non-consensual adoption, an important consideration underlying judicial decision-making is whether or not children's and parents' rights can be reconciled with the best interests principle. This chapter will consider how fleshing out children's rights in adoption cases – as against a pure best interests analysis – can improve the judicial decision-making process, thereby improving case outcomes. This chapter plays an important role by providing a detailed description of the best interests principle and its relationship with rights under the European Convention on Human Rights (ECHR)[1] and the United Nations Convention on the Rights of the Child (UNCRC).[2] It explains fundamental legal and rights-based frameworks, which will be applied and analysed throughout this book.

The concept of best interests and the concept of rights both require further explanation. Best interests are the basis for the making of an adoption order, while rights, typically those of the parents, provide the basis for an appeal against a non-consensual adoption. 'Best interests' is the determinative principle in England and Wales when the courts are making decisions in relation to children.[3] Since the enactment of the Human Rights Act 1998,[4] the courts in England and Wales have at times had to consider the relationship between the best interests of children and the rights of children and birth parents, because the Act brought the principles of the ECHR into English law. Furthermore, domestic courts must take into account decisions from the European Court of Human Rights (ECtHR),[5] and ought to

[1] European Convention for the Protection of Human Rights and Fundamental Freedoms, as amended by Protocols nos 11 and 14, 4 November 1950 (European Convention on Human Rights (ECHR)), ETS 5, available at https://www.refworld.org/docid/3ae6b3b04.html.

[2] United Nations Convention on the Rights of the Child, 20 November 1989, 1577 UNTS 3, available at https://www.refworld.org/docid/3ae6b38f0.html.

[3] *J v C* [1970] AC 668.

[4] This statute came into force on 2 October 2000. It incorporates many key rights under the ECHR into domestic law, most notably Arts 6 and 8.

[5] See *ANS and another v ML (AP) (Scotland)* [2012] UKSC 30.

consider international treaties such as the UNCRC, which has been ratified by the United Kingdom (UK) but not incorporated into domestic law.[6]

This chapter will consider the best interests test in English law, the ECHR (which will be discussed in more detail in other parts of the book, and the relationship between the application of the best interests and the ECHR. This chapter will also discuss UNCRC rights that are relevant in non-consensual adoption cases, and whether the UNCRC could be said to regard non-consensual adoption as a proportionate measure. A central argument is that, despite its weak legal status, the UNCRC can and ought to form an important part of the process when the courts determine the proportionality of non-consensual adoptions. The aforementioned principles stemming from the best interests test, the ECHR and the UNCRC will then be applied throughout to determine the circumstances in which a non-consensual adoption may be a proportionate measure.

A. The Welfare Principle in England and Wales: Definition and Interpretation

Both the Children Act 1989 (CA 1989) and the Adoption and Children Act 2002 (ACA 2002) refer to the child's 'welfare' rather than the child's 'best interests' when the courts decide which court order to make. In practice, though, the terms 'best interests' and 'welfare' are interchangeable.[7] Reference to 'welfare' in key legislation is therefore interpreted as referring to the need for a determination of the child's best interests. Welfare, broadly speaking, refers to ensuring the child's physical, social, emotional and moral well-being. There is no definition of 'well-being' in English legislation.[8] A useful definition can, however, be found in Welsh law. Well-being is defined in section 2(3) of the Social Services and Wellbeing (Wales) Act 2014 as including the child's 'physical, intellectual, emotional, social and behavioural development'.

Regardless of how welfare, or well-being, is defined, it encompasses a range of considerations based on the child's age and level of intelligence and understanding, including interests in being healthy,[9] being protected from harm[10] and being heard in court proceedings.[11] 'Welfare' is multi-faceted. It reflects the value,

[6] There have, however, been attempts to incorporate the UNCRC into English Law. See, eg, the Children's Rights Bill at http://www.publications.parliament.uk/pa/ld200910/ldbills/008/10008.1-7.html#j01.

[7] M Taylor-Sands, *Saviour Siblings: A Relational Approach to the Welfare of the Child in Selective Reproduction* (New York, Routledge, 2013) 48.

[8] E Sutherland and L-A Barnes Macfarlane (eds), *Implementing Article 3 of the United Nations Convention on the Rights of the* Child (Cambridge, Cambridge University Press, 2016) 21 at 49.

[9] *Re C (Welfare of Child: Immunisation)* [2003] 2 FLR 1095.

[10] C Breen, *Age Discrimination and Children's Rights: Ensuring Equality and Acknowledging Difference* (Leiden, Martinus Nijhoff, 2006) 7.

[11] *Mabon v Mabon* [2005] EWCA Civ 634.

importance and vulnerability of children[12] and is a largely paternalistic notion.[13] In general, the courts take the approach that statutory provisions will be presumed to be 'consistent with the general principles relating to the "best interests" of the children'.[14]

Under section 6 of the Adoption Act 1976 (the 'old' law that governed adoption in England and Wales), the child's welfare was the court's 'first' consideration rather than its 'paramount' consideration. The use of 'first' rather than 'paramount' assumed that there might be considerations other than the child's welfare that might have relevance in deciding whether or not to make an adoption order (eg the parents' interests). The change from 'first' to 'paramount' consideration in the ACA 2002 reflected government concern that adults' interests (ie parents') were being treated as paramount in the adoption process, rather than those of children.[15] Furthermore, section 6 of the 1976 Act stated that an adoption order should be made where it would 'safeguard and promote the welfare of the child throughout his childhood'. The ACA 2002 changed the law to bring the welfare test into line with the paramountcy test in section 1(1) of the CA 1989. Section 1(2) of the ACA 2002 thus states that in making an adoption order, the 'paramount consideration of the court or adoption agency must be the child's welfare, throughout his life'. Munby LJ has made it clear that how far into the future the court will need to consider this will be dependent on the context and nature of the issue.[16]

The phrasing 'paramount consideration' means that when the courts consider the interests of others (eg parents[17] or siblings[18]), the interests of the child (or children) in the case will be treated as the court's main consideration and will outweigh those others' interests. Several cases illustrate this point, highlighting that if adoption is deemed to be in a child's best interests but clashes with the interests of the child's birth family, the child's best interests will prevail.[19] In *J v C*[20] it was thus emphasised that paramountcy involved taking a course 'which is most in the interests of the child'.[21]

In *Re P (Contact: Supervision)*,[22] it was emphasised that 'the court is concerned with the interests of the mother and father only in so far as they bear on the welfare of the child'. Thus, when the court treats the child's welfare as its paramount

[12] J Herring, 'Farewell Welfare' (2005) 27 *Journal of Social Welfare and Family Law* 159, 168.
[13] Breen (n 10) 7.
[14] *KO (Nigeria) and Others v Secretary of State for the Home Department* [2018] UKSC 53.
[15] Adoption and Children Bill Special Standing Committee Discussion, 21 November 2001 (afternoon).
[16] *Re B-S (Children)* [2013] EWCA Civ 1146.
[17] *London Borough of Sutton v Gray and Butler* [2012] EWHC 2604 (Fam).
[18] *A and S v Lancashire County Council* [2012] EWHC 1689 (Fam); *D-O'H (Children)* [2011] EWCA Civ 1343.
[19] *Webster and another v Norfolk County Council and others* [2009] EWCA Civ 59.
[20] *J v C* (n 3).
[21] ibid 710–11, *per* Lord MacDermott.
[22] *Re P (Contact: Supervision)* [1996] 2 FLR 314, 328.

consideration, it indicates that the welfare of the child should be the court's *sole* consideration.[23] Although the welfare checklist in section 1(4) of the ACA 2002 is similar to the checklist under section 1(3) of the CA 1989, the main difference is that the child's relationship with his or her birth family is explicitly recognised within the ACA 2002 (see section 1(4)(f)).

Section 1(4) (the welfare checklist) states that:

> The court or adoption agency must have regard to the following matters (among others)—
>
> (a) the child's ascertainable wishes and feelings regarding the decision (considered in the light of the child's age and understanding),
> (b) the child's particular needs,
> (c) the likely effect on the child (throughout his life) of having ceased to be a member of the original family and become an adopted person,
> (d) the child's age, sex, background and any of the child's characteristics which the court or agency considers relevant,
> (e) any harm (within the meaning of the Children Act 1989 (c. 41)) which the child has suffered or is at risk of suffering,
> (f) the relationship which the child has with relatives, and with any other person in relation to whom the court or agency considers the relationship to be relevant, including:
>   (i) the likelihood of any such relationship continuing and the value to the child of its doing so,
>   (ii) the ability and willingness of any of the child's relatives, or of any such person, to provide the child with a secure environment in which the child can develop, and otherwise to meet the child's needs,
>   (iii) the wishes and feelings of any of the child's relatives, or of any such person, regarding the child.

Section 1(4) provides the courts in England and Wales with the discretion to consider the value of the child's relationship with his or her birth family, the birth family's ability to meet the child's needs, and the wishes and feelings of the birth family in determining whether or not a non-consensual adoption ought to take place. These are lists the courts have a broad discretion[24] in applying.

Principles from case law on the CA 1989, section 1(3) welfare checklist are also relevant to the ACA 2002, section 1(4) welfare checklist. For example, Staughton LJ stated in *H v H (Residence Order: Leave to Remove from the Jurisdiction)*,[25] that the welfare checklist under the CA 1989, section 1(3) is not to be treated 'like the list of checks which an airline pilot has to make' but as the considerations that are important in a specific case. Arguably, then, this principle also applies to adoption cases.

[23] J Herring, 'Forging a relational approach: Best interests or human rights?' [2013] 12 *Medical Law International* 32.

[24] *Re G (Children)* [2006] UKHL 43; R Tolson, 'The Welfare Test and Human Rights – where's the beef in the sacred cow?' at http://www.familylawweek.co.uk/site.aspx?i=ed307.

[25] *H v H (Residence Order: Leave to Remove from the Jurisdiction)* [1995] 1 FLR 529, 532.

The welfare test has been criticised for being 'vague and indeterminate',[26] and for the lack of guidance on how much weight to afford to each factor under the test. However, any disadvantages that the best interests assessment may have are amplified in non-consensual adoption cases because of the severity and permanence of adoption for children and birth parents. In fact, in the Court of Appeal decision of *Re B-S (Children)*,[27] Munby LJ went beyond the traditional best interests assessment and stated that a balancing approach[28] ought to be used in considering different options for children in care, including adoption. Munby LJ explained that the balance sheet approach involved a global, holistic evaluation,[29] weighing up the pros and cons of each available option (eg long-term foster care versus adoption), so that the most proportionate option could be chosen. This is in contrast to the traditional best interests assessment, where emphasis is placed on making one type of order (ie adoption) and whether it can be justified after applying the welfare checklist under section 1(4) of the ACA 2002.

The value of using a balance sheet type of analysis in determining a child's best interests in *any* complex matter has been endorsed in the UK Supreme Court by Lady Hale.[30] Jones has warned, however, that applying a balance sheet approach is by itself insufficient to improve the quality of judgments. Application of the balance sheet approach by judges, as well as by professionals such as social workers and guardians, would need to be accompanied by detailed analysis of the facts before balancing the different options and reaching a final decision.[31] Furthermore, the use of a balance sheet approach does not guarantee consideration of the interests of others, such as birth parents or siblings, or their rights under Article 8 ECHR for example. It is thus argued that while the balance sheet analysis is a valuable tool, the benefits of its use would be enhanced by routine reference to UNCRC rights[32] in judgments on adoption matters (see section III.D for further discussion).

B. The Welfare Principle and the ECHR – Can they be Reconciled?

After the enactment of the Human Rights Act 1998, the courts needed to provide a more detailed explanation of how the application of the ECHR could be reconciled with the paramountcy principle, since the former seemed to suggest a

[26] RH Mnookin, 'Child Custody Adjudication: Judicial Functions in the Face of Indeterminacy' (1976) 39 *Law and Contemporary Problems* 226, 229.

[27] *Re B-S (Children)* (n 16).

[28] First enunciated in the UK by Thorpe LJ in *Re A (Medical Treatment: Male Sterilisation)* [2000] 1 FLR 549.

[29] *Re B-S (Children)* (n 16) [44].

[30] *Re ZH (Tanzania) v Secretary of State* [2011] UKSC 4 [51].

[31] M Jones, 'Re B-S and the Perils of the 'Balance Sheet' Approach' at http://www.familylawweek.co.uk/site.aspx?i=ed129743.

[32] H Stalford, K Hollingworth and S Gilmore, *Rewriting Children's Rights Judgments: From Academic Vision to New Practice* (London, Bloomsbury, 2017).

need to consider the rights of the parents (and children) whereas the latter did not.[33] In *Payne v Payne*,[34] a relocation case in which the parents disagreed about whether the child should continue to live in the UK or move abroad, it was held by Thorpe LJ that courts should uphold the child's welfare as the paramount consideration and that the child's own rights could be encompassed within consideration of the child's welfare.

Although in *Payne v Payne* the UK Court suggested that the ECtHR applies the paramountcy principle, in *Johansen v Norway*[35] the ECtHR treated the child's welfare as having particular importance and did not regard it as the sole consideration of the Court that would automatically justify an interference with a parent's right under Article 8 ECHR. Indeed, according to *Johansen*, welfare may in some cases override the parents' rights, but this depends on the nature and seriousness of breach of parents' rights and the relative strength of the child's interests. Herring has rejected the Court of Appeal's interpretation of Strasbourg jurisprudence in *Payne v Payne*, suggesting that the ECtHR has always clearly emphasised a balancing exercise in which the welfare of the child may, but will not always, override parental rights.[36] Since the case of *Payne v Payne* was decided, further clarification has been provided in *Re F (A Child) (International Relocation Cases)*[37] on the analysis to be undertaken by the courts in international relocation cases. Ryder LJ has observed that:

> The questions identified in *Payne* may or may not be relevant on the facts of an individual case and the court will be better placed if it concentrates not on assumptions or preconceptions but on the statutory welfare question.[38]

He went on to state the appropriate approach to be taken in international relocation cases, placing an emphasis on the need to undertake an analysis with reference to proportionality:

> Where there is more than one proposal before the court, a welfare analysis of each proposal will be necessary. That is neither a new approach nor is it an option. A welfare analysis is a requirement in any decision about a child's upbringing. The sophistication of that analysis will depend on the facts of the case. Each realistic option for the welfare of a child should be validly considered on its own internal merits (ie an analysis of the welfare factors relating to each option should be undertaken). That prevents one option (often in a relocation case the proposals from the absent or 'left behind' parent) from being sidelined in a linear analysis. Not only is it necessary to consider both parents' proposals on their own merits and by reference to what the child has to say but it is also necessary to consider the options side by side in a comparative evaluation. A proposal

[33] C Henricson and A Bainham, *The child and family policy divide: Tensions, convergence and rights* (York, Joseph Rowntree Foundation, 2005).
[34] *Payne v Payne* [2001] EWCA Civ 166 [57], *per* Thorpe LJ.
[35] *Johansen v Norway* [1996] 23 EHRR 33.
[36] J Herring, 'Moving Forward?' (2011) 161 *NLJ* 1011.
[37] *Re F (A Child) (International Relocation Cases)* [2015] EWCA Civ 882.
[38] ibid [18], *per* Ryder LJ.

> that may have some but no particular merit on its own may still be better than the only other alternative which is worse.
>
> … [A] step as significant as the relocation of a child to a foreign jurisdiction where the possibility of a fundamental interference with the relationship between one parent and a child is envisaged requires that the parents' plans be scrutinised and evaluated by reference to the proportionality of the same … international relocation cases engage articles 6 and 8 of the European Convention for the Protection of Human Rights and Fundamental Freedoms 1950 [ECHR].[39]

The ECtHR has presumed that the rights of parents and children carry equal weight but that interference with a parent's right may be justified in the light of the child's welfare.[40] Indeed, as Simmonds has observed, the domestic courts have traditionally applied a different approach to decision-making, a different method of reasoning, and may potentially reach a different conclusion because the courts use the welfare principle instead of applying a proportionality analysis under Article 8 ECHR.[41] This means that the Court's emphasis is on children's best interests rather than on the rights of children and their parents. However, recent case law demonstrates a shift in the approach of the courts in England and Wales towards proportionality. A greater emphasis on the child's best interests can be seen in the approach of the ECtHR when considering parental rights and children's welfare in adoption cases (see section II.C and chapter 3).

II. Non-Consensual Adoption and the European Convention on Human Rights

A. An Overview of the European Convention on Human Rights

In England and Wales, section 6 of the Human Rights Act 1998 imposes a positive obligation on public authorities (including but not limited to the courts and social workers) to protect the ECHR rights of individuals affected by state action (eg children and their parents separated by the adoption process). Under section 2 of the Act, the courts in England and Wales must take ECtHR jurisprudence into account in the course of decision-making. The ECHR is therefore considered by the courts in England and Wales in many cases, including adoption proceedings.[42] Furthermore, when domestic remedies have been exhausted, parents may decide to argue before the ECtHR that their Convention rights have been violated.

[39] ibid [30]–[31], *per* Ryder LJ.

[40] *Johansen v Norway* (n 35).

[41] C Simmonds, 'Paramountcy and the ECHR: A Conflict Resolved?' (2012) 71 *CLJ* 448, 498.

[42] For example, see *ANS and another v ML (AP) (Scotland)* (n 5) (Supreme Court); *Re B-S (Children)* (n 16) (Court of Appeal).

The ECHR has an important role to play in cases where parents have argued that non-consensual adoption has violated their own human rights. Children in adoption cases are typically too young to allege violations of ECHR rights, and so it is only in rare instances such as *P, C and S v UK*,[43] where parents argue that their children's rights have also been violated, that the ECtHR (or indeed the courts in England and Wales) will examine children's rights in adoption cases. In practice, the most important ECHR rights in such cases are Article 6 (the right to a fair hearing)[44] and Article 8 ECHR (the right to respect for private and family life).[45] Other applicable ECHR rights may be Article 2 (the right to life) and Article 3 (the right to freedom from torture or inhuman or degrading treatment),[46] and there may in some circumstances be a need to balance children's rights under Articles 2 and 3 against their parents' rights under Articles 6 and 8. The aforementioned provisions of the ECHR and relevant European jurisprudence will be considered in more detail in chapter 3. This chapter will now consider the way in which the ECtHR has interpreted and applied the best interests principle.

B. The European Interpretation of Best Interests of Children in Adoption Cases

This section explains how the best interests principle has been interpreted and applied by the ECtHR generally and in particular adoption cases. An adoption order that amounts to an interference with parents' right to respect for private and family life under Article 8(1) may, in some cases, be justified under Article 8(2), which states:

> There shall be no interference by a public authority with the exercise of this right except such as in accordance with law and is necessary in a democratic society …

Article 8(2) will be satisfied, for example, if adoption is found to be in the child's best interests, since this will demonstrate that interference with the parents' rights has been proportionate.[47] It is worth examining the Court's approach to the best interests principle since, as Ifezu and Rajabali have suggested,[48] the differences between the decision-making in the UK Supreme Court and the ECtHR are most apparent when looking at adoption cases. These differences are seen not necessarily in terms of the case outcomes (see chapters 3 and 6) but in the approach to the best interests principle.

[43] *P, C and S v UK* App no 56547/00 (ECHR, 16 July 2002).

[44] ibid.

[45] *Neulinger and Shuruk v Switzerland* App no 41615/07 (ECHR, 6 July 2010) para 135.

[46] *A v UK* App no 29392/95 (ECHR, 10 May 2001); *Z v UK* App no 29392/95 (ECHR, 10 May 2001).

[47] S Choudhry and H Fenwick, 'Taking the Rights of Parents and Children Seriously: Confronting the Welfare Principle under the Human Rights Act' (2005) 25 *OJLS* 453.

[48] G Ifezu and M Rajabali, 'Protecting the interests of the child' [2013] *Cambridge Journal of International and Comparative Law* 81, 83.

The ECtHR has recognised the important role the best interests test plays in adoption cases. In *Scott v UK*,[49] for example, the Court considered whether a mother's Article 8 rights had been breached by a local authority that had applied to free the child for adoption, and held that 'the best interests of the child is always of crucial importance' in determining when a violation of a parent's right under Article 8(1) may be justified under Article 8(2). Again in *Johansen v Norway*,[50] the Court recognised the importance of the best interests test and how it can override parental rights, emphasising:

> [A] fair balance has to be struck between the interests of the child in remaining in public care and those of the parent in being reunited with the child … In carrying out this balancing exercise, the Court will attach particular importance to the best interests of the child, which, depending on their nature and seriousness, may override those of the parent. In particular … the parent cannot be entitled under Article 8 of the Convention … to have such measures taken as would harm the child's health and development.[51]

In *Johansen*, the Court acknowledged that removing a child into care and placing a child for adoption 'should only be applied in exceptional circumstances and could only be justified if [such actions] were motivated by an overriding requirement pertaining to the child's best interests'.[52]

Despite the fact that the ECtHR has always considered the best interests principle, in *Neulinger and Shuruk v Switzerland*[53] the Court provided, for the first time, a detailed explanation of how it examines the best interests of the child. In *Neulinger*, the father had successfully obtained (in the Swiss court) an order under the 1980 Hague Convention on the Civil Aspects of International Child Abduction,[54] directing the return of his son to Israel. The mother and son took their case to Strasbourg, where they argued that there had been a breach of their rights to respect for their family life under Article 8 ECHR, as the Swiss court had failed to accept the mother's defence under Article 13(b) of the Hague Convention that the child would suffer a grave risk of harm if he was returned to Israel. The Court in *Neulinger* observed that the concept of 'best interests' under Article 3(1) UNCRC had not been developed[55] (see section III.B) and that there were no proposed criteria for the assessment of best interests.[56] The ECtHR has

[49] *Scott v UK* [2001] 1 FLR 958.

[50] *Johansen v Norway* App no 17383/90 (ECHR, 7 August 1996).

[51] ibid para 78.

[52] ibid.

[53] *Neulinger and Shuruk v Switzerland* App no 41615/07 (ECHR, 6 July 2010).

[54] Hague Convention on the Civil Aspects of International Child Abduction, 25 October 1980, Hague XXVIII, available at https://www.refworld.org/docid/3ae6b3951c.html. Art 1(a) indicates that the purpose of the Convention is to 'secure the prompt return of children wrongfully removed to or retained in any Contracting State'.

[55] It should be noted that since this decision, the UNCRC has issued General Comment 14, which provides a more comprehensive explanation of what is meant by the term 'best interests' and what a best interests assessment will entail.

[56] *Neulinger and Shuruk v Switzerland* (n 53) para 51.

emphasised the importance of children's relationships with family members and has stated that

> the child's ties with its family must be maintained, except in cases where the family had proved particularly unfit. It follows that family ties may only be severed in exceptional circumstances and that everything must be done to preserve personal relations and, if and when appropriate, to 'rebuild' the family … [I]t is clearly also in the child's interests to ensure its development in a sound environment, and a parent cannot be entitled under Article 8 to have such measures taken as would harm the child's health and development …[57]

The Court made it clear in *Neulinger* that the issue was whether there was a fair balance between the competing interests of the child, parents and of public order, within the state's margin of appreciation, but with the child's best interests being treated as the Court's primary consideration. It stated that depending on the nature and seriousness of the child's interests, these may override the rights of the parents.[58] The Court said that this approach was supported by the consensus of Member States and by international law (such as the UNCRC), which also emphasises the paramountcy of the child's best interests.[59] The outcome in *Neulinger* was that the ECtHR ruled that the boy did not need to return to Israel. It was not in his best interests, because several years had passed since litigation had commenced and the child was settled in Switzerland. The Court in *Neulinger* assessed both its role in determining the best interests of the child and what the substance of these interests would be. It stated that the child's best interests would depend on a range of factors such as the child's age, maturity, the presence or absence of his parents, and the child's environment and experiences, and emphasised that best interests should be assessed on a case-by-case basis.[60] However, the Court held that it needed to establish whether the national authorities had

> conducted an in-depth examination of the entire family situation and of a whole series of factors, in particular of a factual, emotional, psychological, material and medical nature, and made a balanced and reasonable assessment of the respective interests of each person, with a constant concern for determining what the best solution would be …[61]

Although in previous ECtHR jurisprudence, the concept of 'best interests' was not clearly defined, it is argued that the ECtHR has fleshed out its own definition, for the purposes of case law, in *Neulinger*. In fact, it has been suggested by Boschiero et al that the criterion of best interests now has a 'precise and concrete interpretation',[62] which could potentially be applied in international law. It is

[57] ibid para 136.
[58] ibid para 134.
[59] ibid para 135.
[60] ibid para 138.
[61] ibid para 139.
[62] N Boschiero, T Scovazzi, C Pitea, C Ragni, *International Courts and the Development of International Law* (The Hague, TMC Asser Press, 2013) 607.

not simply the Court's intention to define best interests that makes this decision significant and potentially relevant in adoption cases. The Court held that instead of deferring to the national authorities' assessment of best interests, the Court could perform its own assessment of the child's best interests, and proceeded to do so in this case.

The Court's approach in *Neulinger* was therefore a departure from its usual approach. In fact, according to academics such as Van Bueren, assessing the best interests of the child has typically been seen as a matter within the state's margin of appreciation, rather than a matter for the ECtHR.[63] The question, then, is whether the Strasbourg Court should use its discretion to perform its own assessment in adoption cases. Unlike the approach taken in *Neulinger*, it has been rare for the ECtHR to offer express criticism of the merits of a domestic court decision in adoption proceedings,[64] including a domestic court's assessment of best interests. Despite the fact that the Court has acknowledged that this discretion applies in all cases, it has not been followed in adoption cases (see chapter 3 for further discussion).

C. Application of the Proportionality Criteria in the European Court of Human Rights

As was considered in the introduction to this book (chapter 1), proportionality refers to whether or not a measure taken in the furtherance of a state objective is commensurate to that objective.[65] When a violation of the Article 8(1) ECHR[66] right to respect for private and family life is alleged, the ECtHR determines whether state interference is 'necessary in a democratic society' under Article 8(2). Although the terminology used sometimes differs, there is broad agreement among academics[67] that there are four stages or tests in the proportionality process: a 'legitimate objective'; a 'rational connection'; 'minimal impairment'; and an 'overall balance'.[68] The application of these tests serves to establish whether it can be justifiable to limit rights. Each of these tests can be regarded as distinct steps in determining the proportionality of measures, including adoption orders. Considering the fact that the ECHR is a binding Convention and that decisions of the ECtHR are binding upon the UK, it is essential to explain the criteria applied

[63] G Van Bueren, *Child Rights in Europe* (Strasbourg, Council of Europe Publishing, 2007) 35.
[64] *Haase v Germany* [2004] 2 FLR 39.
[65] N Forman, *Constitutional Change in the United Kingdom* (London, Routledge, 2002) 263.
[66] Arts 8–11 are constructed similarly and justify state interference if it is 'necessary in a democratic society'.
[67] See, eg, G Letsas, 'Proportionality as Fittingness: The Moral Dimension of Proportionality' [2019] *Current Legal Problems* 53.
[68] A Brady, *Proportionality and Deference under the UK Human Rights Act* (Cambridge, Cambridge University Press, 2012) 7. Also see generally A Barak, *Proportionality: Constitutional Rights and their Limitations* (Cambridge, Cambridge University Press, 2012).

by the ECtHR in determining whether measures, such as adoption orders, are necessary and proportionate.

A legitimate objective means that there needs to be a sufficiently important reason to justify a limitation of a right under Article 8(2). For example, an interference with the birth parents' rights under Article 8 due to non-consensual adoption may, in some cases, be justified based on the need to protect the child's rights, health or morals. Removal of the child into care and placement for adoption are measures that have the aim of protecting the child in question. The ECtHR has stressed that taking a child into care for the child's own protection may be legitimate but that it ought to be a temporary measure, to be discontinued as soon as possible. This demonstrates that the state cannot use an objectively legitimate goal to justify its conduct. In respect of non-consensual adoption, for example, it can be argued that just because such adoption satisfies a legitimate objective, it does not mean that it will be regarded as a proportionate measure. This is where the next aspect of the proportionality analysis becomes important.

A 'rational connection' means that there must be a link between the objective and the measure taken by the state in pursuit of that objective. *RK and AK v UK*[69] suggests that when children are taken into care, the imposition of a care order by a domestic court will be rationally connected to the state's aim of protecting the child. The same could be said to be true of adoption orders, which may in many cases protect the rights and freedoms of the child. This could be argued, for example, in the case of *Aune v Norway*,[70] where the child had been settled with his prospective parents for several years and regarded them as his parents.

Brady has observed that very few cases have hinged upon establishing a rational connection, but he has suggested that in order to satisfy this limb, the proposed measure must actually be capable of satisfying the objective pursued.[71] Certainly, in some cases adoption will meet the objective pursued; it will protect the health and morals of the child, or indeed the child's best interests. The difficulty is that an objective of protecting the health and morals and the overall best interests of the child is such a vague yet all-encompassing objective that adoption is automatically likely to satisfy this limb. In other words, while adoption may be rationally connected to the aim of protecting a child's long-term welfare, there may be other less intrusive measures that are rationally connected to the state's aim. This is why the next limb of the proportionality analysis ('minimal impairment') is of particular importance to this book.

Minimal impairment means that the measure taken (ie adoption) did not go further than necessary to meet the state's objective. This is sometimes referred to as the 'least restrictive alternative test', and it can be regarded as the most onerous form of review available to the court since it requires that the state take the

[69] *RK and AK v UK* App no 380001/05 (ECHR, 30 September 2008).
[70] *Aune v Norway* App no 52502/07 (ECHR, 28 October 2010).
[71] Brady (n 68) 54.

least restrictive alternative available to it[72] that will be an equally effective means of achieving the state's aim. Adoption may mean, for example, that children lose not only legal ties with their parents and other birth family, but also the opportunity to develop or to continue to develop relationships with their birth parents, grandparents, siblings and other family members. In *Pontes v Portugal*,[73] the Court considered that alternatives to non-consensual adoption might have been available (including returning the child home), and that these alternatives should have been considered because they would have been just as effective at protecting the welfare of the child.

It is suggested that there may be cases (such as *Zhou v Italy*,[74] *RMS v Spain*[75] and *SH v Italy*[76]) where a child's best interests will dictate providing assistance to the parent instead of placing the child for adoption. If children have not been neglected or abused by their parents (as in the aforementioned cases), if they express a desire to remain with their parents (eg see *YC v UK*[77]) or if parents have changed their circumstances dramatically in a short period of time (see *R and H v UK*[78]) then these are factors that may suggest that adoption does not serve the children's best interests and that the least restrictive alternative to adoption has not been chosen.

The difficulty with ensuring that the least restrictive alternative to adoption is chosen is that, while this may protect the parents' rights, the least restrictive alternative will not necessarily be in the child's best interests. This can be seen in *Aune v Norway*, noted above. Considering the severity of the consequences of adoption, it is important to ensure that a less intrusive measure than non-consensual adoption is as effective at ensuring long-term protection of a child's welfare. In adoption cases, however, it is argued that less restrictive alternatives that are equally effective at meeting children's needs, including the need for stability and permanence, can be found, thereby improving the protection for children's rights under the UNCRC, in particular Articles 7, 8 and 9. It can be implied, from various provisions of the UNCRC, that it is probable an adoption should be the least restrictive measure available for an adoption to be compliant with key provisions of the UNCRC and the UN Guidelines for the Alternative Care of Children.[79]

These alternatives to taking a child into care and placing a child for adoption could include; sole care by one parent,[80] kinship care (care by relatives), special

[72] Y Arai-Takahasi, *The Margin of Appreciation Doctrine and the Principle of Proportionality in the Jurisprudence of the ECHR* (Cambridge, Intersentia, 2002) 88.

[73] *Pontes v Portugal* App no 19554/09 (ECHR, 10 April 2012).

[74] *Zhou v Italy* App no 33773/11 (ECHR, 21 January 2014).

[75] *RMS v Spain* App no 28775/12 (ECHR, 18 June 2013).

[76] *SH v Italy* App no 52557/14 (ECHR, 13 October 2015).

[77] *YC v UK* App no 4547/10 (ECHR, 13 March 2012).

[78] *R and H v UK* [2011] ECHR 844.

[79] UN General Assembly, Resolution 64/142 of 24 February 2010 (reissued 13 April 2010), Guidelines for the Alternative Care of Children 2010.

[80] This tends to be suggested where the concern is with the conduct of one parent only, eg in *P, C and S v UK* (n 43) and *YC v UK* (n 77).

guardianship orders or assistance including financial help, counselling and advice (see further in chapter 5). Also, as adoption orders rarely make provision for contact – and if they do, only indirect contact – adoption with direct contact may be a less restrictive alternative. It is arguable that any measure that prevents parents from raising their children could still have the potential to violate parental rights. However, this book examines whether measures of intervention that are less restrictive than adoption are more likely to protect parental rights (not only under Article 8 of the ECHR but also those protected by the UNCRC, under Articles 5 and 18), and whether alternatives to adoption may be equally effective in protecting children's best interests and rights.

An 'overall balance' involves examining the rights of the individual and weighing them against the interests of the community and/or the rights of other individuals. An example of how this operates can be seen in *Harroudj v France*.[81] In this case, it was held that there was no violation of Article 8 when the French authorities refused to allow a French national to adopt a child who was already in her care under an Islamic form of guardianship known as 'kafalah'. The Court held that the balance had been struck in recognising the public interest in pluralism and integration of children under kafalah, without severing ties with the children's country of origin. This case demonstrates that a balance can be achieved through acknowledging the de facto relationship between an adult and child, without the need for an adoption to take place. In this case, adoption would not have been a proportionate measure. In a non-consensual adoption case, an overall balance would potentially involve balancing parental rights against children's rights and best interests.

Choudhry and Herring have argued that, rather than providing a formal analysis of whether or not Article 8 has been violated (which is based on a legitimate objective, a rational connection, a minimal impairment, a least restrictive alternative and overall balance), the ECtHR instead should apply one of three analytical approaches based on these stages. They have suggested that the Court ought to apply either the least restrictive alternative test or the overall balance test, or consider whether or not the reasons used to justify the State's measure (ie removal of the child from his or her parents or non-consensual adoption) were 'relevant' and 'sufficient' as a whole.[82] Choudhry and Herring have suggested that this is sometimes referred to as the 'sufficiency' standard, which is usually applied by the Court in Article 8 cases concerning family law matters – especially as far as children are concerned.[83]

It is argued that this 'sufficiency' standard is less rigorous than the minimal impairment or least restrictive alternative test, because the Court need not consider whether equally effective but less restrictive methods could have

[81] *Harroudj v France* App no 43631/09 (ECHR, 4 October 2010).

[82] S Choudhry and J Herring, *European Human Rights and Family Law* (Oxford, Hart Publishing, 2010). See ibid 28–34 for further discussion.

[83] ibid 31.

been used, other than removal from the home or even adoption, to best serve children's needs. There is, however, an insufficient body of case law on adoption in the ECtHR to draw any firm conclusion on the type of analysis favoured by the Court in adoption proceedings. In general, the Court appears to have focused on whether or not adoption has struck the overall balance.[84] However, in cases where poverty and insufficient housing have led to adoption, the Court seems to have focused on minimal impairment, while in other family law cases it has applied the 'sufficiency' standard. It is suggested that the serious and irreversible consequences of adoption are such that the existence of a less restrictive alternative, which may perhaps be equally effective when compared with adoption, ought to be taken into account not only by the ECtHR but also by the family courts in England and Wales.

D. The Margin of Appreciation and its Impact on Adoption

The margin of appreciation is the latitude or discretion[85] enjoyed by the national government in its decision-making process.[86] It is sometimes said to stem from the principle of subsidiarity,[87] which means that the ECtHR acknowledges the diversity of national authorities, thereby deferring to them as best placed to make determinations on the needs of their own people.[88] The margin of appreciation amounts to an acknowledgement that although Member States will afford protection to Convention rights, they are able to take into consideration their own unique circumstances when balancing the different interests at stake.

In determining the scope of the margin of appreciation, the ECtHR is influenced by the nature of the right at stake. The more important the right, the narrower will be the margin of appreciation. The mutual rights of children and parents, to have a relationship with one another, are protected under Article 8 ECHR. States may be permitted a wide margin of appreciation when a child is initially taken into care, even though this may violate parents' and children's Article 8 rights.[89] In general, the Court tends to afford Member States a wide margin of appreciation in respect of children's welfare and in determining what will be in children's best interests,[90] including taking a child into care if the child has suffered or is at risk

[84] *Harroudj v France* (n 81).

[85] E Macdonald, F Matscher and H Petzold, *The European System for the Protection of Human Rights* (Leiden, Martinus Nijhoff Publishers, 1993) 55; G Kleijkamp, *Family Life and Family Interests* (London, Kluwer International, 1999) 52.

[86] Arai-Takahasi (n 72) 2. Also see generally for discussion of the margin of appreciation.

[87] Macdonald, Matscher and Petzold (n 85) 59.

[88] D Hoffman and J Rowe, *Human Rights in the UK: An Introduction to the Human Rights Act* (Harlow, Pearson Education Ltd, 2006) 48–49.

[89] *L v Finland* [2000] 2 FLR 118; *Johansen v Norway* (n 50).

[90] Arai-Takahasi (n 72) 64; U Kilkelly, *The Child and the European Convention on Human Rights* (Aldershot, Dartmouth Publishing Company, 1999) 10.

of suffering significant harm,[91] and in determining when children may be placed for adoption.[92]

In adoption cases, however, the wide margin of appreciation is tempered by a more intense standard of proportionality. This can be seen in *Keegan v Ireland*,[93] where an adoption order had been made without the natural father's knowledge or consent. Here, the ECtHR stated that notwithstanding the wide margin of appreciation, a high level of proof was needed to establish that there were relevant reasons for the adoption. An application of this high level of proportionality can also be seen in *Johansen v Norway*.[94] In this case, the Court acknowledged that a wide margin of appreciation existed when the child was taken into care, but found that it had been disproportionate to remove the parental rights of the mother and place her child in a foster home, with a view to the making of an adoption order. Despite the Court's rulings in *Keegan* and *Johansen*, the ECtHR does not always apply a high standard of proportionality in adoption cases that have originally been heard in the UK.[95]

O'Halloran has stated that non-consensual adoption is increasing in England and Wales but that it is an unusual[96] approach when compared with the rest of Europe, where adoption is typically a 'consensual process'.[97] This is significant, since the width of the margin of appreciation may be influenced by the level of consensus amongst Member States about a particular issue. Non-consensual adoption may, in practice, be permitted in many Member States, but it is less commonly used by other states.[98] According to Jones, the application of the consensus principle can be unpredictable in practice and may ultimately grant states a wide freedom of action.[99] The ECtHR has also been criticised for lack of sufficient comparative research, which is problematic, since the Court often uses the consensus criterion as a means of determining what the margin of appreciation will be.[100] However, both scholars[101] and judges[102] have acknowledged that the UK's policy on non-consensual adoption is out of line with the rest of Europe. In fact, the ECtHR has yet to directly address the fact that the UK's policy of

[91] *L v Finland* App no 25651/94 (ECHR, 27 April 2000).

[92] *Keegan v Ireland* (1994) 18 EHRR 342, para 47.

[93] ibid.

[94] *Johansen v Norway* (n 50) para 78.

[95] For further discussion, see K O'Halloran, *The Politics of Adoption: International Perspectives on Law Policy and Practice*, 3rd edn, (Brisbane, Springer, 2015).

[96] ibid. Also see *N (Children) (Adoption: Jurisdiction)* [2015] EWCA Civ 1112 [7], *per* Munby LJ.

[97] O'Halloran (n 95) 110.

[98] C Fenton-Glynn, 'The Child's Voice in Adoption Proceedings: A European Perspective' (2014) 22 *International Journal of Children's Rights* 135.

[99] TH Jones 'The Devaluation of Human Rights under the European Convention' [1995] *PL* 430, 441.

[100] I de la Rasilla del Moral, 'The Increasingly Marginal Appreciation of the Margin-of-Appreciation Doctrine' (2006) 7 *German Law Journal* 611, 618.

[101] For general discussion, see O'Halloran (n 95).

[102] *Down Lisburn Health and Social Services Trust and another v H and another* [2006] UKHL 36 [34], *per* Baroness Hale; and *D (A Child)* [2014] EWHC 3388 (Fam) [35], *per* Mostyn J.

adoption for children in care is inconsistent with the rest of Europe, despite the fact that several non-consensual adoption cases flowing from the UK have been heard by the ECtHR.[103]

III. The United Nations Convention on the Rights of the Child

A. The UNCRC, the Courts in England and Wales and the European Court of Human Rights

The UNCRC is an important Convention that is tailored specifically to the rights of children[104] and is regarded as the most important international document addressing children's rights.[105] The overall ethos of the UNCRC is to emphasise the happiness and well-being of children. Children should be raised in accordance with the ideals listed within the Convention, in an atmosphere of love and understanding. Furthermore, it can be implied from the UNCRC that the family unit should be provided with assistance so that it can fully assume its responsibilities, thereby maximising the well-being of children.[106] The UNCRC attempts to strike a balance between respecting a child's individual rights while also recognising and protecting the child's wider interest in rights derived from being part of a family unit. It is important to consider which UNCRC provisions may be relevant in adoption cases, and if any provisions might emphasise the use of less restrictive alternatives to non-consensual adoption. This discussion will consider which of these UNCRC rights may be in alignment and which may clash with the others.

The UK ratified the UNCRC on the 20 November, 1989, but it has yet to incorporate the UNCRC into domestic legislation.[107] Upon the advice of the UN Committee on the Rights of the Child, the post of Children's Commissioner was created to promote the rights of children[108] (including UNCRC rights), and attempts have been made to introduce the UNCRC more formally in the

[103] O'Halloran (n 95); and Fenton-Glynn (n 98).

[104] In contrast to the ECHR, which is worded primarily to address the rights of adults (discussed in detail in ch 3).

[105] E Verhellen, 'Children's rights in Europe' [1993] 1 *International Journal of Children's Rights* 357, 376; L Stuart, 'Interpreting and Limiting the Basic Socio-Economic Rights of Children in Cases where they Overlap with the Socio-Economic Rights of Others' (2008) 24 *South African Journal on Human Rights* 472, 484; N Ferreira, *Fundamental Rights and Private Law in Europe: The case of tort law and children* (Oxford, Routledge, 2011) 120; T Liefaard and JE Doek (eds), *Litigating the Rights of the Child: The UN Convention on the Rights of the Child in Domestic and International Jurisprudence* (London, Springer, 2015) 1.

[106] See the Preamble to the UNCRC.

[107] Mr Justice Cobb, 'Seen but not heard?' [2015] 45 *Family Law* 144.

[108] The post of Children's Commissioner for Wales was created by the Children Act 2004, s 5.

policy-making process. Compared with England, Wales has taken more measures to emphasise the importance of the UNCRC in law and policy.

Wales incorporated the UNCRC in legislation through the Rights of Children and Young Persons (Wales) Measure 2011, to strengthen the rights-based approach of Welsh Government policy-making for children. The Measure places a duty on Welsh Ministers to have regard to specified UNCRC rights and the Convention's optional protocols. Thus, the Children's Commissioner for Wales was involved in developing a Children's Rights Scheme in Wales,[109] whereby Welsh ministers are duty-bound to have regard to the rights and obligations in the UNCRC in the exercise of their functions.[110] Furthermore, under the Social Services and Well-being (Wales) Act 2016, any persons exercising functions in relation to looked-after or accommodated children under the Act must have regard to Part 1 of the UNCRC. In other words, policy-makers must have regard to a range of rights that may militate against non-consensual adoption.

Despite having a Commissioner to promote children's UNCRC rights in England,[111] England has not followed the approach taken in Wales and has not introduced a similar scheme on Children's Rights. The Children's Commissioner, nevertheless, still has an important role to play in ensuring that UNCRC rights are protected,[112] and in fact the Commissioner has expressed concerns about adoption law in England and Wales.[113] Furthermore, the Children and Families Act 2014 has strengthened the powers of the Children's Commissioner, which may lead to increased consideration of UNCRC rights in judicial decision-making and in government policy in general, and specifically in adoption law and policy.

The potential use of UNCRC as an interpretive tool by the courts (and potentially other professionals) in determining whether or not a non-consensual adoption is a proportionate measure, cannot be understated. In practice, however, because the UNCRC is not incorporated into English legislation, its enforcement mechanism is still widely regarded as weak,[114] and there has been pessimism about the likelihood of incorporation of the UNCRC in the foreseeable future.[115]

[109] The Children's Commissioner for Wales was involved in this process.

[110] 'Children's Rights in Wales' at http://www.childrensrightswales.org.uk/uncrc-rights.aspx. For further discussion, see generally J Fortin, 'Children's rights – flattering to deceive?' (2014) 26 *Child and Family Law Quarterly* 51; and J Williams, 'England and Wales' in Liefaard and Doek (eds) (n 105) 55. The scheme was brought into effect on 27 March 2012, and the Children's Commissioner for Wales was involved in this process.

[111] See ss 1–4 of the Children Act 2004.

[112] Liefaard and Doek (eds) (n 105) 54.

[113] Children's Commissioner, *A Child Rights Impact Assessment of Parts 1–3 of the Children and Families Bill (HC Bill 131)*, 27 February 2013.

[114] L LeBlanc, *The Convention on the Rights of the Child* (Lincoln, NE, University of Nebraska Press, 1995) 186; U Kilkelly, 'The Best of Both Worlds for Children's Rights? Interpreting the European Convention on Human Rights in the Light of the UN Convention on the Rights of the Child' (2001) 21 *Human Rights Quarterly* 308, 311; Ferreira (n 105) 121.

[115] A James, 'Children, 'The UNCRC, and Family Law in England and Wales' (2008) 46 *Family Court Review* 53.

Mr Justice Cobb has argued that the UNCRC ought to have primary or secondary legislative status,[116] which would strengthen the influence of the Convention. Incorporation of the UNCRC – or key provisions such as Articles 7–9 at the very least – into domestic law is essential to ensure implementation of its key provisions by the courts, policy-makers and other decision-makers.[117]

Lady Hale has made repeated assertions that the UNCRC amounts to international law with which domestic courts must comply.[118] For instance, in *R v Durham Constabulary*[119] she stated that '[t]he UNCRC is not only binding in international law; it is reflected in the interpretation and application by the ECtHR of the rights guaranteed by the European Convention'.

Although treaties are not justiciable without incorporation, the Convention on the Law of Treaties (Vienna Convention),[120] which the UK has ratified, makes it clear at Article 26 that 'Every treaty in force is binding upon the parties to it and must be performed by them in good faith.' It could therefore be argued that if one reads the UNCRC in conjunction with the Vienna Convention, greater scrutiny of the UNCRC may be required in judicial decision-making. However, the courts in England and Wales do not scrutinise the extent to which legislation and policy-making respects children's UNCRC rights. The UK has a dualist approach,[121] and at present the courts can choose to consider relevant articles of the UNCRC in their judgments[122] but they are not obliged to do so, and they are not in the habit of considering the UNCRC in adoption cases. Despite the UNCRC's current limitations, it is referred to in an increasing number of domestic law cases[123] if the court must apply the ECHR,[124] as well as in Strasbourg jurisprudence.[125]

[116] Mr Justice Cobb (n 107) 147.

[117] L Lundy, U Kilkelly and B Byrne, 'Incorporation of the United Nations Convention on the Rights of the Child in Law: A Comparative Review' [2013] *International Journal of Children's Rights* 442, 442–46.

[118] *Re ZH (Tanzania) v Secretary of State* [2011] UKSC 4.

[119] *R v Durham Constabulary* [2005] 1 WLR 1184, para 26. Also see *Re ZH (Tanzania)* (n 118).

[120] United Nations, Vienna Convention on Consular Relations, 24 April 1963, available at https://www.refworld.org/docid/3ae6b3648.html.

[121] Liefaard and Doek (eds) (n 105) 53.

[122] See, eg, *R (on the application of SG and others) v Secretary of State for Work and Pensions* [2015] UKSC 16. In particular, see [78] and [86].

[123] For example, see *Re H and A (Paternity: Blood Tests)* [2002] 1 FLR 1145; *Mabon v Mabon* [2005] EWCA Civ 634; and, more recently in the context of adoption proceedings, *RA (Baby Relinquished for Adoption – Case Management)* [2016] EWFC 25. For further discussion also see S Gilmore, 'Use of the UNCRC in Family Law Cases in England and Wales' [2017] *International Journal of Children's Rights* 500.

[124] Gilmore (n 123) 501–02.

[125] *Neulinger and Shuruk v Switzerland* (n 53); *Odièvre v France* App no 53176/99 [2002] 1 FCR 720; *Gaskin v UK* App no 10454/83 (1989) 12 EHRR 36. Kilkelly (n 114) 315, observes that the Commission and the ECtHR have both referred to the UNCRC since it came into existence. It has also been suggested by Stalford and Drywood that the EU is referring to the UNCRC with increasing frequency, either directly or indirectly, in policy and legislative documents. See H Stalford and E Drywood, 'Using the CRC to Inform EU Law and Policy-Making' in A Invernizzi, and J Williams (eds), *The Human Rights of Children: From Visions to Implementation* (Farnham, Ashgate, 2011) 206.

Kilkelly has described the relationship between the UNCRC and the ECHR as having 'created an intricate web of standards that is mutually reinforcing'.[126] In practice, this means that when the ECtHR is making decisions about whether or not ECHR rights have been violated, the UNCRC is referred to, and the content of the UNCRC may potentially become included within particular ECHR rights.[127] Liefaard and Doek have asserted that the ECtHR has 'established a prominent and persuasive children's rights jurisprudence which is grounded very much in the CRC'.[128] Thus UNCRC rights have been and may be considered when a claim is made, for example, under Articles 6 or 8 of the ECHR.[129] According to Lady Hale in the UK Supreme Court, the UK is bound to apply the UNCRC in keeping with its international obligations.[130] It is therefore important to explain and consider the relevance of the UNCRC in non-consensual adoption cases. Furthermore, it is important to consider UNCRC rights under the scope of best interests to highlight that rights form an important part of the best interests test, in contrast to the approach taken by English law, which appears to rest on the assumption that children's rights are at odds with a child's best interests (see section III.B).

B. The UNCRC and the Best Interests Principle

Article 3 UNCRC is a central provision of the Convention, which is considered and applied by the ECtHR and by the UK Supreme Court in adoption cases. Article 3 provides that a child's best interests should be a 'primary' consideration in determining State action:

> 1. In all actions concerning children, whether undertaken by public or private social welfare institutions, courts of law, administrative authorities or legislative bodies, the best interests of the child shall be a primary consideration.
> 2. States Parties undertake to ensure the child such protection and care as is necessary for his or her well-being, taking into account the rights and duties of his or her parents, legal guardians, or other individuals legally responsible for him or her, and, to this end, shall take all appropriate legislative and administrative measures.
> 3. States Parties shall ensure that the institutions, services and facilities responsible for the care or protection of children shall conform with the standards established by competent authorities, particularly in the areas of safety, health, in the number and suitability of their staff, as well as competent supervision.

[126] U Kilkelly, 'Using the Convention on the Rights of the Child in Law and Policy: Two Ways to Improve Compliance' in Invernizzi, and Williams (eds) (n 125) 183.

[127] *Sahin v Germany* [2002] 1 FLR 119.

[128] Liefaard and Doek (eds) (n 105) 225.

[129] *Keegan v Ireland* (n 92); *Odièvre v France* App no 42326/98 (ECHR, 13 February 2003).

[130] For example, see *ZH (Tanzania)* (n 118); *H (P) v Deputy Prosecutor of the Italian Republic v H (P) v F-K v Polish Judicial Authority* [2012] UKSC 25.

Hodgkin and Newell have argued that the best interests principle recognises the possibility of conflict between the interests of the child and those of his or her parents and the wider community.[131] This can be seen most acutely in the context of adoption proceedings where birth parents who have neglected or abused their children oppose an adoption, when it is not possible for their children to be returned to their care and the children themselves may be opposed to or indifferent to a relationship with their parents (see discussion in chapter 4). Despite the existence of this potential conflict, Henricson and Bainham have claimed that the UNCRC nonetheless recognises the importance of parents in several of its provisions, including the best interests principle itself.[132]

The best interests principle in Article 3 is a substantive right, a fundamental interpretative legal principle and a rule of procedure. It is one of the UNCRC 'general' principles,[133] which should be applied in legislation and decision-making in relation to all the other Convention rights.[134] The principle has been regarded as vague yet flexible,[135] and as a 'gateway'[136] to children's rights. The UN Committee has emphasised that there is no hierarchy of rights and that the best interests principle exists to ensure a child's 'effective enjoyment'[137] of all UNCRC rights. The Committee has stated:

> The full application of the concept of the child's best interests requires the development of a rights-based approach, engaging all actors, to secure the holistic, physical, psychological, moral and spiritual integrity of the child and promote his or her human dignity.[138]

In other words, the UNCRC's conception of best interests involves a consideration of a wide range of human rights, arguably including several rights that are relevant in adoption cases (including but not limited to Articles 5, 7, 8 and 9 UNCRC). Thus it is relevant to consider a range of different UNCRC provisions that are relevant in the context of the best interests principle and within adoption proceedings. Although the best interests principle is relevant in respect of all of the Convention Rights, explicit reference to 'best interests' can be found within a

[131] R Hodgkin and P Newell, *Implementation Handbook for the Convention on the Rights of the Child*, 3rd edn (Geneva, United Nations Publications, 2007) 38.

[132] Henricson and Bainham (n 33) 21.

[133] The other three are Art 2 non-discrimination, Art 6 maximum survival and development, and Art 12 participation of the child. See UNCRC General Comment No 14 (2013) on the right of the child to have his or her best interests taken as a primary consideration (Art 3, para 1); A Daly, *A Commentary on the United Nations Convention on the Rights of the Child, Article 15 the Right to Freedom of Association and the Freedom of Peaceful Protest* (Boston, MA, Brill Nijhoff, 2016) 16.

[134] General Comment No 5 (2003) General measures of implementation for the Convention on the Rights of the Child.

[135] Sutherland and Barnes Macfarlane (eds) (n 8) 36–37.

[136] U Kilkelly 'The Best Interests of the Child: A Gateway to Children's Rights' in Sutherland and Barnes Macfarlane (n 8) 51, 65.

[137] UNCRC General Comment No14 (n 133) (Art 3, para 1).

[138] ibid.

number of UNCRC rights, including Articles 9, 18, 20, 21, 37 and 40.[139] Article 3 provides that the child's best interests must be 'a primary consideration' in the decision-making process. In other words, the child's best interests will not necessarily take priority over others' rights, such as, for example, those of the child's birth parents. The exception to the principle that children's best interests will not take precedence over the rights of others, is Article 21 UNCRC on the right to adoption (considered in section III.C).

C. The UNCRC and Adoption

Article 21 UNCRC outlines the circumstances in which adoption may be permitted:

> States Parties that recognize and/or permit the system of adoption shall ensure that the best interests of the child shall be the paramount consideration and they shall:
>
> (a) Ensure that the adoption of a child is authorized only by competent authorities who determine, in accordance with applicable law and procedures and on the basis of all pertinent and reliable information, that the adoption is permissible in view of the child's status concerning parents, relatives and legal guardians and that, if required, the persons concerned have given their informed consent to the adoption on the basis of such counselling as may be necessary.

Although there is no explicit reference to non-consensual adoption, the wording states that parental consent to adoption will only be required where it is also required under domestic legislation. By implication, then, provisions enabling adoption without parental consent will be lawful, if such an adoption is in a child's best interests. It can therefore be concluded that non-consensual adoption under section 52(1)(b) of the ACA 2002 is permitted by Article 21.[140] In fact, the child's best interests can be viewed as a determining factor, dictating when an adoption should or should not take place. The fact that the child's best interests are paramount in adoption cases has been interpreted to mean that they should be placed above those of the prospective adopter(s) as well as those of the birth parents.[141] These best interests arguably necessitate reference to a range of UNCRC rights, particularly those that make explicit reference to the best interests of the child.

The UNCRC also emphasises the paramountcy of children's best interests in adoption cases. At first glance, then, an analysis of the proportionality of adoption might not be dissimilar to a bare welfare analysis. However, it has been argued that the welfare analysis required under Article 21 may be more extensive than

[139] See the discussion in P Alston, 'The Best Interests Principle: Towards a Reconciliation of Culture and Human Rights' in M Freeman (ed), *Children's Rights*, vol II (Farnham, Ashgate, 2004) 183, 185.

[140] See also the brief analysis of Art 21 in *RA (Baby Relinquished for Adoption – Case Management)* (n 123).

[141] N Cantwell, 'Are Children's Rights Still Human?' in Invernizzi and Williams (eds) (n 125) 49.

first thought. Sloan, for example, has argued that Article 21(a) of the UNCRC may 'point in a different direction'[142] from a simple welfare test. This is important in the context of this book, since a simple welfare test has, since the enactment of the ACA 2002, been applied by the courts when deciding whether or not an adoption ought to take place under section 52(1)(b) of the Act. In fact, cases can be found where adoptions have taken place based on a simple welfare analysis, with no direct reference to the welfare checklist under the ACA 2002, section 1(4).[143]

Furthermore, Munby LJ has expressed concern about the quality of judicial reasoning in adoption proceedings in England and Wales[144] (see chapter 4 for further detail). If more than a simple welfare test is, in fact, required under Article 21 then it could be argued that the approach taken by the courts in England and Wales in determining whether or not it is in the child's best interests to be adopted is at best insufficient and at worst amounts to a violation of other UNCRC rights (for example, Articles 7, 8 and 9). Thus, this may mean there are cases where an adoption order is made where this is disproportionate and potentially also a violation of Article 8 ECHR.

The simple welfare-based approach towards decision-making does not fit in well with the UNCRC's proposed approach for dealing with conflicting rights, particularly in the context of adoption. UN General Comment No 14 has made it clear that where the child's best interests may conflict with the rights of other children (eg in cases where the mother is under-age or sibling relationships are likely to be affected by adoption), a careful balancing process must take place so as to find a 'suitable compromise',[145] and that the same approach must be taken

> if the rights of other persons are in conflict with the child's best interests. If harmonization is not possible, authorities and decision-makers will have to analyse and weigh the rights of all those concerned, bearing in mind that the right of the child to have his or her best interests taken as a primary consideration means that the child's interests have high priority and are not just one of several considerations.[146]

The welfare checklist under the ACA 2002, section 1(4)(f) refers to the 'relationship which the child has with relatives', which can loosely be interpreted as referring to interests of individuals other than the child in the context of deciding whether to make an adoption order. However, parents' interests/rights do not appear to be assessed explicitly in the context of adoption, despite the severity of the consequences, unless parents decide to challenge final rulings (see chapters 3 and 4). The UN Committee on the Rights of the Child is not opposed to the adoption of children in care, with explicit reference to adoption appearing within the

[142] B Sloan, 'Fostering and Adoption as a Means of Securing Article 6 Rights in England' (2015) 26 *Stellenbosch Law Review* 363, 370–71.
[143] *YC v UK* (n 77).
[144] *Re B-S (Children)* (n 16).
[145] UNCRC General Comment No 14 (2013) (n 133) (Art 3, para 1) 10.
[146] ibid.

UN Guidelines for the Alternative Care of Children. However, it does not actively promote adoption as a favoured option for children in care.

This assertion is supported by Sloan, who has suggested that the UNCRC can be regarded as neutral[147] on the subject of adoption. Further support for this argument can be found within the UNCRC itself, and also in the UN Guidelines for the Alternative Care of Children.[148] In fact, both the UNCRC and the Guidelines emphasise the importance of keeping children and birth parents together, and of reuniting children with their parents where a separation has occurred. The Guidelines mention foster care and kinship care as alternatives to children's living with birth parents who may be unable to provide adequate care for their children,[149] while Article 20(3) of the UNCRC explicitly mentions alternatives to adoption for children in care.[150]

Article 20 was reviewed in a consensual adoption case, *RA (Baby Relinquished for Adoption – Case Management)*,[151] where it was argued that all states need to comply with Article 20 UNCRC and the Court needed to consider 'the desirability of continuity in a child's upbringing and to the child's ethnic, religious, cultural and linguistic background'. In this case, it was argued by counsel that the alternative of a maternal grandmother in Latvia willing to care for the child meant that an adoption order would violate the child's Article 20 UNCRC right. If such a case were to reach the ECtHR, it would be interesting to see the extent of the measures the state would need to undertake, to satisfy the child's right under Article 20 UNCRC (likely argued within the scope of Article 8 ECHR).

Under Article 6 UNCRC (see section III.E), states must protect the child's 'inherent right to life' and the right to maximal 'survival and development'. Thus, Article 6 is a relevant consideration under the best interests analysis to be undertaken by the courts in adoption cases. According to Sloan, it may 'provide clues'[152] as to the meaning of best interests (under Article 3 UNCRC) and how they ought to be applied under Article 21. Prioritising non-consensual adoption for children in care has consequences for various UNCRC provisions[153] (such as Articles 5, 7, 8, and 9) that emphasise the importance of maintaining children's relationships with their birth parents. It can be argued, then, that the UNCRC may in fact be consistent with a conception of proportionality, which routinely incorporates the assessment of less restrictive alternatives to non-consensual adoption.

[147] B Sloan, 'Conflicting Rights: English Adoption Law and the Implementation of the UN Convention on the Rights of the Child' (2013) 25 *Child and Family Law Quarterly* 40.

[148] UN Guidelines for the Alternative Care of Children (n 79).

[149] ibid, para 29.

[150] Art 20(3) UNCRC states that 'care could include … foster placement, kafalah of Islamic law, adoption or if necessary, placement in suitable institutions for the care of children. When considering solutions, due regard shall be paid to the desirability of continuity in a child's upbringing and to the child's ethnic, religious, cultural and linguistic background'.

[151] *RA (Baby Relinquished for Adoption – Case Management)* (n 123).

[152] Sloan (n 142) 363. Also see Hodgkin and Newell (n 131) 303.

[153] Sloan (n 142) 374.

Another relevant consideration when determining whether or not an adoption ought to take place is the extent to which a child has had a say in the adoption process. It is argued that, where possible, the child should be able to participate in the adoption process,[154] although within Article 21 there is no explicit reference to the child's views, or whether or not the child should be able to consent to adoption. Article 21 could nevertheless be construed alongside Article 12. In this sense, taking children's views into account in adoption cases may be regarded as an implied requirement under Article 12 UNCRC (considered in section III.D).[155]

D. The UNCRC and the Child's Right to be Heard

Article 12 (the right of the child to be heard) concerns children's right to participate in court proceedings and provides that the child's views should be 'given due weight in accordance with the age and maturity of the child', thereby acknowledging the importance of children's right to autonomy in the context of court proceedings.[156] It provides:

> 1. States Parties shall assure to the child who is capable of forming his or her own views the right to express those views freely in all matters affecting the child, the views of the child being given due weight in accordance with the age and maturity of the child.
> 2. For this purpose, the child shall in particular be provided the opportunity to be heard in any judicial and administrative proceedings affecting the child, either directly, or through a representative or an appropriate body, in a manner consistent with the procedural rules of national law.

There are three aspects to Article 12 – the ability to be heard, the ability to be heard in official proceedings, and the right for the child's views to be given due weight – but there is no guarantee that a child's views and wishes will be followed, because the balance between the child's participatory rights and the child's best interests needs to be respected. Article 12 was developed because of the scant attention paid to the views of children.[157]

Article 12 has been influential[158] and is the most frequently cited UNCRC right in cases in England and Wales,[159] but this is usually in the context of the making of child arrangement orders rather than in adoption proceedings. It can be argued, nonetheless, that it has the potential to be an important right that may be used in

[154] F Ang et al, *Participation Rights of Children* (Cambridge, Intersentia, 2006) 163.
[155] Hodgkin and Newell (n 131) 296; Ang et al (n 154) 164–65.
[156] See also UNCRC General Comment No 12 (2009) The right of the child to be heard.
[157] Cantwell (n 141) 55.
[158] *Mabon v Mabon* [2005] EWCA Civ 634; *ZH (Tanzania)* (n 118); *R (on the application of SG) and Others v Secretary of State for Work and Pensions* [2015] UKSC 16.
[159] Gilmore (n 123) 509.

support of the child's right to have a say in the adoption process, or even to provide or withhold consent to adoption. In general, children in care want to have a determinative say in what happens in their lives, and when they do not feel that they have been heard, Daly suggests that this can increase their distress levels[160] and create negative feelings stemming from 'autonomy repression'.[161]

As the law currently stands, however, while the wishes and feelings of the child are a factor courts may consider generally and in the context of adoption, they are not compelled to do so.[162] In practice, children in England and Wales have a very limited role to play in expressing themselves in court proceedings generally, let alone in adoption proceedings. This is even though UNCRC General Comment 12, note 161, paragraph 21 states that 'non-verbal forms of communication including play, body language, facial expressions' ought to be considered when making decisions in relation to children. It could be argued, then, that the wishes of even very young children could be considered in adoption proceedings. However, as Daly points out, there is no requirement that children's wishes are prioritised in court proceedings.[163] It is asserted that the more intrusive the state action (ie adoption), the greater the emphasis ought to be on children's participatory rights.

Fortin has argued that even though Article 12 does not explicitly refer to the rights of parents, it nonetheless promotes children's autonomy while respecting parents' authority.[164] This can be demonstrated by the relationship between Article 12 and Article 5 (on respect for parents' rights, duties and responsibilities), since parents must take into account the evolving capacities of the child when making decisions in relation to the child. It is important under Article 12 for adults – including parents and policy-makers – to facilitate the participation of children in matters that affect their lives,[165] including the draconian step of adoption.

Other rights that may balance against Article 12 include that under Article 3 (the best interests principle), which arguably takes precedence over Article 12 in legal proceedings in some countries,[166] such as in England and Wales. Articles 3 and 12 are interrelated, since a best interests determination (including but not limited to adoption cases, for example) should mean that decision-makers take into account the child's own views as to what will be in his or her best interests.[167]

[160] A Daly, *Children, Autonomy and the Courts: Beyond the Right to be Heard* (Leiden, Brill, 2018) 41 and 137.

[161] ibid 358.

[162] CA 1989, s 1(3)(a).

[163] Daly (n 160) 55.

[164] J Fortin, *Children's Rights and the Developing Law*, 3rd edn (Cambridge, Cambridge University Press, 2009) 43.

[165] T Buck, *International Child Law* (New York, Routledge, 2011) 130.

[166] A Parkes, *Children and International Human Rights Law: The Right of the Child to be Heard* (New York, Routledge, 2013) 58.

[167] S Detrick, *A Commentary on the United Nations Convention on the Rights of the Child* (Leiden, Martin Nijhoff Publishers, 1999) 89.

However, there can be a tension between Articles 3 and 12,[168] given that a child might wish to remain with his or her birth parents or not to be adopted, when in practice adoption may be the best way to meet a child's emotional needs and ensure stability and permanence for that child. In England and Wales, children's participatory rights are limited because, as Tisdall et al[169] have recognised, the wider implementation of Article 12 in children's proceedings in England and Wales has been hindered by the belief that listening to children might clash with their best interests.[170] This might be seen, for example, where a child wishes to be reunited with his or her parents, and this may not be possible due to the parents' severe neglect and/or abuse of the child (relevant rights in this context are Articles 6, 19 and 34 of the UNCRC).

E. The UNCRC and Child Protection

Under Article 6 UNCRC it is stated that:

> 1. States Parties recognize that every child has the inherent right to life.
> 2. States Parties shall ensure to the maximum extent possible the survival and development of the child.[171]

This right overlaps with Article 3 of the Convention on the child's best interests, in the sense that Article 6 also aims to ensure that children grow up in a healthy and safe environment and reach their full potential.[172] Thus, there is a need for the state to consider children's safety and development when drafting laws and policies.[173] Rights under Article 6 can be bolstered by Article 19, which protects children from abuse. Therefore, removal of a child into care would be justified based on these rights, but adoption would not necessarily be a proportionate measure in such cases (for further discussion, see chapters 3 and 4).

However, the positive educational, social and emotional outcomes that may be attributed to adoption are relevant considerations when developing an appropriate and effective way of protecting children in care. It should be noted, though, that the state must consider 'the least intrusive intervention as warranted by the circumstances',[174] and under Article 20 must give 'special protection and assistance' to children who cannot be raised by their birth parents. Although at first glance,

[168] K Marshall, *Children's Rights in the Balance: The Participation–Protection Debate* (Edinburgh, The Stationery Office, 1997) 14.

[169] E Kay et al, 'Listening to the views of children? Principles and Mechanisms within the Children (Scotland) Act 1995' (2002) 24 *Journal of Social Welfare and Family Law* 385, 394.

[170] For general discussion, see Daly (n 160).

[171] For further discussion, see Daly (n 133) 28.

[172] ibid 27.

[173] ibid.

[174] UNCRC General Comment No 13 (2011) The right of the child to freedom from all forms of violence, para 54.

Articles 6 and 19 could be regarded as relevant considerations when determining whether or not non-consensual adoption is a proportionate measure, the emphasis on the need for less intrusive intervention (also found in the UN Guidelines for the Alternative Care of Children) implies that the state ought to avoid 'intrusive' measures (eg non-consensual adoption) where possible.

This may suggest that there is a greater need for the state to put more resources into supporting families (see chapters 3 and 5). Furthermore, Sloan has asserted that, 'given the other requirements of the UNCRC,[175] the right to development must ordinarily relate to development *within* one's home environment'.[176] Thus, the need for state intervention is insufficient by itself to justify a restrictive measure such as non-consensual adoption. The provision of state assistance may, in some circumstances, improve the likelihood that children can continue to develop relationships with their parents via a range of alternatives to adoption. Non-consensual adoption ought to be a measure reserved for circumstances in which less restrictive alternatives are unavailable.

F. The UNCRC and the Child's Relationship Rights

Article 7 (the right to know and be cared for by one's parents) and Article 8 (the right to know one's identity) alone or in conjunction with each other emphasise that children ought to be raised by their birth parents, and that they ought to know who they are and where they come from.

Article 7

1. The child shall be registered immediately after birth and shall have the right from birth to a name, the right to acquire a nationality and, as far as possible, the right to know and be cared for by his or her parents.
2. States Parties shall ensure the implementation of these rights in accordance with their national law and their obligations under the relevant international instruments in this field, in particular where the child would otherwise be stateless.

Article 8

1. States Parties undertake to respect the right of the child to preserve his or her identity, including nationality, name and family relations as recognized by law without unlawful interference.
2. Where a child is illegally deprived of some or all of the elements of his or her identity, States Parties shall provide appropriate assistance and protection, with a view to re-establishing speedily his or her identity.

Article 7 can be read along with other articles of the UNCRC in addition to Article 8, such as Articles 5, 9, 10 and 20 and 27.[177] Articles 7 and 8, like Article 12,

[175] Brian Sloan referred to Arts 7, 8 and 9 of the UNCRC. See Sloan (n 142) 366.
[176] ibid.
[177] Hodgkin and Newell (n 131) 97.

could also be seen as constituting participation rights that are relevant to making decisions in adoption cases, since children may wish to have information about[178] or contact with their birth parents. Articles 7 and 8 have been referred to briefly in some adoption cases heard by the ECtHR,[179] as well as by the UK Supreme Court,[180] but have not been considered in depth. Also, the ECtHR made no reference at all to the UNCRC in two important ECtHR cases concerning non-consensual adoption (*P, C and S v UK*[181] and *Kutzner v Germany*[182]), despite the importance of the Convention in international law.

There is disagreement about the scope of Article 7 UNCRC and whose rights it protects. This is significant in the context of adoption proceedings because it could be interpreted as applying to all types of parent (birth, foster and adoptive parents for example),[183] or solely to relationships between children and their birth parents.[184] The right to identity and the preservation of family relationships under Article 8 UNCRC is most 'at risk' when an adoption order is made.[185] As O'Donovan has argued, a person's identity exists at birth, and our childhood, life experiences[186] and our genetics[187] all form part of our identity. Regardless of the age at which a child is adopted, he or she has an identity that comes from his or her birth family based on genetics and experiences up to the point of adoption, which will influence children even after the adoption process.

This can be seen most acutely in *RA (Baby Relinquished for Adoption – Case Management)*.[188] There, a child was to be adopted with the consent of his Latvian birth parents. The Latvian Central Authority[189] supported the maternal grandmother as a carer for the child and sought for her to be assessed. Counsel for the Latvian Authority argued that adoption in England would violate Article 8 of the UNCRC, because it would 'deny [RA]'s rights to grow up in his inherited culture and will cause violations to the rights of the child to preserve his identity'.[190]

[178] *Odièvre v France* (n 125); *Gaskin v UK* (n 125).

[179] *Keegan v Ireland* App no 16969/90 (ECHR); *Odièvre v France* (n 125); *Saviny v Ukraine* App no 39948/06 (ECHR, 18 December 2008); *Kearns v France* App no 35991/04 (ECHR, 10 January 2008); *EB v France* App no 43546/02 (ECHR, 22 January 2008).

[180] *In the Matter of B (A Child)* [2013] UKSC 33.

[181] *P, C and S v UK* (n 43).

[182] *Kutzner v Germany* App no 46544/99 (ECHR, 26 February 2002). For further discussion on reference to UNCRC provisions in ECtHR cases, see J Moloney, S Symonds and E Harper, *Consideration by the European Court of Human Rights of the UN Convention on the Rights of the Child 1989* (London, ILPA, 2008).

[183] Hodgkin and Newell (n 131) 97.

[184] A Bainham, 'Honour Thy Father and Thy Mother: Children's Rights and Children's Duties' in G Douglas and L Sebba (eds), *Children's Rights and Traditional Values* (Aldershot, Dartmouth Publishing, 1998) 104.

[185] G Lansdown and P Newell, *UK Agenda for Children* (London, Child Rights Development Unit, 1994) 43.

[186] K O'Donovan, 'Interpretations of Children's Identity Rights' in D Fottrell (ed), *Revisiting Children's Rights* (The Hague, Kluwer Law International, 2000) 73.

[187] *Re H and A (Paternity: Blood Tests)* [2002] 1 FLR 1145.

[188] *RA (Baby Relinquished for Adoption – Case Management)* (n 123).

[189] The Latvian equivalent of Social Services.

[190] *RA (Baby Relinquished for Adoption – Case Management)* (n 123) [20].

The Court determined that the child's right under Article 8 of the UNCRC was not violated, but indicated that it was desirable to consider alternative carers as early as possible, and acknowledged that a child's nationality formed an important part of the court's welfare assessment. The grandmother was assessed, but it was later decided that it was in the child's best interests for the adoption order to be made. This case raised other significant issues that will be considered in more depth in chapter 4. Adoption of children of non-UK nationals is particularly controversial, and we could see more adoption cases involving non-UK nationals with Article 8 UNCRC argued in conjunction with other Convention rights, such as Article 20.

When parents face poverty and housing problems, this increases the likelihood of public care and raises issues under Articles 7, 8 and 9.[191] This is because children are more likely to be separated from their parents, siblings and other family members in such circumstances. This has the potential to lead to the loss of continuance of such relationships and the ongoing development of cultural identity. Where less restrictive alternatives are available to the state that will keep children and parents together, states may have a positive obligation under the ECHR and the UNCRC to intervene in family life, not simply to protect children from harm or the risk of harm but to be proactive and provide assistance to families in need. This could include, for example, practical assistance with housing, or help from social workers or financial assistance (see chapter 3, section IV.C and chapter 5, section II for further discussion). Where such assistance is likely to help children to remain with their birth parents while simultaneously protecting them from harm, this affords protection of children's rights under Articles 7 and 8. Thus it may be argued that in some circumstances, state assistance and the use of other, less restrictive alternatives to non-consensual adoption may be required to protect children's rights under Articles 7 and 8 of the UNCRC. The use of less restrictive alternatives may also be required to protect children's and parents' rights under Article 18 UNCRC (see discussion in section III.G) and under Article 8 ECHR (see chapter 3, section IV.C).

In fact, Sloan has argued that Articles 7 and 8 of the UNCRC serve as a reminder that adoption may not be proportionate even where it is appropriate to separate parent and child.[192] In the light of these Convention articles, Sloan has rightly expressed concern that the judicial approach towards adoption in England and Wales is not necessarily compatible with Article 7 UNCRC, or with the emphasis on 'family relations' in Article 8 UNCRC.[193] The next section will consider in further detail how the UNCRC protects familial rights and may in fact support the use of less restrictive but equally effective alternatives to non-consensual adoption.

[191] Lansdown and Newell (n 185) 83.
[192] Sloan (n 147).
[193] ibid.

G. The UNCRC and the Family Unit

Article 5 aims to respect the role of parents and others in the child's upbringing, and to provide limited protection of parents' rights to make decisions in relation to their children:

> **Article 5**
>
> States Parties shall respect the responsibilities, rights and duties of parents or, where applicable, the members of the extended family or community as provided for by local custom, legal guardians or other persons legally responsible for the child, to provide, in a manner consistent with the evolving capacities of the child, appropriate direction and guidance in the exercise by the child of the rights recognized in the present Convention.

Article 5 is not routinely referred to in adoption cases but, like other Convention articles considered in this book, it may suggest the need for less restrictive alternatives than non-consensual adoption. There is an absence of a paramountcy principle in Article 5, which means it places an emphasis on the interests of adults as well as those of children, and Article 5 also recognises the possibility of conflict between the best interests of the child and the interests of the birth parents and the wider community.[194] Furthermore, it refers to 'extended family' or the 'community', thereby acknowledging that other persons involved in the child's life, and who care for the child, may also have rights.[195] This could include siblings, aunts and uncles, grandparents and extended family with or without biological ties. In fact, despite the emphasis on kinship care (see chapter 4) adoption is often a preferred option in England and Wales, despite the availability of other family members who may be willing to care for children who are placed for adoption.[196]

According to Ferreira, Article 5 UNCRC reflects 'progressive autonomy',[197] since it acknowledges that the evolving capacity of the child will have a bearing on the discharge of parental rights and responsibilities. For example, Article 5 could be used in support of providing children with the opportunity to be involved in the adoption decision-making process,[198] which will ultimately impact on the extent to which their birth parents may have a say in their lives. Recognition of the importance of parents' rights and duties under Article 5 implies that where possible, children should be raised by their parents, who ought to be able to make decisions about their children's lives. Implicit in Article 5, then, is the notion of minimal intervention[199] and a recognition of the importance of the birth family's

[194] J Tobin, 'Judging the Judges: Are they Adopting the Rights Approach in Matters Involving Children?' (2009) 33 *Melbourne University Law Review* 579, 587–89; Daly (n 133) 59.
[195] LeBlanc (n 114) 113.
[196] This can be seen in *Webster v Norfolk County Council* [2009] EWCA Civ 59, for example.
[197] Ferreira (n 105) 122.
[198] Fenton-Glynn (n 98).
[199] The emphasis on minimal state intervention is inherent in the CA 1989 too.

guiding role in a child's life. In fact, it has been observed by McGillivray that the Convention refers to parents 36 times, with 19 of its substantive articles deferring to parents.[200] Nevertheless, despite the reference in Article 5 to parents' rights, it is not clear what the scope of these rights is and how they are to be balanced against the rights of children.[201]

Another relevant article when considering the family unit as a whole is Article 18 UNCRC. This Convention right states that parents have 'common responsibilities for the upbringing and development of the child', and Article 18(2) provides that states need to 'render appropriate assistance to parents and legal guardians in the performance of their child-rearing responsibilities'. This provision is significant,[202] because it implies that less restrictive alternatives, such as state assistance (see chapter 5, section II), ought to be considered before more serious measures, such as non-consensual adoption, take place. Hodgkin and Newell, for example, have suggested that to satisfy Article 18, this may mean that the state should help with financial benefits, housing, day care, home help, and psychiatric and professional support where needed.[203] The role of increased assistance for parents in potentially decreasing the need for non-consensual adoption will be considered in more depth in chapters 3–5 of this book.

The case law on adoption in both the courts in England and Wales and the ECtHR does not often refer to Article 5 or Article 18 of the UNCRC.[204] However, both of these articles could be considered in cases where parents allege that their own rights under Article 8 ECHR, and potentially those of their children, have been violated. It could be argued that if the state fails in its positive obligation under Article 8 of the UNCRC to provide 'appropriate assistance' to the birth parents or wider birth family to help them care for a child (eg by the provision of financial or practical support from the state), this may violate the rights of children, birth parents and members of the wider birth family.

Article 9 UNCRC is another important right that refers to the family unit. Article 9 recognises a principle of family integrity,[205] and acknowledges that a child should only be separated from his or her parents when it is 'necessary for the best interests of the child'.[206] This may apply in situations where children are

[200] A McGillivray, 'The Long Awaited: Past Futures of Children's Rights' (2013) *21 International Journal of Children's Rights* 209. This includes Art 18, for example, which emphasises that parents have responsibilities 'for the upbringing and development of the child'. Also see the Preamble to the UNCRC.

[201] A Quennerstedt, 'Balancing the rights of the Child and the Rights of the Parent in the Convention on the Rights of the Child' [2009] *Journal of Human Rights* 162, 173.

[202] Sloan (n 142) 371.

[203] Hodgkin and Newell (n 131) 237.

[204] Gilmore (n 123).

[205] Buck (n 165) 137.

[206] See reference to Art 9 and Art 21 of the UNCRC in a ECtHR decision on adoption without parental consent: *X v Croatia* App no 11223/04 (ECHR, 17 July 2008).

neglected or abused by their parents, or where their parents live apart.[207] Article 9 provides as follows:

Article 9

1. States Parties shall ensure that a child shall not be separated from his or her parents against their will, except when competent authorities subject to judicial review determine, in accordance with applicable law and procedures, that such separation is necessary for the best interests of the child. Such determination may be necessary in a particular case such as one involving abuse or neglect of the child by the parents, or one where the parents are living separately and a decision must be made as to the child's place of residence.
2. In any proceedings pursuant to paragraph 1 of the present article, all interested parties shall be given an opportunity to participate in the proceedings and make their views known.
3. States Parties shall respect the right of the child who is separated from one or both parents to maintain personal relations and direct contact with both parents on a regular basis, except if it is contrary to the child's best interests.
4. Where such separation results from any action initiated by a State Party, such as the detention, imprisonment, exile, deportation or death (including death arising from any cause while the person is in the custody of the State) of one or both parents or of the child, that State Party shall, upon request, provide the parents, the child or, if appropriate, another member of the family with the essential information concerning the whereabouts of the absent member(s) of the family unless the provision of the information would be detrimental to the well-being of the child. States Parties shall further ensure that the submission of such a request shall of itself entail no adverse consequences for the person(s) concerned.

Article 9 is most commonly referred to in relation to contact with non-resident parents,[208] but it could also be interpreted to apply to contact with parents whilst in care. It may further be read in conjunction with Article 27, which recognises 'the right of every child to a standard of living adequate for the child's physical, mental, spiritual, moral and social development'. Protection of children's Article 27 rights may, for example, include keeping children with their parents where it is safe to do so. So it may be said that homelessness or poverty should not be grounds for removal of children from their parents[209] (eg where the living conditions of the parents may justify a child's or children's being taken into care). Furthermore, even where such removal may be necessary to protect a child's right under Article 27 (or in fact Articles 6 and 19), this does not mean that non-consensual adoption

[207] Hodgkin and Newell (n 131) 122.

[208] Gilmore (n 123). See, eg, *Re R (A Minor) (Contact)* [1993] 2 FLR 762, 767, where the Court of Appeal commented that 'It is the right of a child to have a relationship with both parents wherever possible. This principle has been stated again and again in the appellate courts. It is underlined in the United Nations Convention on the Rights of the Child and endorsed in the Children Act 1989.'

[209] Hodgkin and Newell (n 131) 123.

will be a necessary or proportionate measure.[210] UN General Comment No 14, on the best interests principle, states:

> Given the gravity of the impact on the child of separation from his or her parents, such separation should only occur as a last resort measure, as when the child is in danger of experiencing imminent harm or when otherwise necessary; separation should not take place if less intrusive measures could protect the child. Before resorting to separation, the State should provide support to the parents in assuming their parental responsibilities, and restore or enhance the family's capacity to take care of the child, unless separation is necessary to protect the child. Economic reasons cannot be a justification for separating a child from his or her parents.[211]

Thus, it could be argued, in cases where economic factors (eg inadequate housing) have an adverse impact on a parent's ability to raise his or her child (see *Zhou v Italy*[212] in chapter 3 for example), the removal of a child into care and the subsequent non-consensual adoption of a child may be in violation of Article 9 UNCRC. Articles 5, 9 and 18 not only acknowledge parental interests, but also suggest that a less restrictive alternative to non-consensual adoption must be chosen, where possible, for the state to satisfy its obligations under the UNCRC.

Article 9 UNCRC states that separation will be justified when it is in a child's best interests under Article 3 UNCRC, where the child has been subjected to neglect or abuse.[213] This means that removal of a child into care is clearly consistent with the spirit of Article 9. However, if a less restrictive alternative to adoption is available (including but not limited to state assistance, kinship care or special guardianship) that is equally effective as adoption, then it could be argued that the separation of the child from his or her parents and wider family is potentially a disproportionate measure and, when read in conjunction with other rights (such as Articles 5, 7 and 8), then Article 9 becomes relevant in non-consensual adoption cases. In other words, in cases where a less restrictive and equally effective alternative is available, adoption is not a 'necessary' step. In fact, an adoption in such circumstances may be contrary to the child's best interests, and may even violate Article 9.

The word 'necessary' in Article 9, interpreted along with the Article 3 best interests principle, suggests similarity to the approach taken by the ECtHR, which employs a test of proportionality when assessing rights violations and the best interests of children (for further discussion see chapter 3). The ECtHR referred to Article 9 in *Saviny v Ukraine*,[214] and emphasised the need to provide assistance so as to enable birth parents to parent more effectively, thereby ensuring

[210] *SH v Italy* App no 52557/14 (ECHR, 13 October 2015).

[211] UNCRC General Comment No 14 (n 133) 10. See also the UN Guidelines for the Alternative Care of Children (n 79) para 15.

[212] *Zhou v Italy* (n 74).

[213] Detrick (n 167) 172.

[214] *Saviny v Ukraine* (n 179) (for further detail see ch 3, section IV).

that families are kept together where possible.[215] Lansdown and Newell have interpreted Articles 7 and 9 of the UNCRC as requiring every possible effort to be made to seek security for a child within his or her own family, and where this is not possible, for the child to at least have contact and be able to maintain relationships with family members.[216] This interpretation suggests that the UNCRC requires the least restrictive but equally effective alternative to non-consensual adoption to be chosen.

H. The UNCRC and the Third Optional Protocol

The United Nations Committee on the Rights of the Child aims to ensure that countries that have signed the UNCRC respect, protect and fulfil the rights in the Convention, via a reporting mechanism whereby the Committee produces a report on each Member State, which must be responded to within a specific timeframe. The UNCRC General Assembly approved a Third Optional Protocol, entitled 'Optional Protocol to the Convention on the Rights of the Child on a Communications Procedure', which enables children to make complaints to the UN Committee on specific violations of their Convention rights by their state.[217] This measure has the effect of addressing criticisms that the Committee is currently limited in what it can do to address violations of children's rights,[218] and it fills a 'lacuna'[219] in the law by creating a mechanism for aggrieved children to raise rights' violations.[220]

Although the Third Optional Protocol has not been signed, let alone ratified, by the UK, it is hoped by Fortin that this may, one day, make the UNCRC more effective for children.[221] The Protocol raises the potential for adoption cases to be examined by the Committee. However, there are still issues that may affect the effectiveness of the Optional Protocol. Thus, for instance, children may be unaware that they have rights, or if they are aware, they may not have the practical means to enforce them. Also, children may still face the arduous task of having to exhaust

[215] ibid paras 35–36. The Court refers to recommendations of the Council of Europe on 'positive parenting'. See Recommendation Rec (2005)5 of the Committee of Ministers on the rights of children living in residential institutions (adopted 16 March 2005); and Recommendation Rec (2006)19 of the Committee of Ministers to Member States on policy to support positive parenting (adopted 13 December 2006).

[216] Lansdown and Newell (n 185) 43.

[217] See UN General Assembly A/RES/66/138 66th session agenda item 64, at https://treaties.un.org/doc/source/signature/2012/a-res-66-138-english.pdf (this came into force on 14 April 2014).

[218] W Binford, 'Utilizing the Communication Procedures of the ACERWC and the UNCRC' at http://papers.ssrn.com/sol3/papers.cfm?abstract_id=2209507.

[219] More properly, 'loophole'.

[220] R Smith, 'The Third Optional Protocol to the UN Convention on the Rights of the Child? – Challenges Arising Transforming the Rhetoric into Reality' (2013) 21 *International Journal of Children's Rights* 305, 305.

[221] J Fortin, 'Children's rights – flattering to deceive?' (2014) 26 *Child and Family Law Quarterly* 51.

domestic remedies first before making use of the Optional Protocol.[222] Despite these limitations, there is at least potential for children, or their birth parents as representatives of their children, to use the Optional Protocol to challenge an adoption order made without parental consent, on the basis of one or more of the rights already mentioned.

I. UN Guidelines for the Alternative Care of Children

The overall purpose of the Guidelines is to 'enhance the implementation'[223] of the UNCRC and other relevant international instruments concerning the protection and well-being of children who have been deprived of parental care, or who are at risk of being deprived of such care. The Guidelines aim at striking the appropriate balance by ensuring that children are not removed from their family homes unnecessarily; but that where such a measure of intervention is necessary, the method of alternative care is the best option for the child. These alternatives could include placement with other family members (kinship care), foster care or adoption.

The Guidelines may be regarded as an instrument that does not impose binding obligations on the state. However, state governments are encouraged to provide better implementation of their responsibilities and obligations, with regard to the prevailing 'economic, social and cultural conditions'.[224] In other words, the Guidelines provide further protection to children's best interests and rights in the context of care proceedings and, potentially, non-consensual adoption proceedings as well, to ensure that removal of a child from the care of his or her birth family is 'a measure of last resort'.[225] This mirrors the wording used in domestic law proceedings to consider when a non-consensual adoption may or may not be a proportionate measure (see chapter 4 for further discussion).

In particular, the Guidelines are meant to 'support efforts to keep children in, or return them to, the care of their family or, failing this, to find another appropriate and permanent solution, including adoption and kafalah'.[226] The Guidelines further emphasise that permanent care solutions ought to be sought, where possible, and that 'the most suitable forms of alternative care are identified and provided, under conditions that promote the child's full and harmonious development'.[227]

Although the Guidelines apply to the UNCRC as a whole, there are specific rights that are referred to indirectly within the instrument. The Guidelines can be perceived, in particular, to emphasise the importance of the protection of

[222] Smith (n 220) 311.
[223] UN Guidelines for the Alternative Care of Children (n 79) para 1.
[224] ibid para 2.
[225] ibid para 14.
[226] ibid para 2.
[227] ibid para 2.

children's right to know and be cared for by their parents (Article 7 UNCRC), children's right not to be separated from their parents (protected under Article 9 UNCRC), children's right to be heard (Article 12 UNCRC), the right to special protection and help for children who cannot live with their families (Article 20 UNCRC) and the right to adoption (Article 21 UNCRC), all of which are important Convention rights for the purposes of this book.

IV. Conclusion

The purpose of this chapter has been to explain and analyse children's best interests and children's and parents' rights, and to show how they may be applied and argued in non-consensual adoption cases. In doing so, this chapter has served to lay down foundations for the discussion and analysis in subsequent chapters of the circumstances in which non-consensual adoption may be regarded as a proportionate measure. As considered in chapter 1 and in this chapter, the welfare (or best interests) of the child under section 52(1)(b) of the ACA 2002 determines whether or not a non-consensual adoption takes place. Therefore, it has been relevant to explain what is meant by the 'welfare principle', and the way in which it may be applied by the courts in England and Wales.

In the ECtHR, the application of the best interests principle (under Article 8(2)) may, in some cases, justify interference with parental rights to respect for private and family life under Article 8 ECHR. Thus this chapter has considered the best interests principle applied by the ECtHR and enshrined within the UNCRC (in Article 3). The best interests principle, which is recognised internationally, is similar to the welfare principle in England and Wales, and may justify the making of an adoption order without parental consent. This chapter has provided a detailed discussion and analysis of children's rights, in particular under the UNCRC. It has also referred to parental rights under the ECHR and the UNCRC.

The chapter has drawn several important conclusions about the relevance of the UNCRC. While the UNCRC is non-binding in the courts in England and Wales, and is considered intermittently by the English courts and the ECtHR in adoption matters, it has been argued that many UNCRC rights are relevant in non-consensual adoption cases (eg Articles 3, 5, 6, 7, 8, 9, 18, 19, 20 and 21). Article 20 UNCRC, for example, explicitly states that where possible, the least restrictive measures available to states to protect children from harm ought to be taken.

Furthermore, it is suggested that it is implied within Articles 5, 7, 8, 9 and 18 (as well as the UN Guidelines for the Alternative Care of Children) that the least restrictive measure available to the state must be taken so as to ensure that, where possible, families stay together. While it appears that Article 21 may permit non-consensual adoption solely on the basis of the child's welfare, a bare welfare test is not necessarily sufficient to justify non-consensual adoption. In fact, due to the indivisible and interdependent nature of the Convention, the interpretation of welfare must encompass consideration of other UNCRC rights.

Thus, state measures such as non-consensual adoption, which are chosen when alternatives are available, may not be in children's best interests under Article 3 UNCRC. Furthermore, in some cases non-consensual adoption may be regarded as a disproportionate measure in the light of these provisions of the UNCRC.

This chapter has provided an overview of children's best interests and children's parental rights, which may be relevant in non-consensual adoption cases, and has also considered the wider implications and potential influence of the UNCRC on non-consensual adoption. Having explained the main rights that arise in cases before the ECtHR, and having considered the approach the Court takes towards the best interests principle, the following chapter discusses how ECHR rights, the best interests principle and UNCRC rights have influenced the decision-making process of the ECtHR.

3

Adoption Cases in the European Court of Human Rights

I. Introduction: Last Port of Call and Last Portal of Hope?

The European Court of Human Rights (ECtHR) in Strasbourg is the last port of call for parties – typically birth parents – who seek to challenge adoption proceedings in England and Wales. This chapter outlines the legal rights birth parents and children have under the European Convention on Human Rights (ECHR)[1] to establish whether the Court's interpretation of these rights is sufficient, or if the scope of these rights ought to be widened. Second, this chapter considers the Court's assessment of alleged ECHR rights in adoption cases. In doing so, it considers the way in which the Court applies the proportionality principle. Third, this chapter will consider articles of the United Nations Convention on the Rights of the Child (UNCRC)[2] that would have been potentially relevant in these cases, as reference to the UNCRC is made only in a small number of judgments.[3] The chapter will address these issues via detailed discussion of Strasbourg case law and the legal principles which can be extrapolated from the Court's decisions.

The Court's role is not to act as a final court of appeal[4] and set aside adoption orders, but to assess whether or not the birth parents' rights have been violated either by the making of an adoption order itself,[5] or by an error with regard to the decision-making process leading up to the adoption.[6] In these cases, the birth parents may allege that the adoption itself was a disproportionate measure, or that measures taken prior to the adoption (such as the making of care orders or the removal of a child into care) violated their rights under Article 6 ECHR

[1] European Convention for the Protection of Human Rights and Fundamental Freedoms, as amended by Protocols nos 11 and 14, 4 November 1950 (European Convention on Human Rights (ECHR)), ETS 5, available at https://www.refworld.org/docid/3ae6b3b04.html.

[2] United Nations Convention on the Rights of the Child, 20 November 1989, 1577 UNTS 3, available at https://www.refworld.org/docid/3ae6b38f0.html.

[3] A Jacobsen, 'Children's Rights in the European Court of Human Rights – An Emerging Power Structure' (2016) 24 *International Journal of Children's Rights* 548, 556.

[4] *Malone v UK* (1984) 7 EHRR 14.

[5] *Aune v Norway* App no 52502/07 (ECHR, 28 October 2010).

[6] *P, C and S v UK* App no 56547/00 (ECHR, 16 July 2002).

(the right to a fair hearing) and/or Article 8 ECHR (the right to respect for private and family life).

This chapter considers the articles identified above, which are argued routinely in non-consensual adoption cases. This discussion also provides a brief analysis of areas for possible development in Strasbourg case law in the context of adoption proceedings. This includes the potential relevance of children's rights under Article 2 ECHR (the right to life) and Article 3 ECHR (the right to freedom from torture or inhuman or degrading treatment), and how these rights may be balanced against other rights children and their parents may claim under Articles 6 and 8 of the Convention. Articles 2 and 3 are not currently discussed and applied by the domestic courts and the ECtHR in cases where children have been separated from their parents and have been subject to non-consensual adoption, even though it would be relevant and appropriate for the courts to do so. Although the Court is not bound to consider arguments put before it, this chapter looks at how examining children's rights could enrich existing Strasbourg jurisprudence generally and, in particular, in adoption cases.

An examination of these different ECHR rights and how they have been and may be applied to adoption by the ECtHR and by courts and policy-makers in England and Wales, will provide a way of evaluating the proportionality of non-consensual adoption.

II. The Protection of Children: The ECHR, the UNCRC and Proportionality

A. Article 2: Right to Life

> Everyone's right to life shall be protected by law. No one shall be deprived of his life intentionally save in the execution of a sentence of a court following his conviction of a crime for which this penalty is provided by law.

Article 2 ECHR is a relevant consideration in non-consensual adoption cases, since adoption typically serves the purpose of protecting the child from harm and may also protect the child from risks to his or her life. Article 2 comprises both positive and negative obligations. The state has a positive obligation to protect life[7] and a negative obligation to refrain from taking life. Implicit in Article 2 is a positive obligation on the part of the state to protect children from significant harm.

It is useful to consider some factual circumstances in which Article 2 has been argued to demonstrate that a failure to provide adequate resources to sustain

[7] *Dink v Turkey* App no 2668/07 (ECHR, 14 September 2010); *Paul and Audrey Edwards v UK* App no 46477/99 (ECHR, 14 March 2002); *Centre for Legal Resources on Behalf of Valentin Câmpeanu v Romania* App no 47848/08 (ECHR, 17 July 2014).

the lives of children may constitute a breach of Article 2. Thus, for instance, in *Nencheva and others v Bulgaria*,[8] 15 children and young adults living in a state institution died because of a shortage of food, medicine and other basic necessities, as well as from the effects of the cold. The ECtHR held that Article 2 ECHR had been violated because the state had failed in its positive obligation to protect vulnerable children from a serious and immediate threat. States have a positive obligation to be proactive and to intervene to protect the lives of children by taking measures of investigation and/or protection.

In *Kontrova v Slovakia*,[9] the police's response to reports of domestic violence was held to be inadequate as it had resulted in the death of the female victim and her children, at the hands of her husband. The ECtHR held that the Slovakian authorities were in breach of their positive obligation under Article 2 as the deaths were a direct consequence of police failings. Thus, to meet its positive obligation to act to protect children's lives, the state will sometimes have a duty to intervene in cases where children are experiencing severe neglect or abuse – whether it be at the hands of the state (such as in the care of an institution) and/or at the hands of a family member (such as a parent). It is possible that a state's failure to intervene when children are at risk at the hands of specific individuals[10] (including their parents) could give rise to an arguable case under Article 2 if the child's death was foreseeable,[11] and if the authorities knew or ought to have known of the existence of a real and immediate risk to the life of an identified individual and did not do all that could be reasonably expected of them to avoid that risk.[12]

The difficulty is in establishing what might be reasonable to expect of authorities, and in ensuring that state intervention is necessary and proportionate to protect the child's life. It is probable that such an assessment would depend on the specific facts of each case, as in many cases harm to the child might be foreseeable but death might not. It is clear, however, that an obligation under Article 2 ECHR could apply to authorities such as social services, the police and potentially even medical professionals. These authorities must also consider other Convention rights that may seem to run counter to Article 2.

When children have been removed into care, for instance, the ECtHR has commented that there is an obligation under Article 8 ECHR to reunite these children with their parents where this is possible.[13] However, in cases of severe neglect and/or abuse, where a child's life is endangered, returning the child to his or her birth parents would be unthinkable. Such a step would potentially threaten the child's right to life under Article 2 of the Convention, since in the most serious of cases a child who is returned to an abusive parent (or parents) could

[8] *Nencheva and others v Bulgaria* App no 48609/06 (ECHR, 18 June 2013).
[9] *Kontrova v Slovakia* App no 7510/04 (ECHR, 31 May 2007).
[10] *Osman v. United Kingdom* (1999) 29 EHRR 245.
[11] The difficulty is that there must be an interested party able to proceed with the cases. However, in practice, there may be no one who is willing or able to bring a case on behalf of the deceased child.
[12] *Osman v United Kingdom* (1999) 29 EHRR 245.
[13] *Hokkanen v Finland* [1996] 1 FLR 289, para 55.

be killed. This occurred in the Ellie Butler case,[14] where a child was released back into the care of her father, Ben Butler,[15] who was exonerated of the charges he had faced for causing injuries to his daughter. This was despite the father's numerous convictions for violent offences. Despite a Serious Care Review acknowledging the mistakes made by professionals, Ellie's grandparents plan to take the case further. Here, it can be argued that the return of Ellie into the care of her father amounted to a violation of her rights under Article 2 ECHR and under Article 6 UNCRC (the right to life) and Article 19 UNCRC (protection from mental and/or physical violence).

If it is decided that a child should not be reunited with his or her parents because of the risk of the child's suffering from life-threatening neglect and/or abuse, adoption may be in the child's best interests under Article 3 UNCRC. In other words, as Sloan has argued, for some children, adoption could be a way of protecting a child's right to life and be part of the state's obligation to ensure the child's optimal development.[16] Thus, the violation of the birth parents' right to respect for private and family life under Article 8 ECHR may be trumped by the child's Article 2 ECHR right in life-threatening cases of neglect and/or abuse. There may be cases where children's lives may not be endangered but they may still have suffered from (or be likely to suffer from) parental neglect or abuse that will harm the child physically and/or emotionally. In such cases, then, any rights-based arguments in favour of adoption would instead stem from Articles 3 and 8 ECHR (considered in section II.B and section IV.A respectively). Ultimately, even a positive obligation flowing from Article 3 should be 'interpreted in a way which does not impose an impossible or disproportionate burden on the authorities'.[17]

B. Article 3: Right to Freedom from Torture or Inhuman or Degrading Treatment or Punishment

> No one shall be subjected to torture or to inhuman or degrading treatment or punishment.

Many non-consensual adoptions in England and Wales take place after children have been removed into care because they were neglected and/or abused by their parents. Such removal may be appropriate and necessary to protect children's Article 3 ECHR rights, making it important to assess the relevance of Article 3 to the question of the proportionality of adoption.[18] Under Article 3, there is an

[14] Sutton Local Safeguarding Children Board, *Child D: A Serious Case Review Overview Report* (Sutton LSCB, 2016).

[15] *London Borough of Sutton v Gray and Others* [2016] EWHC 1608 (Fam).

[16] B Sloan, 'Conflicting Rights: English Adoption Law and the Implementation of the UN Convention on the Rights of the Child' (2013) 25 *Child and Family Law Quarterly* 40.

[17] *Osman v United Kingdom* (1999) 29 EHRR 245.

[18] Note that Art 37(a) UNCRC is similar in scope to Art 3 ECHR and states that '[n]o child shall be subjected to torture or other cruel, inhuman or degrading treatment or punishment'.

absolute right to freedom from torture or inhuman or degrading treatment. Case law of the Strasbourg Court on Article 3 has emphasised the state's duty to intervene to protect children from abuse or neglect at the hands of their parents.[19] This can be seen, for example, in *Z and Others v UK*,[20] where a local authority failed to intervene early enough to protect four children from severe neglect and abuse. The local authority had known about the serious neglect and ill-treatment for five years but, despite having the means to do so, had failed to take any effective steps to bring the children's distress to an end. The social workers were reluctant to intervene because they had not established that physical abuse had occurred but only what they regarded as 'neglectful parenting'.[21]

The children brought a case against the UK, alleging that the state's failure to intervene to protect them had violated their Article 3 rights. The ECtHR found that the children had suffered from emotional and physical abuse and neglect, and that the harm the children suffered had reached the level of severity prohibited under Article 3 ECHR. The Court stated that 'the severity of the damage suffered by the children is inextricably linked to the long period of time over which the abuse persisted'.[22] The Court held that the state had a positive obligation under Article 3 to protect the children from being harmed by their parents. The state had not satisfied its obligation through its failure to intervene sooner, and consequently the ECtHR held that the children's Article 3 right to freedom from torture or inhuman or degrading treatment had been violated.

As the above case shows, neglect and/or abuse or risk of abuse may justify removing children into the care of the state, even though this will amount to an interference with the parents' Article 8 right. In some cases, non-consensual adoption may be a necessary and proportionate measure to prevent further abuse and further potential violations of Article 3 ECHR. In particular, adoption may serve to protect the Article 3 rights of children who have been abused by their parents and who risk further abuse if they are returned to their parents or maintain relationships with them. Thus, adoption may sometimes be the most effective measure to protect children's Article 3 right and rights under the UNCRC, including, but not limited to, Article 19 of the UNCRC (protection from physical or mental violence). Therefore, in some cases, adoption without parental consent may be a necessary and proportionate measure that protects children from further needless distress, which may be caused by further attempts to reunite children with their birth parents or by attempting measures other than non-consensual adoption.

[19] U Kilkelly, 'Protecting children's rights under the ECHR: the role of positive obligations' (2011) 61 *Northern Ireland Legal Quarterly* 245, 248. This is borne out by case law such as *A v UK* App no 29392/95 (ECHR, 10 May 2001); *Z v UK* App no 29392/95 (ECHR,10 May 2001); *O'Keeffe v Ireland* App no 35810/09 (ECHR, 28 January 2014).

[20] *Z v UK* (n 19).

[21] ibid para 14.

[22] *Z and Others v UK* [2001] 2 FLR 612, para 121.

Clearly, the state has a positive obligation to act to protect children from harm, as demonstrated by *Z and Others v UK*. However, there may be cases where the harm is less severe. In such circumstances, the threshold under Article 3 ECHR will not be satisfied and the harm may instead be considered within the scope of Article 8. Alternatively, there may be cases where even though the threshold under Article 3 may be satisfied and it is necessary and proportionate to remove children from the care of their parents, such children have the potential to be able to benefit from relationships with their parents. In cases where children have been subjected to neglect and/or abuse, not all of them will be harmed by maintaining relationships with their parents, or even, in some circumstances, being reunited. It depends on the facts in individual cases (as shown throughout this book).

Alternatively, in some cases, parental circumstances may change so significantly as to make it arguable that it is appropriate for children to be returned to their parents (see section V). In other cases, it may be desirable to seek a less restrictive measure that may be just as effective as adoption (such as kinship care or special guardianship – see chapter 5). As demonstrated in chapter 2, Article 7 UNCRC (the right to know and be cared for by one's parents), Article 8 UNCRC (the right to preservation of one's identity, which includes family relations) and Article 9 UNCRC (the right not to be separated from one's parents unless it is necessary) are rights that could be argued on the child's behalf, against non-consensual adoption.

However, it can be a challenge to ensure that the appropriate balance is achieved in protecting children's rights under Article 3 ECHR on the one hand and children's rights to respect for private and family life under Article 8 ECHR and under Articles 7, 8 and 9 of the UNCRC, on the other. At one end of the spectrum, state intervention, whereby a child is removed from his or her family home, may be a necessary and proportionate measure that protects a child from experiencing further neglect or abuse, thereby protecting his or her rights under Article 3.[23] However, at the other end of the spectrum, taking a child into care may, in some cases, be a disproportionate measure that violates both the rights of the child under Article 3 and/or Article 8 and his or her parents' right to respect for private and family life under Article 8.[24] To date, Article 3 has not been considered by the ECtHR in adoption proceedings. However, Article 3 has been argued by the state as a justification for intervening in family life (which potentially violates Article 8 ECHR).

This can be seen in *P, C and S v UK*,[25] where a newborn baby (S) was removed into care because she was determined by the High Court in England to be at risk of significant harm, and was placed for adoption without parental consent. Here, the UK Government argued Article 3 ECHR in its defence.[26] In fact, if the state

[23] *In the Matter of J (Children)* [2013] UKSC 9 [1], *per* Lady Hale.
[24] *Haase v Germany* App no 11057/02 (ECHR, 8 April 2004).
[25] *P, C and S v UK* (2002) 35 EHRR 31.
[26] ibid para 108.

had not taken sufficient precautions to protect S, and if S had been subjected to significant harm by her mother in the future, she could have argued the existence of an Article 3 violation. The UK Government argued that the state had a positive obligation to intervene to protect a newborn child from harm, and risked falling foul of Article 3 if it did not do so. This is a right of S, which is distinct from the rights and interests of the parents. An important question, however, would be whether removal of S at birth, preventing contact between S and her parents, and S's adoption were necessary and proportionate measures to protect her right under Article 3 of the Convention. It is at least arguable that S could have been protected from harm and that the state could have discharged its positive obligation via less restrictive measures, such as state assistance, a supervision order or even open adoption.[27]

Article 3 may have further relevance in non-consensual adoption cases. It could be relevant in cases where children face trauma due to being taken into care and/or due to the experience of the adoption process itself. Although parental distress and humiliation, which may occur when a child is taken into care, will not cross the necessary threshold for an Article 3 obligation to arise,[28] it is arguable that such distress and humiliation in the context of adoption cases might engage children's and parents' rights under Article 3 ECHR. Thus, if parents and/or their children suffer physical or emotional harm due to the children's being taken into care and subsequently placed for adoption without parental consent, this may satisfy the threshold required to engage Article 3, since the ECtHR has recognised that severe mental distress can reach a threshold that satisfies the provision.[29] Alternatively, in cases where the threshold under Article 3 is not satisfied, parents and children can argue potential violations of their right to private life under Article 8 ECHR, as well as of their right to family life.

Article 3 could also be argued by children who have been abused in care (or by adoptive parents) when it would have been possible to reunite the children with their parents or to place them with birth relatives. Such an argument has been successful before the Court of Appeal in England and Wales,[30] and it could be raised before the ECtHR. Although neglect and/or abuse which is severe enough to engage Article 3 may be a very persuasive factor in favour of adoption, in cases where non-consensual adoption has the potential to be traumatic for a child and potentially violate the child's Article 3 right, a less restrictive alternative to adoption ought to be found. This is argued, for example, in respect of *YC v UK*[31] (see chapter 6, section II), where a young boy was removed from his mother and placed for adoption, despite the fact that the mother had not directly harmed her son and there was evidence of a strong bond between mother and son.

[27] See section III for further discussion of *P, C and S v UK* App no 56547/00 (n 6) and chapter 5 for further discussion of less restrictive alternatives to non-consensual adoption.

[28] *MAK v UK* App no 45901/05 [2010] 2 FLR 451 (ECHR).

[29] *Kurt v Turkey* App no 24276/94 (ECHR, 25 May 1998).

[30] *A and S v Lancashire County Council* [2012] EWHC 1689 (Fam).

[31] *YC v UK* App no 4547/10 (ECHR, 13 March 2012).

III. Procedural Protection of Rights in Adoption Proceedings

A. The Relationship between Article 6(1) and Article 8

Birth parents have argued, in some cases, that the procedures for the care proceedings and/or the adoption proceedings have violated their rights under Article 6(1) ECHR and/or Article 8 ECHR. This section first discusses the relevance of Article 6(1), which provides:

> In the determination of his civil rights and obligations … everyone is entitled to a fair and public hearing within a reasonable time by an independent and impartial tribunal established by law …

Before considering how Article 8 of the Convention can also provide procedural protection to parents' (and potentially children's) rights in adoption cases, this section discusses the protection that these rights provide for children and parents.

Under Article 6(1) ECHR, children's and parents' rights to a fair hearing must be protected, and this includes protection in adoption cases. There are four different procedural rights in Article 6(1): a right to a court,[32] a right to be heard by an independent and impartial tribunal established by law,[33] a right to have fairness in the court process[34] and a right for the hearing to take place within a

[32] The first express right concerns whether there has been access to court and whether or not there is legal certainty. Lack of access to court is where the applicant complains that he or she was unable to submit a claim to a court to examine the facts and law relevant to his or her case. This principle was first recognised in *Golder v UK* App no 4451/70 (ECHR, 21 February 1975), where the Court acknowledged that right to a fair hearing was meaningless without the means to gain access to a court.

[33] In terms of an independent and impartial tribunal established by law, the qualities of independence and impartiality are distinct characteristics. A tribunal established by law is one that has the powers to consider matters within its competence and the power to make binding decisions. See *Belilios v Switzerland* (1988) Series A, no 132 (ECHR); *Sramek v Austria* (1985) 7 EHRR 351. The body should be established and regulated by law and the scope of discretion should be specified by law. See *Lavents v Latvia* App no 58442/00 (ECHR, 28 November 2002); *Posokhov v Russia* (2004) 39 EHRR 21. Independence typically refers to independence of both the parties in the case and the executive, while impartiality involves considering subjectively whether the members of the tribunal are free of personal bias. See *Belukha v Ukraine* App no 33949/02 (ECHR, 9 November 2006). Also, whether objectively there was sufficient appearance of impartiality and whether justice was seen to be done. See *Piersack v Belgium* App no 8692/79 (ECHR, 1 October 1982).

[34] Fairness in the court process is regarded as covering the legal proceedings as a whole. It includes the right to observe and comment upon evidence produced by the other party. The nature of the evidence and the way in which it was taken are also relevant considerations for the court. Inherent within the principle of fairness in the court proceedings is the notion of procedural equality or 'equality of arms'. Fairness also encompasses the right to a public hearing, which means that the party should be present in court and able to participate in proceedings, to do so in public and for judgments to be made public. In terms of fairness, Art 6 ECHR is concerned with ensuring that the court process as a whole is fair, and not with factual findings. This is why in some adoption cases, even though an appeal judge might disagree with the final outcome of the adoption process, the adoption order will be regarded as valid.

reasonable time.[35] Jurisprudence of the ECtHR has established many procedural protections that are relevant to parents in adoption proceedings. There must be fair and effective access to the court and decision-making must be transparent, with parents being informed of evidence against them in the proceedings.[36] Parents have the right to an oral hearing,[37] they must be included in the decision-making process, they have the right to legal representation[38] and the decisions must be free from bias.[39]

Since the late 1980s, the ECtHR has developed a procedural aspect to Article 8 that focuses on protecting the substantive rights encapsulated in the article (the right to respect for private and family life). This was articulated in *W v UK*,[40] where the ECtHR stated that 'the Court is entitled to have regard to that process by which it has been decided that an adoption order should be made, to determine whether it has been conducted in a manner that, in all the circumstances, is fair and affords due respect to the interests protected by Article 8'.[41]

W v UK has created procedural safeguards for parents whose children are removed from them by the state,[42] and the protection under Article 8(1), in this case, bears similarities to that under Article 6(1). This procedural component of Article 8 ECHR has received further elaboration in subsequent cases, such as in *McMichael v UK*[43] (on the need to release official documents to parents) and *TP and KM v UK*[44] (on the need for local authorities to disclose information to parents and involve them in the decision-making process).

In *X v Croatia*,[45] the Court emphasised that the applicant, a mother excluded from adoption proceedings due to lack of capacity, should have had the opportunity to be heard. This exclusion from the proceedings leading up to the adoption amounted to a violation of Article 8 ECHR. Article 8 not only offers substantive protection of the right to respect for private and family life, but may in some cases offer procedural safeguards for those substantive rights. This can be seen in *P, C and S v UK*, where the applicants' lack of legal representation and the short period of time between the care and adoption hearings meant that the parents were unable to be involved in the decision-making process. This was held to be a breach of the parents' rights under Article 8 ECHR because there

[35] The hearing must also take place within a reasonable timeframe to satisfy the requirements of Art 6(1). In determining what will be 'reasonable', this will depend on the facts of the case and the nature of the proceedings.

[36] *Buchberger v Austria* [2001] ECHR 873.

[37] *L v Finland* [2000] 2 FLR 118.

[38] *P, C and S v UK* App no 56547/00 (n 6).

[39] *Buscami v Italy* [1999] ECHR 70.

[40] *W v UK* (1987) 10 EHRR 29.

[41] ibid para 62.

[42] Mowbray expresses his approval of this development. See A Mowbray, *The Development of Positive Obligations under the European Convention on Human Rights by the European Court of Human Rights* (Portland, OR, Hart Publishing, 2004) 156.

[43] *McMichael v UK* (1995) Series A no 307-B (ECHR).

[44] *McMichael v UK* A.307-B (1995) [2001] 2 FLR 549.

[45] *X v Croatia* App no 11223/04 (ECHR, 17 July 2008).

had been insufficient procedural protection of their right to respect for private and family life.[46]

B. The Relationship between Article 6(1) and Article 8: *P, C and S v UK*

In *P, C and S v UK*,[47] an important case concerning the procedural protection of family life, the applicant's child (S) was taken into care and placed for adoption without the mother's consent. In the UK, P (the mother) had to bring her own case on behalf of herself, her husband and daughter, before the English court without legal representation. When P's legal representatives withdrew from her case, she requested an adjournment to find new counsel, but this was denied by the court. She was given a brief adjournment of four days and the High Court indicated that she would need to conduct her own case. P went ahead with the case with the assistance of a 'McKenzie Friend'.[48] The court held it was not in S's best interests to be returned to her parents because of the risk of harm, and freed S for adoption.

The ECtHR held that there were violations of Articles 6 and 8 ECHR. Article 6(1) was engaged because obtaining advice from a lawyer relates to the right of access to a court. The Court emphasised that the need for permanence did not justify the 'draconian' action of conducting complex care proceedings followed by an order freeing S for adoption just one week later. The ECtHR criticised the English court's approach, describing it as a 'somewhat inflexible and blanket approach, applied without particular consideration of the facts of this individual case'.[49] The Court also observed that despite being freed for adoption, it was five-and-a-half months later that S was placed with a family. The final adoption order was then made another six months after S's placement. Thus, the procedures used had been unfair and did not enable the applicants to participate in the decision-making process in an effective manner. The Court concluded that the applicant had not had fair and effective access to court, and there had been an Article 6(1) breach of her right and the right of her child.[50]

The ECtHR took what Hewson et al have described as an 'unusual'[51] step, by allowing the parents to argue on the child's behalf. In fact, most cases concerning the separation of parent and child tend to be brought by the parents in respect of violations of their own rights. It has been described as 'striking'[52] by Hewson et al that the ECtHR stated that the child's Article 6 and 8 rights had been violated

[46] See discussion in *P, C and S v UK* App no 56547/00 (n 6) paras 134–38.
[47] ibid.
[48] This is the name of a non-lawyer who acts as a representative in court; it may be someone with some basic knowledge of the law and court proceedings.
[49] *P, C and S v UK* App no 56547/00 (n 6) para 98.
[50] ibid para 100.
[51] B Hewson, D Casey and N Mole, 'The Appearance of Fairness' (2002) 152 *NLJ* 1245.
[52] ibid.

due to the fact that her parents were not legally represented, despite the fact that S herself was legally represented throughout the proceedings. However, the ECtHR's reasoning demonstrates how it can sometimes be difficult to separate the rights of the parents from those of the child.

Although there was no direct violation of S's right, it would have been difficult for S to maintain a legal tie with her parents and to have her Article 8 rights protected if her parents had not had adequate legal representation in the process of care and adoption proceedings. For S to obtain the best possible chance of having a relationship with her parents and having her Article 8 right protected, it would therefore be necessary for her parents to have proper legal representation (for further detail, see section IV).

This section has considered the procedural protection that may be provided to birth parents and children in non-consensual adoption cases. The following section considers how substantive rights may be protected under Article 8 ECHR.

IV. Proportionate Protection of Substantive Rights in Care and Adoption Proceedings

A. Article 8 Right to Respect for Private and Family Life: Overview

The discussion following will provide an overview of whose rights are protected by Article 8 ECHR, and in what circumstances these rights will be protected. In particular, it will consider cases where Article 8 has been argued in care and adoption proceedings. Although different issues may be raised in care proceedings when compared with adoption proceedings, the focus of this chapter is on whether the initial removal was a justified interference with parents' Article 8 rights, and whether children's continued presence in care is a necessary and proportionate interference with parents' Article 8 rights.

Typically, care proceedings precede the making of adoption orders without parental consent, and (as seen from *P, C and S v UK*[53]) arguments raised in Article 8 cases, alleging that non-consensual adoption is not a proportionate measure, may require a consideration of whether the particular state intervention was a necessary and proportionate measure. Furthermore, both care and adoption proceedings cases raise issues concerning if and when children ought to be reunited with their parents, and if and when it is appropriate for children to have contact with their parents.

Article 8 ECHR states:

> (1) Everyone has the right to respect for his private and family life, his home and his correspondence.

[53] *P, C and S v UK* (2002) 35 EHRR 31.

(2) There shall be no interference by a public authority with the exercise of this right except such as is in accordance with the law and is necessary in a democratic society in the interests of national security, public safety or the economic well-being of the country, for the prevention of disorder or crime, for the protection of health or morals, or for the protection of the rights and freedoms of others.

Article 8 is not an absolute right but a 'qualified' right. Article 8(2) provides that in specified circumstances it may be justifiable and proportionate for a State to interfere with individual rights and thus impose limits on them. Under Article 8(2), the Court performs an analysis to determine whether a rights violation is necessary and proportionate. An adoption order that amounts to an interference with the parents' rights under Article 8(1) may be justified under Article 8(2) by reference to the child's best interests. For instance, in an adoption case, the family court may decide that the child has suffered such terrible abuse that he or she should be placed for adoption without parental consent.

Article 8 is argued frequently in non-consensual adoption cases in relation either to the adoption itself, or to measures that preceded the adoption, such as the removal of a child into care or a reduction in or termination of contact. It is in the context of Article 8 where issues of proportionality typically arise. This chapter will consider when Article 8 may be argued, and when interference with this right may constitute a necessary and proportionate measure from the ECtHR's perspective. Although the state has a negative obligation not to unnecessarily intervene in family life, it has a positive obligation towards the child to intervene to prevent neglect or abuse. According to the ECtHR, there must be pressing reasons for the interference with family ties,[54] and intervention must be necessary in a democratic society and proportionate to the legitimate aim of child protection. This means that the state must strike a fair balance between the interest of protecting children on the one hand and protecting family life on the other.[55] Any state intervention that takes place should protect the child's best interests and be proportionate. The discussion in the next section will consider the content of Article 8(1) and the process whereby rights argued by parents and/or other individuals may be limited by reference to Article 8(2).

B. Article 8 Right to Respect for Private and Family Life: Interpretation and Definition

Respect for a private and family life means that the state is duty-bound to take positive steps to protect these rights.[56] Under 'family life' a range of different relationships are protected.[57] This includes relationships between children

[54] *X & Y v Germany* App no 8059/77 (3 October 1978).

[55] *Neulinger and Shuruk v Switzerland* App no 41615/07 (6 July 2010).

[56] *Sheffield and Horsham v United Kingdom* (1999) 27 EHRR 163.

[57] See, eg, *Johnston v Ireland* App no 9697/82 (1987) 9 EHRR 203; and *X, Y and Z v United Kingdom* App no 21830/93 (1997) 24 EHRR 143.

and birth parents[58] and other 'de facto "family ties" where sufficient constancy is present'.[59] The jurisprudence of the ECtHR emphasises the importance of the 'reality' of family life rather than the strict legal and/or biological relationships that exist between parties, and therefore foster parents,[60] adoptive parents[61] and prospective adoptive parents who have developed a relationship with a child can also fall within the scope of family life.[62] The ECtHR has, in some cases, also protected the relationship between children and other family members, including siblings,[63] aunts and uncles,[64] and grandparents.[65]

Private life is a broad concept that refers to 'aspects of an individual's physical and social identity',[66] 'personal development'[67] and 'the right to establish relationships with other human beings'.[68] This means that in adoption cases, where fathers find themselves unable to establish the right to 'family life' with their children, it may nonetheless be possible to argue instead that there is a right to a 'private life'.[69] The right to a private life is important for the child too, as it covers the extent to which an adoption order can impact on the child's own social and personal identity, since the child[70] will join another family and may have his or her surname and even forename changed.

The right to respect for private and family life protects a person's physical and psychological well-being.[71] A sound mental state is also included within the scope of 'private life'.[72] It has been held by the ECtHR that measures that affect an individual's physical integrity or mental health must reach a certain degree of severity to amount to an interference with the right to private life.[73] However, even minor interferences that are against a person's will may fall within the scope of Article 8 ECHR.[74] In evaluating physical integrity within Article 8, there is overlap with Article 3. The distinction between the two seems to be related to

[58] *Hokkanen v Finland* (n 13).

[59] *Mikulić v Croatia* (2002) 11 BHRC 689, para 51; and *Kroon v Netherlands* App no 18535/91 (ECHR, 27 October 1994) para 30.

[60] *X v Switzerland* App no 8257/78 (EComHR, 10 July 1978); *Moretti and Benedetti v Italy* App no 16318/07 (ECHR, 27 April 2010); *Kopf and Liberda v Austria* App no 1598/06 (ECHR, 17 January 2012).

[61] *Ageyevy v Russia* App no 7055/10 [2013] ECHR 122.

[62] *Harroudj v France* App no 43631/09 (ECHR, 4 October 2012).

[63] *Boughanemi v France* (1996) 22 EHRR 228; and *Moustaquim v Belgium* (1991) 13 EHRR 802.

[64] *Boyle v United Kingdom* App no 16580/90 (1995) 19 EHRR 179.

[65] *L v Finland* App no 25651/94 (2001) 31 EHRR 30; *Beccarini and Ridolfi v Italy* App no 63190/16 (ECHR, 7 December 2017).

[66] Including various aspects of one's sexual life and sexual orientation – see *Dudgeon v UK* App no 7525/76 (ECHR, 22 October 1981); and *EB v France* App no 43546/02 (ECHR, 22 January 2008).

[67] *X v Iceland* App no 6825/74 [1976] 5 DR 86.

[68] *Mikulić v Croatia* (n 59) para 53.

[69] *Anayo v Germany* App no 20578/07 (ECHR, 21 December 2010).

[70] *Odièvre v France* App no 42326/98 (ECHR, 13 February 2003) para 29.

[71] *X and Y v The Netherlands* (1985) 8 EHRR 235; *Glass v UK* App no 61827/00 (ECHR, 9 March 2004).

[72] *Bensaid v UK* App no 44599/98 (ECHR, 6 February 2001) para 47.

[73] ibid, para 46.

[74] *Storck v Germany* App no 61603/00 (ECHR, 16 June 2005) para 143.

the severity of the interference. Therefore, even where the alleged child abuse or neglect may not be grave enough to reach the threshold required to engage Article 3, it may nevertheless come under Article 8. For example, Article 8 may be engaged where a child is not washed, sleeps in soiled sheets, is not appropriately dressed or receives inadequate nourishment, as such treatment interferes with the child's right to respect for his or her physical integrity.[75]

Usually, the birth mother will have a right to family life engaged in relation to her child, regardless of whether she has ever raised the child.[76] In *X v Croatia*,[77] the applicant suffered from schizophrenia and gave birth to a daughter. She was divested of her legal capacity because of her mental illness. It was found that she would be unable to care for the child because of this illness and her drug addiction, neither of which had showed signs of improvement. She agreed to being placed under guardianship, regarding it as in her own best interests and those of her child. The legal consequence of being divested of capacity was that she was deprived of her parental rights. A decision was made that the child should be placed in foster care and that the applicant needed a carer. Although the applicant was deemed to be unfit to care for her child, contact was arranged between them by the national authorities. Proceedings for adoption were commenced without the applicant's knowledge. Under Croatian law, as she had been divested of her capacity, she was not a party to the adoption proceedings and the authorities had no obligation to inform her about the adoption.

The applicant alleged a violation of Article 8 ECHR because her daughter had been placed for adoption without her knowledge, consent or participation in the adoption proceedings. There were no domestic remedies available to her under Croatian law, because the law was such that once she was regarded as lacking mental capacity, her acts were incapable of producing legal effects. The Croatian Government argued that Article 8 did not apply because the relationship between mother and daughter had deteriorated to such a level that it no longer represented family life, and that a blood relationship was insufficient for this. The ECtHR disagreed and held that, under Article 8, the applicant had the right to family life with her daughter, because the applicant had lived with her child after the birth and visited her until contact was stopped. This case shows that the right to a family life under Article 8 is not lost due to removal of a child into care or a parent's lack of mental capacity.

The ECtHR has been inconsistent in its approach towards unmarried fathers. The Court has stated previously that a biological relationship between a father and child is insufficient to establish the existence of family life.[78] However, the Court will often recognise the existence of a right to private life even where it is reluctant

[75] *X and Y v Netherlands* (n 71).
[76] *P, C and S v UK* App no 56547/00 (n 6).
[77] *X v Croatia* (n 45).
[78] *Lebbink v The Netherlands* (2004) 40 EHRR 417; *M v The Netherlands* (1993) 74 DR 120.

to acknowledge a right to family life.[79] This can be seen in *Anayo v Germany*,[80] where the applicant had fathered twins with a married woman, who had raised the children with her husband but had not allowed the applicant to have contact with them. The Court held that it could not 'exclude' the possibility of a family tie, since it was not the applicant's fault that he did not have a relationship with the twins. However, it focused primarily on the applicant's right to a private life, observing that having contact with his children still formed an important part of the applicant's identity and, thus, his right to a private life.

In other cases, the Court has been prepared to recognise the existence of family life between an unmarried father and his child. For instance, in *Keegan v Ireland*,[81] the claimant was an unmarried father whose child was placed for adoption without his knowledge or consent. The Court held that, under Article 8 ECHR, family life could be established between a father and child even where he was not married to the mother and was no longer in a cohabiting relationship with the mother at the time of the child's birth. The Court held that the father's Article 8 right was engaged, and that Irish law enabling the adoption to take place in secret amounted to an interference with his Article 8 rights.

As considered in the paragraph above, in family proceedings including adoption proceedings, fathers will be able to argue that their right to a 'family' or 'private' life is engaged under Article 8. Similarly, in cases where a mother has not raised her child, it is likely that she will be able to argue that a right to a private life has been engaged, even if the right to a family life is not applicable. In *IS v Germany*,[82] for example, the mother argued that her right to 'family life' was engaged when she sought contact with and information about her children who were placed for adoption. The Court held that although she had previously had a 'family life' with her children, the act of voluntarily giving up her newborn children meant that family life had ceased and that a claim under the right to 'private life' was more appropriate.

These cases are important because they demonstrate that birth parents can argue that non-consensual adoption may violate their Article 8 right, regardless of whether they have managed to establish a relationship with their child. This means that in cases where children are removed from their parents immediately after birth, the birth parents can nonetheless assert rights under Article 8.

C. State Intervention to Assist Families: Article 8 ECHR

It can be argued that in some cases, the state may have a positive obligation under Article 8 ECHR to provide assistance to families before placing a child for adoption.

[79] *Mikulić v Croatia* (n 59); and *DO v Switzerland* App no 24545/94 (EComHR, 31 August 1994).
[80] *Anayo v Germany* (n 69).
[81] *Keegan v Ireland* (1994) 18 EHRR 342.
[82] *IS v Germany* App no 31021/08 (ECHR, 5 June 2014).

This is, it is argued, emphasised throughout the UNCRC and the UN Guidelines for the Alternative Care of Children (considered in chapter 2).[83] Although neither of these is binding on the state, they are influential international documents that emphasise the importance of keeping children and parents together, where it is possible to do so. In cases where children are at risk of harm but have not been harmed by their parents, it is arguable that with appropriate practical and/or financial assistance from the state, some children could remain with their parents. In other words, the availability and provision of measures less restrictive than adoption may be equally effective and less likely to violate the Article 8 rights of children and their parents.

There are cases that suggest that there may be a positive obligation under Article 8 ECHR to provide practical and/or financial assistance to help children and parents stay together. One such case is *Wallova and Walla v Czech Republic*.[84] There, the parents were unemployed; and as the state authorities regarded their housing as being unsuitable, they put in place a supervision order so as to encourage the parents to find suitable housing. When the parents failed to do so, their children were taken into care. The parents alleged violations of Article 8 because they had been separated from their five children and because the state had failed to assist them. The Court held that the separation had been caused by difficulties the authorities could have addressed in another way, which would have avoided having to split up the family. The Court suggested alternatives (such as monitoring the applicants' living and hygiene conditions, and providing advice) the state had failed to consider.

The Court found that although the reasons provided by the state were relevant to intervention, these reasons had been insufficient to justify the removal of the children into care. Accordingly, it held that there had been a violation of the applicants' Article 8 rights. Potentially, this case could be used to support the notion of a wider positive obligation under Article 8 to keep families together,[85] particularly when Article 8 and this case are considered in conjunction with Articles 7–9 UNCRC. These provisions emphasise the importance of children's relationships with their parents and their identity.

It is argued that Article 8 ECHR should be interpreted more expansively so as to protect children's and parents' rights to continue to live together, or at least to be able to maintain relationships with one another. As considered in section II in the context of Article 2 (the right to life) and Article 3 (the right to freedom from torture or inhuman or degrading treatment), the state has a positive obligation to intervene to safeguard life and to protect children from harm. However, the scope of the positive obligation under Article 8 to help

[83] UN General Assembly, Resolution 64/142 of 24 February 2010 (reissued 13 April 2010), Guidelines for the Alternative Care of Children 2010.

[84] *Wallova and Walla v Czech Republic* App no 23848/04 (ECHR, 26 October 2006).

[85] *Redefining and Combating Poverty: Human Rights, democracy and common goods in today's Europe* (Strasbourg, Council of Europe Publishing, 2012) 137.

keep birth families together remains unclear.[86] What is clear, however, is that there are often social problems that lie behind the need for state intervention in the first place. These problems are acute in the UK, where, according to the Special Rapporteur on extreme poverty and human rights, the 'social safety net has been badly damaged by drastic cuts to local authorities' budgets, which have eliminated many social services'.[87] Furthermore, there is concern that measures of austerity will continue to adversely impact children, with it being predicted that 40 per cent of children in the UK will be living in poverty by 2021.[88] It is argued that the state must provide more assistance to children and their families to ensure protection of their rights under Article 8 ECHR and other provisions of the Convention.

There are cases, for example, where social factors such as poverty lead to neglect.[89] Parents may lack financial resources, which will impact on their ability to find appropriate housing or child care, and in extreme cases it may impact on their ability to feed and clothe their children. Poverty, and the stress that this may cause to parents, combined with other factors such as learning disabilities, mental illness or drug and alcohol addiction, may exacerbate these problems. In such cases, timely state assistance might have prevented children from being harmed. It has been argued by Kilkelly that if Article 8 were to be interpreted widely, requiring State intervention to assist families, this would make protection for children and their families practical and effective.[90] It is also argued that provisions of the UNCRC and the UN Guidelines for the Alternative Care of Children would augment protection of children and their parents. Expanding the scope of Article 8 ECHR could have the potential to decrease neglect and abuse and lead to greater utilisation of measures that might be just as effective as non-consensual adoption but less restrictive. There is increasing evidence of this type of approach being taken in European jurisprudence, which may, in time, influence the law on non-consensual adoption in England and Wales.

In *RMS v Spain*,[91] for example, the Court needed to consider the extent to which the scope of the positive obligation under Article 8 extends towards the provision of state assistance. In this case, a child had been removed into care and placed for adoption because of her mother's poverty and uncertain living arrangements. The Court stated that whereas in some cases children in poor living conditions or suffering from material deprivation have been removed into care, this had never been the sole reason.[92] Such removal was only justified alongside other factors,

[86] ibid.

[87] Human Rights Council, *Visit to the United Kingdom of Great Britain and Northern Ireland: Report of the Special Rapporteur on extreme poverty and human rights* (UN, 2019) 1.

[88] ibid.

[89] U Kilkelly, *The Child and the European Convention on Human Rights* (Aldershot, Dartmouth Publishing Co, 1999) 174.

[90] ibid.

[91] *RMS v Spain* App no 28775/12 (ECHR, 18 June 2013).

[92] ibid para 84.

such as the parents' psychological state or inability to provide their children with emotional and educational support.[93]

Other factors that, by themselves, could justify intervention might include physical or psychological ill-treatment,[94] sexual abuse,[95] lack of emotional development,[96] the child's having health problems or the psychological instability of the parents.[97] The removal and adoption of the child in *RMS v Spain* was therefore held by the Court to be a disproportionate interference with the mother's Article 8 right to respect for private and family life, as the state had failed to take sufficient and appropriate measures to secure the mother's right to live with her child. The Court held that the state could have taken less restrictive alternative measures, such as advising the mother on how to obtain benefits and to secure social housing. The decision in *RMS v Spain* indicates that poverty and uncertain living arrangements are insufficient grounds for taking a child into care and placing the child for adoption. Some other factor, such as abuse or neglect, is needed to justify a measure like adoption, which may be a serious interference with the Article 8 rights of the birth parents. This type of case is also an example of potential violation of children's rights under the UNCRC and the UN Guidelines for the Alternative Care of Children.

A similar approach was taken in *Zhou v Italy*,[98] where the Court again needed to consider whether there were sufficient grounds to justify interference with parental rights under Article 8 ECHR. Here, the applicant was a working mother who had placed her child in the care of a neighbouring couple while she went to work. As social services did not regard the couple as suitable carers for the child, the child was taken into care and placed for adoption. Because of the choices the mother had made, she was regarded as being incapable of exercising her parental role and supporting her son's emotional and intellectual development. The Italian court made an adoption order. The mother argued that placing her child for adoption and preventing her from seeing the child had violated her right to respect for private and family life under Article 8 ECHR. The Strasbourg Court held that the mother's Article 8 right had been violated, and that the state ought to have taken tangible measures to attempt to reunite the mother with her son before placing him for adoption. Such measures could have included helping the mother find alternative forms of care, or the provision of financial assistance enabling the mother to care for her child. Therefore, non-consensual adoption was not the least restrictive option available to protect the child's welfare and rights. The approach taken by the state in this case is also

[93] *Rampogna and Murgia v Italy* App no 40753/98 (ECHR, 11 May 1999); *MG and MTA v Italy* App no 17421/02 (ECHR, 28 June 2005).

[94] *Zakharova v France* App no 53706/00 (ECHR, 13 December 2005).

[95] *Covezzi and Morselli v Italy* App no 52763/99 (ECHR, 9 May 2003).

[96] *Kutzner v Germany* App no 46544/99 (ECHR, 26 February 2002).

[97] *Bertrand v France* App no 57376/00 (ECHR, 19 February 2002); and *Couillard Maugery v France* App no 64796/01 (ECHR, 1 July 2004).

[98] *Zhou v Italy* App no 33773/11 (ECHR, 21 January 2014).

inconsistent with many of the UNCRC provisions considered in chapter 2, in particular, Articles 7–9.

In *SH v Italy*,[99] the state intervened and removed three children into care, whose mother was suffering from depression and was struggling to raise her children. The parents accepted that they needed assistance from the child's grandfather and the Italian social services, but they maintained that it was not necessary for the children to be taken into foster care. The Italian equivalent of a children's guardian recommended, in the light of the strong emotional bond that existed between the mother and her children and the fact that the mother was willing to have psychotherapy, that the children ought to be reunited with their parents. The children were returned to their mother, but were removed into foster care again because the mother was hospitalised and the grandfather was too ill to assist the family.

Despite a court-ordered expert report suggesting that the children should remain in care and that contact between the children and their parents ought to continue (albeit with a support package from social services in place), the Italian court ordered that contact should cease and that the children ought to be placed for adoption, on the basis of the mother's mental health problems and the father's inability to show his children affection. This conclusion is clearly not congruent with the ethos of the ECHR or the UNCRC, which emphasises the importance of maintaining relationships between children and their birth parents, particularly Articles 7–9 UNCRC.

After having appeals rejected by the superior Italian courts, the mother argued before the ECtHR that her right under Article 8 ECHR had been violated, as the Italian authorities had failed to satisfy their positive obligation to provide support in order to keep the family together. The three children were placed separately, which meant that not only did they lose their relationships with their parents, but they also lost the opportunity to maintain relationships with one another. The Court considered that Member States must equip themselves with legal powers to ensure compliance with their positive obligations under Article 8.[100] The Court observed that, despite the existence of emotional bonds, the family's willingness to collaborate with social services and the existence of an expert report recommending that the family should be kept together, the Italian court had ordered the adoption of the three children.[101] The Court determined that the Italian court's failure to consider less radical solutions, such as the support package recommended by expert testimony, demonstrated that the national authorities had not made sufficient attempts to protect the mother–child bond, and thus the mother's Article 8 right had been violated. The Court further emphasised that state agencies must, in particular, protect, guide and advise vulnerable persons such as those

[99] *SH v Italy* App no 52557/14 (ECHR, 13 October 2015).
[100] ibid para 41.
[101] ibid para 47.

suffering from mental health problems.[102] An interesting aspect of this decision is that the Court emphasised the importance of state intervention in this case, despite the resource implications of providing such support to families.

The ECtHR is increasingly emphasising the importance of the need for states to use measures less restrictive than non-consensual adoption that may be equally effective. A wider implication of these decisions, in particular the decision in *SH v Italy*, is that the positive obligation owed by the state to families may mean that it will become necessary for state authorities to attempt to reunite families by the use of less restrictive alternatives to non-consensual adoption. This decision may have a wider impact in non-consensual adoption cases in England and Wales, where the state has not sufficiently explored the possibility of keeping families together via state assistance (see the discussion in chapter 5 for further details).

D. Removing Children from the Family Home

Regardless of the state's positive obligation to assist children and their parents, interference with parents' rights may sometimes be justified under Article 8(2) ECHR, for example in cases of severe neglect and abuse (see section II.B). Such circumstances will make it necessary for the state to take action[103] and potentially remove a child from his or her family home. Any interventionist measure must, however, be proportionate,[104] and arguably there may be cases where measures (which are less restrictive and thus less of an interference with children's and parents' rights under Article 8(1)) may be used to protect children's rights under Articles 2 and 3 ECHR and their best interests.

In practice, measures of intervention could include the provision of additional help or support for the family unit where required,[105] the reduction and/or the termination of contact,[106] the termination of parental responsibility/rights[107] and ultimately even adoption. There are several cases, however, where state measures have been held not to be proportionate and the Court has found violations of Article 8.[108] The cases typically challenge the initial separation of the parent and child and any subsequent measures that adversely impacted on the ongoing relationship between parent and child, and the likelihood of their being reunited in the future.

Some cases show that initial state intervention under Article 8(1) ECHR has been justified, but further measures, such as removal of the child from the family

[102] ibid para 54.
[103] *K and T v Finland* App no 25702/94 (ECHR, 12 July 2001).
[104] *Saviny v Ukraine* App no 39948/06 (ECHR, 23 December 2008); *Pontes v Portugal* [2012] ECHR 1573.
[105] *Kutzner v Germany* (n 96).
[106] ibid.
[107] See the discussion in ch 2.
[108] *Eriksson v Sweden* [1989] ECHR 10; *Kutzner v Germany* (n 96); *Saviny v Ukraine* (n 104).

home or adoption, have not. In *Kutzner v Germany*,[109] the children were taken into foster care because the applicants were not considered to have the requisite intellectual capacity to raise their children and because there was emotional under-development in the children. The children had been provided with educational support measures that were inadequate, and the authorities determined that further intervention was required. The Court questioned whether social services and the judiciary had given sufficient consideration to additional measures of support as an alternative to the more serious measure of separating the children from their parents. The parents were not permitted to have contact with their children for six months, and although they were eventually granted the right to have contact, they were allowed to see their children only twice a month for an hour.

The actions taken by the state were held to have been disproportionate, with the Court disapproving of the state's decision to make a care order and, in particular, the manner in which it was implemented.[110] The Court observed that it might have been possible to have protected the children's welfare by offering additional practical support to the family from social services, rather than taking 'by far the most extreme measure'.[111] It also suggested that the limitations on contact would only have served to add to the alienation between the children and their parents.[112] The Court therefore held that even though the reasons for intervention were legitimate, they were insufficient to justify such a serious interference with family life. The Court found that there had been a violation of the parents' Article 8 rights.

The decision in *Kutzner* is an example of a state's failing to satisfy the proportionality test by not considering less restrictive alternatives that would have provided sufficient protection for the children's welfare.[113] *Kutzner* shows that, in particular, where children are removed from parents with learning disabilities, the relevant authorities must consider whether it would be appropriate to provide the family with additional support.[114] A failure to give sufficient consideration to alternative methods of family support that would enable children to remain in the family home would be a disproportionate interference with parental rights. Such an approach is, arguably, inconsistent with the ethos of the UNCRC and the UN Guidelines for the Alternative Care of Children. Furthermore, *Kutzner* also serves as a warning that it is not justifiable to remove children from their parents just because they could be raised in a more beneficial environment than

[109] *Kutzner v Germany* (n 96).
[110] ibid para 70.
[111] ibid para 75.
[112] ibid para 79.
[113] See the discussion in C Hoss, 'Family Matters: European Court of Human Rights Finds German Parenting Rights Decisions to be in Violation of Article 8' [2002] *German Law Journal* at http://www.germanlawjournal.com/article.php?id=146; and J Wallbank, S Choudhry and J Herring, *Rights, Gender and Family Law* (New York, Routledge, 2010).
[114] See the discussion in A Bond, *Care Proceedings and Learning Disabled Parents: A Handbook for Family Lawyers*, 2nd edn (Bristol, Family Law, 2014) 3.

that which their parents could provide.[115] A similar message can be found in *Haase v Germany*,[116] where the Court held:

> The fact that a child could be placed in a more beneficial environment for his or her upbringing will not on its own justify a compulsory measure of removal from the care of the biological parents; there must exist other circumstances pointing to the 'necessity' for such an interference with the parents' right under Art 8 to enjoy a family life with their child … [B]efore public authorities have recourse to emergency measures in such delicate issues as care orders, the imminent danger should be actually established. It is true that in obvious cases of danger no involvement of the parents is called for. However if it is still possible to hear the parents of the children and to discuss with them the necessity of the measure, there should be no room for an emergency action, in particular when, like in the present case, the danger had already existed for a long period.

There are cases where state intervention may be regarded as being justifiable so as to assist parents in raising their children, but not the removal of a child from his or her parents. In *Saviny v Ukraine*, four children were removed from their blind parents on the basis that the children were in 'danger'. The reason for their removal was that the environment the children were living in was regarded as unsatisfactory by the authorities because the children's residence was cold, dirty and untidy. The Court held that the parents' Article 8 right had been violated by removing the children into care, and that while the reasons for removal were relevant, they were insufficient to justify compulsory removal. The Court emphasised that there must be 'weighty considerations in the interests of the child'[117] that would justify the children's being taken into care. Establishing that a child would be removed into a 'more beneficial environment'[118] did not justify the state's action. The Court said that financial assistance and social counselling could have been helpful for the parents in this case, and it stressed the importance of sufficiently exploring 'less far-reaching alternatives'[119] before removing the children into care, a measure that was disproportionate in the circumstances and also inconsistent with many provisions under the UNCRC and the UN Guidelines for the Alternative Care of Children.

As already considered, state intervention may be justified to protect children's welfare under Article 8(2) ECHR, but in some cases care orders may not be a proportionate measure. In other cases, care orders may well be proportionate, but the ECtHR takes the view that they ought to be a temporary measure[120] and that the state ought to take active steps to reunite children with their parents. The state's positive obligation may extend to reuniting parents and children even where separation has been justified under Article 8(2).[121]

[115] *Kutzner v Germany* (n 96) para 69.
[116] *Haase v Germany* [2004] 2 FLR 39, para 95.
[117] *Saviny v Ukraine* (n 104) para 49.
[118] ibid para 50.
[119] ibid para 58.
[120] *K and T v Finland* (n 103).
[121] *KA v Finland* App no 27751/95 (ECHR, 14 January 2003).

Olsson v Sweden (No 2)[122] is an example of a case where the Court has stated that such a positive obligation exists. *Olsson* concerned three children who were taken into care, separated from each other and housed a considerable distance from their parents, which made it difficult for regular contact to take place. The initial removal of the children was held not to be a violation of Article 8(1) ECHR, but the restrictions on access between 1987 and 1990 were violations, as at that time there was no legal provision upon which the restrictions of access could be based.[123] However, the Court took into consideration the lengthy period of separation between the children and their parents, and also the children's objections to being reunited, and held that the restrictions on access from 1990 onwards did not violate the parents' rights.

This case is an important demonstration of how the separation of parents and children and infrequent contact can make reuniting children and parents difficult, or even impossible. As the Court stated in *Ignaccolo-Zenide v Romania*,[124] 'the passage of time can have irremediable consequences for relations between the children and the parent who does not live with them'.[125] The reasoning in cases like *Olsson* and *Ignaccolo-Zenide* is important when assessing the proportionality of adoption orders, since increased efforts by the state to reunite children with their parents prior to adoption is less likely to violate the rights of children and their parents under Article 8(1) ECHR. Nonetheless, it is essential for the state to strike the appropriate balance and not make endless attempts to reunite children with their parents, since this could lead to delay in the adoption process.

P, C and S v UK[126] is one of the most critical judgments that the ECtHR has delivered on the UK's application of procedures on child protection and adoption, and was described by Hewson et al as a groundbreaking case.[127] This judgment makes it clear that the immediate removal of a newborn child at birth is potentially a violation of Article 8 ECHR and a draconian measure, which will rarely be justified. The removal of S at birth was subjected to close scrutiny by the Court, which stated that such removal at birth required 'exceptional justification' as it is 'a step which is traumatic for the mother and places her own physical and mental health under a strain, and it deprives the new-born baby of close contact with its birth mother'.[128]

The Court accepted that the local authority was entitled to apply for an emergency protection order,[129] as there were relevant and sufficient reasons for doing so (ie the fact that P had been convicted in the USA for harming her son raised doubts about the welfare of her unborn child). The intervention and action had

[122] *Olsson v Sweden (No 2)* (1992) Series A no 250 (ECHR).
[123] ibid para 81.
[124] *Ignaccolo-Zenide v Romania* [2000] ECHR 25.
[125] ibid para 102.
[126] *P, C and S v UK* (2002) 35 EHRR 31.
[127] Hewson et al (n 51) 1245.
[128] *P, C and S v UK* (n 126) para 131.
[129] See the Children Act 1989 (CA 1989), s 44.

been 'necessary in a democratic society to safeguard the health and rights of the child'.[130] However, the Court determined that the removal of S at birth was not supported by relevant and sufficient reasons. There was no suspicion that S would be in danger from her mother immediately after birth. According to the Court, it was unnecessary to remove S immediately after birth, and supervision would have been sufficient to protect S from harm. Thus, the Court concluded that the national authorities had not acted in a manner that was proportionate, and it was held that there had been a breach of the Article 8 rights of the mother, P, and of the father, C. Even though Member States have a wide margin of appreciation in taking measures to protect the welfare of children, an intense standard of proportionality will be applied when a 'draconian'[131] measure, such as the removal of a newborn baby occurs. Thus, without compelling reasons for the removal, less restrictive alternatives should be used to protect the child's welfare.

Despite the emphasis the Court placed on the draconian nature of the removal of a child at birth, cases like this continue to be heard in the courts in England and Wales.[132] Mothers have had their babies removed at birth, or shortly after birth, when there is no evidence that the child is at immediate risk of harm, or that his or her Article 2 (the right to life) or Article 3 (the right to freedom from torture or inhuman or degrading treatment) rights are likely to be violated (see the discussion in chapter 4, section IV). In *P, C and S v UK*, a sad aspect of the final decision was that contact between S and her parents was stopped. It will be argued in chapter 5 that non-consensual adoption with direct contact may be a less restrictive but equally effective alternative to non-consensual adoption without direct contact. The following section will now go on to consider how the ECtHR has addressed the issue of contact between children and parents prior to adoption and after an adoption has taken place.

E. Contact between Children and Birth Parents

The ECtHR has emphasised the importance of contact being maintained between children and parents, and that state authorities should give adequate consideration to the question of whether contact is in a child's best interests.[133] In such cases, the principle of 'stricter scrutiny'[134] applies and dictates that whereas initial removal of a child will warrant a wide margin of appreciation, any further measures imposing restrictions on the parent–child relationship (such as by reducing/terminating contact) must be subject to stricter scrutiny, and consequently

[130] *P, C and S v UK* (n 126) para 130.
[131] ibid para 98.
[132] For example, *X Council v B* [2004] EWHC 2015 (Fam), [2005] 1 FLR 341; *R (G) v Nottingham City Council* [2008] EWHC 152 (Admin); *Re NL (A Child) (Appeal: Interim Care Order: Facts and Reasons)* [2014] EWHC 270 (Fam).
[133] *Anayo v Germany* [2010] ECHR 2083; *R and H v UK* [2011] ECHR 844.
[134] *Johansen v Norway* App no 17383/90 (ECHR, 7 August 1996).

a corresponding narrow margin of appreciation will exist since the removal of contact would mean that 'the possibilities of reunification will be diminished and eventually destroyed'.[135] The Court has thus acknowledged that once a child has been removed from his or her parents, any further relationship restrictions (eg reduction/termination of contact) may weaken the bond between them and lessen the likelihood of their being reunited.[136]

In *Eriksson v Sweden*,[137] the child was placed in a foster home one month after birth, because the mother had been sentenced to 14 months in prison for dealing in stolen goods and for the possession of narcotics. In this case, it was undisputed that the child needed to be in care during this time. However, according to the Court, the 'severe and lasting restrictions'[138] on contact violated the mother's right to respect for private and family life under Article 8 ECHR. Although the initial intervention had been necessary, the restrictions on contact were disproportionate in light of the aim of protecting the child from harm.

Another example of the Court's expressing its disapproval of the state's limitation of contact between a parent and child can be seen in *Andersson v Sweden*.[139] In this case, a boy was taken into care because the authorities had concerns about his social and emotional development, which, despite being brought to the attention of his mother, had not been addressed by her. While in care, he was unable to see his mother because contact was prohibited, as it was regarded to be 'necessary in order to achieve the purposes of the care order',[140] which were adversely affected by his mother's attempts to encourage her son to run away from care. The mother had been limited to contact by telephone and letters (which had also been terminated for a certain period). She and her son were successful before the ECtHR in arguing that these restrictions on contact violated their Article 8 rights. The Court held that although national authorities had provided general reasons for these measures, the measures were so far-reaching that there was a need to provide strong reasons for their justification under Article 8(2) ECHR. As the Court found that there were no such reasons, it held that the national authorities had failed to establish it was necessary to deprive the applicants of contact, and had failed to show that these measures had been consistent with reuniting the family. The Court therefore held that there had been a violation of Article 8(1), as the restrictions were disproportionate and were not necessary in a democratic society.

The Court has recently emphasised the importance of preserving relationships between children and their grandparents where they have lived together.

[135] *Görgülü v Germany* App no 74969/01 (ECHR, 26 February 2004) at para 46. Also see *K and T v Finland* (n 103) para 175.

[136] *Scozzari and Giunta v Italy* App no 41963/98 (ECHR, 13 July 2000.

[137] *Eriksson v Sweden* (n 108).

[138] ibid para 71.

[139] *Andersson v Sweden* App no 12963/87 (ECHR, 25 February 1992).

[140] ibid para 16.

In *Beccarini and Ridolfi v Italy*,[141] the grandparents had been caring for their grandchildren and sought the assistance of the Italian social services. The children were removed from their grandparents on the basis that the children's needs had not been met. Nonetheless, the grandparents sought regular contact while the children were in care, and the Italian court directed that such contact should take place. However, social services stopped the contact while the children were in care, and the contact did not resume once the children were returned to their mother. The ECtHR held that social services had not taken 'adequate or sufficient steps' to ensure that contact had taken place, which resulted in a violation of the grandparents' rights under Article 8 ECHR. It is also argued that children's rights to such contact would be protected under Articles 7 and 8 UNCRC.

The case law of the ECtHR emphasises that the state must endeavour to support the reunification of parents and children, but that this obligation is not absolute.[142] In some cases before the Court, state restrictions on contact between child and parent have been justified under Article 8(2) ECHR.[143] In *Levin v Sweden*,[144] for example, the Court suggested that the parents' right to contact could be restricted depending on the 'nature and seriousness of children's interests'.[145] In *Levin*, the national authorities were held to be justified in limiting contact because of the distress the children suffered when contact took place. Distress suffered by the child and an express wish not to have contact appears to be given weight by the Court and will justify limiting parents' rights under Article 8(2). The dissenting judgment of Judge Forde in *Levin* does, however, suggest caution in finding an interference with parents' rights to be proportionate based on a child's distress at seeing a birth parent when in care. Judge Forde suggested that while it may be relevant to consider a child's distress, the manner in which the state facilitates contact may create distress, not the contact per se. She said that the speed and extent to which the contact was reduced was not proportionate. In her opinion, the national authorities had failed to discharge their duty to reunite the children with their birth parents.[146]

The ECtHR has also had to consider whether post-adoption contact ought to be provided, for the state to satisfy its obligation under Article 8 ECHR. *Aune v Norway*[147] provides an example of circumstances in which non-consensual adoption may be a necessary and proportionate measure. In this case, the child was removed from his parents due to the ill treatment he had received because of his parents' drug abuse problems. While in care, he developed a bond with his foster parents, who sought to adopt him. The birth mother argued before the ECtHR that her Article 8 right was violated because of the deprivation of her parental

[141] *Beccarini and Ridolfi v Italy* (n 65).
[142] See, eg, *Hokkanen v Finland* (n 13) para 55.
[143] *Strand Lobben and Others v Norway* App no 37283/13 (ECHR, 30 November 2017).
[144] *Levin v Sweden* App no 35141/06 (ECHR, 15 March 2012).
[145] ibid para 64.
[146] ibid 17–19, at paras 7–8 of Judge Forde's dissenting judgment.
[147] *Aune v Norway* (n 5).

responsibilities and because of the state's consent to her son's being adopted by the foster parents. Although the mother accepted that the child was to remain in foster care, she expressed concern that there would be no guarantee of contact post-adoption.

The Court held that the boy's best interests were an overriding requirement that justified the making of the adoption order. In the light of the boy's interest in stability, the bonds he had formed with his prospective adoptive parents and the fact that they continued to facilitate contact between him and his birth mother, the Court held that it had been reasonable for the Norwegian authorities to decide that the interest in placing him for adoption outweighed the mother's interest in assured contact. The Court therefore held that the mother's Article 8 right had not been violated and it had been a proportionate step for the boy to be adopted. Arguably, adoption was the most effective measure available to protect the boy's own rights under Article 8 ECHR and under Articles 7–9 UNCRC.

Having outlined the general principles of ECtHR case law, the following section will examine how they have been applied in UK cases on non-consensual adoption that have reached the ECtHR.

V. Guidance on Reuniting Children and Parents in Adoption Cases?

A. Overview of the Role of National Authorities

National authorities must take reasonable and necessary steps to reunite children with their parents.[148] There must be exceptional circumstances before the state decides that children should be removed from their parents permanently.[149] *Neulinger and Shuruk v Switzerland*[150] and other cases of its ilk have emphasised that it will be in children's best interests for relationships to be maintained with family members, except where the family is shown to be particularly unfit. It can be argued that the ECtHR has not provided clear guidance on what steps it might be 'reasonable' for state authorities to take in order to facilitate the reunion of children and parents, and what might constitute 'exceptional circumstances' justifying a permanent separation between children and parents. The following section thus outlines what steps are likely to be, and ought to be, regarded as 'reasonable' for states to take in order to satisfy their positive obligation under Article 8 ECHR to reunite children and their parents in cases where adoption is a potential outcome.

[148] *Hokkanen v Finland* (n 13); *Görgülü v Germany* (n 135); *Neulinger and Shuruk v Switzerland* (n 55); *Pini and Others v Romania* App no 78028/01 (ECHR, 22 June 2014).
[149] *Johansen v Norway* (n 134).
[150] *Neulinger and Shuruk v Switzerland* (n 55).

B. Reasonable Steps before Removal and Adoption

It is important to identify whether a state has taken any measures ('reasonable steps') to try to reunite the child concerned with his or her birth parents. It is argued that these reasonable steps could be informed by an examination of the UNCRC, the UN Guidelines for the Alternative Care of Children and a range of practical factors the ECtHR has had to consider in several cases. This section will consider factors that the ECtHR appears to have taken into account in its decision-making process, and will suggest other factors that may also be relevant.

If the state has tried different methods of helping to support the family but has nevertheless decided that non-consensual adoption is the best option, it would be legitimate for the state to argue that reasonable efforts had been made or steps taken to reunite the parents and child. This could include consideration of whether the family had regular visits from a social worker, whether the family was given the opportunity to and did actually participate in state programmes aimed at helping families, whether the child and parents were offered family therapy and/or whether additional financial assistance or housing was available for families living in poverty.

In *RMS v Spain*,[151] for example, the Court held that insufficient efforts had been made on the part of the authorities to help the family obtain suitable housing (see further section IV.C). In *Johansen v Norway*,[152] the authorities had made numerous attempts to assist the mother in caring for her first child before he was taken into care. This information influenced the authorities in deciding to remove the mother's second child into care and to plan for the child's adoption.

Another relevant case example is *Saviny v Ukraine*.[153] There, the Court advised that 'particular attention should be paid to difficult social and economic circumstances, which require more specific support'.[154] It was emphasised at the Conference on Child Removal Proceedings[155] in Prague in October 2014 that the authorities ought to be encouraged by the Council of Europe to be more proactive in providing assistance to families in trouble. Reference to providing families with appropriate support, and keeping families together where possible, can also be found in Articles 7, 8 and 9 UNCRC and in the UN Guidelines for the Alternative Care of Children. The difficulty lies in determining how much assistance a state must supply before it decides to use a restrictive measure like non-consensual adoption.

Assistance could involve a range of practical measures such as financial aid, parenting classes, alcohol or drug rehabilitation programmes, counselling or

[151] *RMS v Spain* (n 91).
[152] *Johansen v Norway* (n 134).
[153] *Saviny v Ukraine* (n 104).
[154] ibid para 36.
[155] This conference was organised by Marica Pirosikova from the Slovak Republic.

regular visits from social workers. Regardless of the level of assistance that it would be desirable to provide, the state ought not be expected to persist if, after assistance has been provided for a reasonable period, measures of intervention have been ineffective. Nevertheless, it is difficult to assess the length of time that might be required to expect to see some improvement in a family's circumstances. It seems probable that this would vary depending on the type of intervention provided and the specific challenges faced by the family in question.

The Court should also consider whether contact had been supported prior to the adoption or the placement for adoption. The lack of contact between children and parents prior to adoption is an issue that has been viewed with concern by the ECtHR. Despite the Court's disapproval, it appears to be accepted practice in English law to terminate or reduce contact between children in care and their parents[156] where adoption is regarded as in the child's best interests. If contact between children and their parents were to be supported throughout the care process, this would make it easier to argue that reasonable efforts to reunite children and parents had been made and that the decision to go ahead with a non-consensual adoption was a proportionate measure. In *Aune v Norway*,[157] for example, the mother still had contact with the child, but because of the bond the child had developed with the prospective adopters, it was determined by the Court that it had been in the child's best interests to be adopted. The positive obligation to reunite children with their birth families under Article 8 ECHR and the importance of facilitating contact would, however, need to be balanced against the child's own rights under Articles 2, 3 and 8 ECHR.

Authorities ought to investigate to discover whether alternatives to adoption may be available (eg kinship care, see chapter 5). The greater the amount of work undertaken by authorities to assess alternatives to adoption and implement them where necessary, the more probable it is that a final adoption decision will be regarded as a reasonable and proportionate measure by the ECtHR. In *Pontes v Portugal*,[158] the Court held that the authorities had violated Article 8 ECHR because the many available alternatives to adoption had not been fully considered, and so the adoption was not justified. In the *Pontes* case, the parents had five children who were monitored by the Portuguese authorities because of the parents' drug use. Due to the parents' negligence, the children were taken into care. Subsequently, the parents' home life improved and their children were returned to them, except for their son P, with regard to whom they had their parental authority removed by the state and who was subsequently placed for adoption. The reasoning of the national authorities was that P had spent three years in care and had developed a close relationship with his foster parents, with no ties to his siblings or biological parents.

[156] See the Children and Families Act 2014, s 8(3).
[157] *Aune v Norway* (n 5).
[158] *Pontes v Portugal* (n 104).

The parents took their case to the ECtHR, arguing that their Article 8 right to respect for their private and family life had been violated as (i) their son had never been allowed to spend holidays or weekends with his family; (ii) contact had been terminated in 2006; (iii) their parental authority had been removed and P had subsequently been adopted. The Court observed that the authorities had failed to consider less radical measures, including returning the child to his parents, and drew attention to the inconsistency whereby all of the children except P had been returned to their parents. The Court doubted that it could be in P's best interests to break up the family or lose a relationship with his parents or siblings, when it was clear that he could have been reunited with his parents. The Court therefore held that Article 8 ECH R had been violated, as the adoption had not been founded on relevant and sufficient reasons and was not proportionate. This case demonstrates that it is crucial that states carry out a thorough analysis of a child's best interests and provide sufficient justification for the termination of contact and subsequent adoption. In *Pontes*, adoption was not in the child's best interests because he had lost the opportunity to be raised by his birth parents and to develop a relationship with his siblings.

Relevant children's rights ought to form a significant part of the Court's analysis. Generally, however, the Strasbourg Court focuses on the rights of the parents and the best interests of children rather than on children's rights. Thus, although in principle a child's rights under the ECHR are also engaged (such as the Article 8 right to respect for private and family life, and in some cases the child's Article 2 right to life and Article 3 right to freedom from torture or inhuman or degrading treatment), these rights are not typically discussed by the ECtHR in adoption cases unless argued directly by legal counsel.[159] Similarly, although there are certain UNCRC rights that it may also be relevant for the Court to consider in the context of adoption, these are not examined. For instance Article 7 (the right to know and be cared for by one's parents), Article 8 (the right to identity – specifically, the right to family relations) and Article 9 (concerning parental separation).

The reason for the lack of consideration of children's rights in adoption cases is that the focus tends to be on the parents' rights and whether the actions or omissions of the state leading to the non-consensual adoption or the adoption itself violate parental rights. It is suggested that in all cases concerning children, it would improve the quality of judicial reasoning and provide greater protection of both parents' and children's rights to determine the proportionality of non-consensual adoption through the lens of children's rights, in particular under the UNCRC. This analysis could also involve scrutiny of whether domestic courts have given explicit consideration to children's rights under the UNCRC and the ECHR in the process of making non-consensual adoption orders.

[159] *P, C and S v UK* App no 56547/00 (n 6) is a rare case in which the child's rights under Arts 6 and 8 ECHR were put to and ultimately considered by the Court. See also *Strand Lobben and Others v Norway* App no 37283/13 (ECHR, 30 November 2017).

In addition to detailed assessment of whether states have taken reasonable steps, by reference to children's rights, it is also relevant to consider whether factors exist that may justify less or more effort from state authorities. The Court should place emphasis on the length of time the child has been raised by his or her birth parents, the quality of the relationship between the child and his/her parents, and the wishes and views of the child in question. Parent–child relationships may range from parents who are unable to provide good quality care for their children but who may still have a well-developed bond with them (this was observed in *YC v UK*[160] for example), to those at the other end of the spectrum who have abused their children severely and/or who do not have strong bonds (eg in *Aune v Norway*[161] and in *Strand Lobben and Others v Norway*[162]).

There may be cases where children state that they do not want to maintain relationships with their birth parents, or where they demonstrate visible signs of distress or regression in behaviour when in their parents' presence. This occurred in *Strand Lobben and Others v Norway*, for example, where the baby was separated from his mother due to concerns about her parenting skills. Initially, the state provided four to six contact sessions per year, during which the baby became distressed due to the mother's emotional outbursts and lack of empathy. In such cases, this might be a factor that justifies making less strenuous efforts to attempt to reunite a child with his or her parents, and which increases the likelihood that a non-consensual adoption would be a proportionate measure. However, this ultimately depends on the facts of the case.

In *Levin v Sweden*,[163] Judge Forde pointed out that sudden removal from a parent by the authorities may be distressing and could contribute to a child's distress at having contact with his or her parents. It should also be noted that in *Strand Lobben*, the lack of frequency of the contact and the tension between the mother and the foster mother may have contributed to the child's distress. Thus, while the child's own explicit and implicit response to his or her parents is an important factor that ought to be considered by the Court, it should not be determinative. Work needs to be undertaken to analyse the reasons for children's distress, rather than to make assumptions about a child's emotional response.

It is relevant for the Court to consider the reasons for removing a child into care in the first place – in other words, prior to adoption. Children may be removed from the family home because their parents have neglected and/or abused them, and in such cases this may have a bearing on the proportionality of non-consensual adoption. The factors that could be examined by the Strasbourg Court might include, for example, the reason for the child's initial removal into care, whether the removal was based on a risk of harm or actual harm, the number of occasions on which the child has been harmed and the severity of the harm that

[160] *YC v UK* (n 31).
[161] *Aune v Norway* (n 5).
[162] *Strand Lobben and Others v Norway* (n 159).
[163] *Levin v Sweden* (n 144) 17–19, paras 7–8 of Judge Forde's dissenting judgment.

may have taken place. In cases where severe abuse has taken place and no effort on the part of the parents has been made to address their own behaviour that led to such abuse (drug or alcohol addiction, for example), it should not be incumbent on states to make strenuous efforts to reunite children with their parents. Indeed, as already stated, it is suggested that in such cases, further consideration of reuniting the family may run counter to the child's rights under Article 2 ECHR (the right to life) and Article 3 ECHR (the right to freedom from torture or inhuman or degrading treatment).

However, in cases where parents' circumstances have affected their ability to raise their child, this should be a relevant consideration when assessing whether or not non-consensual adoption complies with human rights. In *RMS v Spain*,[164] the Court observed that the child who had been removed into care and placed for adoption had not been subjected to physical or psychological harm, nor sexual abuse, had no serious health problems and her emotional development was normal. The main basis for taking the child into care was the parents' poverty and their difficulty in finding accommodation. As a result, there was a breach of the mother's Article 8 right because of the state's failure to make adequate and effective efforts to explore whether or not it was possible to reunite parent and child. It is also important to consider Lady Hale's words *In the Matter of B (A Child)*,[165] where she stated:

> There are cases where the harm suffered or feared is very severe, but it would be disproportionate to sever or curtail the family ties because the authorities can protect the child in other ways … Conversely, there may be cases where the level of harm is not so great, but there is no other way in which the child can be properly protected from it.[166]

In other words, it may be possible in some cases for the state to reunite a child with his or her parents and protect the child from the risk of harm or from further harm occurring. In such cases, then, it may be possible for children's rights under Articles 2 and 3 ECHR to be protected while also protecting the parents' and children's Article 8 ECHR rights. However, if permanent removal of a child from his or her home environment is essential to protect his or her rights under Article 2 and 3 ECHR, a non-consensual adoption is likely to be a proportionate measure that has the effect of protecting the children's Convention rights and which does not breach the parents' rights under Article 8 ECHR.

It is submitted that although the ECtHR has to be careful not to substitute its view for that of the national court in any given case, it should consider in detail less restrictive alternatives and consider children's rights, in particular how the UNCRC may shape children's rights under the ECHR.

[164] *RMS v Spain* (n 91).
[165] *In the Matter of B (A Child)* [2013] UKSC 33.
[166] ibid para 197, *per* Lady Hale.

C. Exceptional Circumstances: When is Non-Consensual Adoption Justifiable?

It is argued that the test of 'exceptional circumstances', which justifies removal of children from their family homes and even adoption, has, in practice, not been a difficult hurdle for domestic authorities to overcome when justifying non-consensual adoption before the ECtHR. It has been suggested by Fenton-Glynn, for example, that the exceptional circumstances test will often be satisfied if the measure (eg an adoption order) is regarded by national authorities to be in the child's best interests.[167] At first glance this appears to have been borne out, for example, by the discussion in the adoption cases of *R and H v UK*[168] and *YC v UK*,[169] considered in more detail in section VI. The fact that this test is so easily satisfied may mean that, in some cases, parents' Article 8 rights are not well protected when the state determines that it is in the child's best interests to be removed into care and placed for adoption. It may also mean that a child's Article 8 ECHR right to have a relationship with his or her parents may be violated. However, it should be observed that the ECtHR appears to have taken a more deferential approach in non-consensual cases arising from England and Wales since the enactment of the Adoption and Children Act 2002 (ACA 2002), when compared with similar cases concerning non-consensual adoption originating from other European countries (see chapters 3 and 6).

While a concrete definition of what amounts to 'exceptional circumstances' carries the risk of creating a straitjacket for Member States, it can be argued that the test is still too vague. Whereas on the one hand it could be regarded as making it easier for the state to intervene to protect children's rights under Articles 2 and 3 ECHR, on the other hand it could be argued that these rights could be protected via less restrictive alternatives to non-consensual adoption. Thus the test of 'exceptional circumstances' at present provides insufficient protection for the rights of children and their parents in non-consensual adoption cases. Removal of children into care and placement for adoption are serious steps that, in the case of adoption, have irreversible consequences. Consequently, children, parents and Member States ought to have a clear idea of when the ECtHR will regard steps such as care or adoption orders as justifiable due to exceptional circumstances. This would be helpful not only at the ECtHR level but also at the domestic level, since many challenges brought by parents (and sometimes also children) may not reach the Court in Strasbourg.

It is argued that although the determination of 'exceptional circumstances' requires flexibility, there is nevertheless a need for greater clarification as to what

[167] C Fenton-Glynn, 'Adoption in a European Perspective' in JM Sharpe (ed), *Research Handbook on European Family Law* (Cheltenham, Edward Elgar Publishing, 2016) 1, 2.

[168] *R and H v UK* (n 133).

[169] *YC v UK* (n 31).

sort of circumstances will be regarded as exceptional for the purposes of Article 8 and other Convention rights. Articles 2 and 3 ECHR, for example, could have a bearing on this analysis. It is argued that the 'exceptional circumstances' test ought to apply only where children's lives are endangered, or where they are at risk of significant physical or emotional harm. In a case where a child was removed into care and placed for adoption due to severe neglect and/or abuse, this would have the effect of protecting the child's right under Article 3 ECHR (prohibition of torture or inhuman or degrading treatment). This can be seen in *Z v UK*,[170] for example, where it was necessary to remove the children from their parents due to the severe neglect that they had suffered. However, children may experience emotional harm under Article 3 if they are removed from parents with whom they have strong bonds.

It can be argued that in *YC v UK*, for example, the separation of 8-year-old K from his mother could have engaged his right under Article 3 ECHR. This case is significant because it is arguable that the circumstances were exceptional enough to justify state intervention and removal of the child, but not so exceptional that non-consensual adoption was a necessary and proportionate measure (see further in section VI.B). Similarly, in cases where the severity of the harm suffered by the child, or that would be suffered by the child, satisfied Article 2 ECHR, such circumstances ought to be regarded as exceptional circumstances that justify non-consensual adoption.

In cases where a child's right to life under Article 2 and his or her right to freedom from torture or inhuman or degrading treatment under Article 3 were engaged as well as his or her parents' rights under Article 8, the child's rights under Articles 2 and 3 would outweigh those of the parents. In those circumstances, taking a child into care and placing him or her for adoption may be justified. It is argued that the test of exceptional circumstances needs to be clear, and ought to apply and provide justification for non-consensual adoptions only in circumstances where it can be demonstrated that the child's rights under Article 2 or 3 are under threat because the risk of significant harm is so severe.

The Court has, in some cases, considered whether less restrictive measures could be taken that fall short of non-consensual adoption, but which may be just as effective in terms of outcomes (ie protection of children's rights and best interests). It is suggested that in all cases, there should be a thorough analysis of whether the state has taken reasonable steps to reunite children and their parents, or whether other less restrictive alternatives may exist that are as effective (as already considered). It is argued that certain factors may be extracted from the case law considered in the previous sections of this chapter, and that the UNCRC rights considered in chapter 2 are relevant considerations that may help state authorities and the ECtHR decide when non-consensual adoption may or may not be proportionate. This is particularly important in adoption cases because of

[170] *Z v UK* (n 22).

the long-term – in fact life-long – consequences adoption has for children and their birth parents.

VI. Two UK Adoption Cases in the European Court of Human Rights

A. *R and H v UK*

R and H v UK[171] concerned an adoption that had originated in Northern Ireland.[172] The final appeal was heard in the House of Lords (now the Supreme Court in the UK), the final domestic court of appeal for Northern Ireland as well as England and Wales. Thus, even though the adoption law is different in Northern Ireland, this case is important because it nonetheless forms part of the law in England and Wales, and may be relevant in cases where courts consider non-consensual adoptions under the ACA 2002. This case also provides an example of how subsequent analysis of an adoption case heard in the highest court in England and Wales has been approached by the ECtHR.

In this case, the applicants were the biological parents of N, a baby girl, who was born in April 2002. The mother had a history of alcohol problems. She was admitted to an addictions centre after the birth of N (who was removed after birth) and attended a parenting centre with N for assessment purposes. The reports were positive and the applicants were allowed to take N home. However, the mother subsequently returned to her drinking and asked for assistance from social services because she was unable to care for her children. N was again taken into care by social workers from Down Lisburn Health and Social Services Trust on a voluntary basis, and was placed with foster carers. The mother had three other children who were placed in trust accommodation but who were eventually returned to their mother. N's care plan was that she would remain with foster parents in the short term, but in the long term she would be freed for adoption. A kinship assessment was made of N's maternal grandmother, but it was decided that the placement with her would not be appropriate. On 31 May 2005, it was determined that adoption was in N's best interests because it was unlikely that the mother would remain abstinent from alcohol, and because of the mother's failure to prioritise the needs of her children and herself over those of her partner. The judge accordingly made the freeing order requested by the authorities.

The applicants took their case to the ECtHR and argued violations of Article 6 ECHR (the right to a fair hearing) and Article 8 ECHR (the right to respect for private and family life). It was argued under Article 6(1) that conducting freeing

[171] *R and H v UK* (n 133).
[172] *Down Lisburn Health and Social Services Trust and another v H and another* [2006] UKHL 36.

order proceedings deprived the parents of the opportunity to participate in the later adoption order proceedings, which breached their right to a fair hearing. In terms of the substantive aspect of Article 8, it was argued that the freeing order was a disproportionate interference with their rights, because the national authorities had not kept the family situation under review and had not given sufficient consideration to kinship assessments for N.

The applicants also argued that the reasons for the freeing order provided by the trial judge were neither relevant nor sufficient, because the order had been based on the prediction that the second applicant would be unable to abstain from drinking alcohol, a prediction that she disputed. The applicants drew attention to the fact that they had subsequently had another child, O, who had not been the subject of care proceedings since birth and with respect to whom no concerns had been expressed about his welfare. They also argued, via the procedural aspect of Article 8, that it was procedurally improper to make a freeing order in advance of an adoption order, and was disproportionate in the light of the mother's lengthy period of sobriety. The Court considered the arguments presented by the applicants and held that there had been no violations of Articles 6 or 8.

The Court did not consider the argument that the freeing order prevented the couple from participating in the adoption proceedings within the scope of Article 6(1); instead it dealt with it as part of its analysis of the procedural requirements of Article 8. The question for the Court was whether the removal and adoption struck a fair balance between the parents' right to have a relationship and contact with N on the one hand and N's best interests in being protected from harm on the other.[173] The Court considered the relationship between the parents' Article 8 right and the best interests of the child. In doing so, it examined the earlier child abduction case of *Neulinger and Shuruk v Switzerland*,[174] which stated that the child's best interests should be treated as paramount even where they clash with the rights of the parent. This emphasis on paramountcy can also be seen in Article 21 UNCRC on the adoption of children.

In *R and H*, the Court held that the principles in *Neulinger* were of general application and could be applied to cases concerning custody and adoption proceedings. In *Neulinger*, it was proposed that there are two limbs to be applied when determining the child's best interests: (i) 'the child's ties with its family must be maintained, except in cases where the family has proved particularly unfit', (ii) 'it is clearly also in the child's interest to ensure its development in a sound environment, and a parent cannot be entitled under Article 8 to have such measures taken as would harm the child's health and development'.[175]

The Court in *R and H* observed that the state had a wide margin of appreciation in matters pertaining to the best interests of the child. However, despite this wide margin, the Court noted that as adoption had the effect of depriving biological

[173] *R and H v UK* (n 133) para 85.
[174] *Neulinger and Shuruk v Switzerland* (n 55).
[175] ibid para 136.

parents of their parental responsibilities, it should be authorised only in exceptional circumstances and would be justified only if the adoption was in the child's best interests.[176] In this case, the Court deferred to the UK court in determining what measure was in the child's best interests. Leaving the state to determine both the best interests *and* the appropriate measure to be taken in pursuit of the child's best interests without further scrutiny is in keeping with the wide margin of appreciation. However, it seems to differ from the approach envisaged in *Neulinger*, which allows the ECtHR to perform its own best interests analysis, which has been acknowledged as being of general application in all cases concerning the child's best interests.[177]

In terms of the procedural aspect of Article 8, which requires fairness in decision-making relating to Article 8 rights, the Court emphasised that this principle applies 'with greater force when those proceedings may culminate in a child being taken away from her biological parents and placed for adoption'.[178] On the facts, however, no Article 8 violation was found. The applicants had been legally represented, had been able to participate and to make their views known, and there were practical reasons for the two-stage procedure involving first the freeing and then the adoption of their child. The Court observed that freeing orders were not made lightly and that well-defined criteria tended to be applied. Although it was noted that it would be more advantageous to biological parents if they were able to participate in adoption proceedings, ultimately, weighing this against the right of the child meant that 'the interests of the biological parents must inevitably give way to that of the child'.[179]

The Court was unable to conclude that the process was unfair or that social services and the UK court had failed to provide sufficient protection to the parents' interests. In balancing the interests of the child against those of the parents, the state had acted in a manner that was proportionate to the aim of protecting the welfare of the child. The mother's problem with alcohol was cited as a reason for N to be freed for adoption rather than being returned to her parents. The Court accepted this as a relevant and sufficient reason for rejecting the applicants' submission against the freeing order, and held that there was no violation of Article 8.

The Court decided that 'exceptional circumstances' justified N's removal into care and her subsequent adoption without parental consent. It is not difficult to establish the existence of 'exceptional circumstances', which will in the eyes of the Court justify the removal and placement of a child for adoption. However, prior to N's removal into care, she had suffered very serious neglect,[180] which arguably engaged her right to freedom from torture or inhuman or degrading treatment under Article 3 ECHR. It is not disputed that the initial state intervention was

[176] *R and H v UK* (n 133) paras 81 and 88.
[177] ibid para 74.
[178] ibid para 76.
[179] ibid para 77.
[180] *Down Lisburn Health and Social Services Trust and another v H and another* (n 172) para 49.

justified, but it is at least questionable as to whether non-consensual adoption was necessary and proportionate.

It has already been suggested that several factors may be relevant in determining whether or not a non-consensual adoption may be regarded as a necessary and proportionate measure. In the first instance in this case, the child entered into the care system with the mother's consent. In the second instance, based on the facts, there was recognisable neglect that warranted state intervention. The state had initially provided assistance to the parents, but once N had been taken into care a second time, it was determined that adoption was in her best interests. In part, this seems to have been based on the 'complex problems'[181] of two of N's older siblings, who were considered to be 'extremely disturbed and damaged young people'.[182] However, one of the older siblings had not been as seriously affected by the mother's issues, and the mother and N's father were raising O effectively, which suggests that the mother had worked hard to address her issues and was able to parent effectively.

As considered previously, the mother's alcohol problem was the main reason used to argue against N's return and to suggest that she was at risk of harm. However, this was never argued in relation to a subsequent child, O, who had never been subject to care proceedings. If anything, the facts seem to suggest that the mother's circumstances had in fact changed and that her continued sobriety had enabled her to raise all her children without the need for support from the state. Further measures of state intervention could have been appropriate here, and that practical assistance (such as ongoing alcohol rehabilitation, therapy or support from social workers) may have addressed concerns about future relapses by the mother. Furthermore, while the trial judge had been concerned about history repeating itself on the part of the mother, the Court of Appeal was less pessimistic in this regard.[183]

The ECtHR appeared to place little weight on particular factors that suggested that the parents were able to raise N. These factors were the parents' ability to raise O, who was born after N, as well as N's three half-siblings. Another relevant factor that ought to have been considered in more depth was the attachments that had been observed during contact sessions between N and her parents. The Court simply described the existence of this fact as 'instructive',[184] and stated that the national authority was entitled to focus on N's individual needs and interests, although the ECtHR did not articulate what these needs and interests were and how they had best been served by adoption. It could be argued here that the national authorities should have considered the impact that the adoption would have had on N's right to know and be cared for her parents under Article 7 UNCRC. In fact, the combined effects of Articles 7 and 8 UNCRC emphasise that the child's

[181] ibid para 11.
[182] ibid para 48.
[183] ibid para 29.
[184] ibid para 86.

identity and knowledge of who his or her parents are can be regarded as weighty factors in a decision-making process. The Court should also have considered how an adoption prevented N from being raised with her three half-siblings and her full sibling, O. These considerations could have been weighed against any potential detriment to N if her mother resumed her drinking. Even if the ECtHR had still ultimately agreed with the state's decision, by providing a detailed assessment of N's best interests, encompassing her rights under the UNCRC, it would have sent a clear message to Member States as to which factors should be emphasised in an assessment of best interests.

In determining the best interests of N, once the national authorities had decided that she could not be returned into her parents' care, they only examined one possible alternative to adoption, which was placing the child with her grandparents. The ECtHR considered this and concluded that social services had been justified in rejecting the kinship placement with the grandmother, based on the allegations of indecent assault made against the grandfather many years before. However, the Court failed to consider the possibility of other less restrictive, but equally effective, alternatives that might have achieved a better balance between the protection of the best interests and the rights of N on the one hand (ie to be protected from harm under Article 3 ECHR and to have a relationship with her parent under Article 8 ECHR) and her parents' Article 8 ECHR rights on the other hand. This would also have provided closer adherence to the UNCRC and to the UN Guidelines for the Alternative Care of Children, which, it is argued, emphasise the importance of making use of alternatives to non-consensual adoption and the protection of parental responsibilities (in particular, under Articles 5 and 18 UNCRC).

In these circumstances, long-term foster care might have been beneficial, as N would have maintained the legal relationship with her birth family but it would have protected her from the potential impact of her mother's alcohol abuse if her mother were to relapse. This would have protected N from potential interferences with her rights under Article 3 ECHR and also under Article 19 UNCRC (protection from physical or mental violence). It would have been a less restrictive alternative to adoption that might have provided sufficient protection of N's welfare.

Although the decision in *R and H v UK* was not necessarily the wrong one, it is arguable that the Court's reasoning and analysis could have been better. The analysis would have been stronger if the ECtHR had provided a more in-depth examination of whether adoption was the most proportionate measure in the light of rights-based considerations (under the UNCRC for example), or whether other less restrictive measures could provide equally effective protection of N's rights and those of her parents. While non-consensual adoption may have been proportionate, it is less clear why non-consensual adoption with direct contact was not considered to be warranted in this case.

The Court accepted the domestic court's assessment that adoption was in N's best interests, without considering how N's rights might have been affected or how these best interests and rights were linked with her parents' rights, both of which are protected under the provisions of the UNCRC. In fact, N not only lost the legal tie with her birth parents and siblings, but also lost the opportunity to be raised within her birth family even though her parents were capable of caring for her (arguably an important right that is protected under Article 7 UNCRC). Based on N's continued relationship with her parents and siblings, it might have been possible for her to have been reintegrated into her family. However, it may no longer have been an equally effective alternative to non-consensual adoption based on the facts of the case coupled with the passage of time.

Interestingly, despite the fact that there was no Article 8 ECHR violation in respect of the aforementioned arguments, the Court considered the issue of post-adoption contact in some depth. In *R and H*, the parents were concerned that there would be no contact with N after the adoption, and it was one reason why the parents refused to consent to N's adoption. Expert witness Professor Triseliotis had made submissions to the Court that direct contact between N and her parents would be beneficial and that direct contact should have been sought. The Court agreed that the parents were justified in refusing to agree to adoption without knowledge of whether contact would occur. However, one factor that may have influenced the Court was an unusual feature in this case, which was that post-adoption contact was still ongoing at the time the case was heard, even though there was no specific legal order in place to enforce this contact.

It could be argued that a contact order might have provided some protection for N and her parents' Article 8 right to maintain their relationship, as a fear of loss of contact was the main reason why the parents disputed the adoption. Such a step would also have been in accordance with the principles of the UNCRC, considered throughout this book, that in some cases non-consensual adoption with direct contact may be an effective way of striking the balance between protecting children's rights and best interests on the one hand and parental rights on the other. However, in *R and H v UK*, while the parents were given assurances by the local authorities that contact would continue, no formal court order was in place protecting N's and her parents' mutual right to contact.

It is interesting that there were some dissenting judgments in this case: one in the ECtHR and the other in the House of Lords. The brief dissenting judgment of Judge Kalaydjieva in the ECtHR referred to Lady Hale's dissenting judgment in the House of Lords. Lady Hale had questioned 'whether it is necessary and proportionate to sever the links with the family of birth if a new (adoptive) family has not yet been identified'.[185] Judge Kalaydjieva held that freeing orders helped authorities to search for prospective adopters but they did not (i) provide a proper assessment of the child's best interests, or (ii) provide an assessment of the parents' rights and how they would be impacted by the freeing order and the likelihood of a subsequent adoption order.

[185] *Down Lisburn Health and Social Services Trust and another v H and another* (n 172) [34].

Simmonds has suggested that *R and H v UK* demonstrates that the Court is placing greater weight on children's rights in the field of child protection and adoption than in other areas of child law. She has argued that in contrast to relocation cases (such as *Neulinger*), for example, the ECtHR does not conduct a substantive analysis of the content or the weight to be given to the child's best interests.[186] Simmonds argues that children's rights are better protected due to the Court's acknowledgement of paramountcy in cases such as *R and H v UK*. She claims that the ECtHR protects parents' rights in contact, residence and relocation cases but that it is 'happy to side-line parental rights' in child protection and adoption cases. Nonetheless, she has approved of the paramountcy approach taken by the Court and has suggested that ECtHR rulings now 'comply more fully' with the UNCRC as far as adoption is concerned,[187] in contrast to the approach in the earlier case of *Johansen v Norway*,[188] which involved balancing the interests of the child in remaining in care on the one hand and the parents' interest in being reunited with their children on the other.

While Simmonds has observed that the Court has side-lined parental rights in child protection and adoption cases, she has emphasised that these cases provide increased protection for children's rights. However, it can be argued that not only did the Court in *R and H v UK* fail to consider N's rights (eg under Articles 5, 7, 8 and 9 UNCRC), but it also failed to give sufficient consideration to her best interests because of the narrow approach it took in accepting that adoption was the best option at the time for N. The evidence suggested that N had formed a good relationship with her birth parents and family, and that loss of contact had the potential to be distressing for her. Adoption would also have had the effect of severing the legal ties with a full sibling who remained with their parents, as well as with half-siblings. Because of the existence of the facts mentioned above, weighing these up alongside the other considerations of the Court, it can be argued that adoption might not have been in N's best interests. Furthermore, if N's rights under Article 8 ECHR and under the UNCRC had been considered by the Court, perhaps it would have given greater consideration to the importance of protecting the legal tie between N and her birth parents and her relationships with her wider birth family. As has been mentioned, N's parents were allowed to look after a younger full sibling, O, who had never been subject to care proceedings.

While it was necessary and proportionate to remove N from her parents' care, it is arguable that freeing N for adoption (which had the effect of severing the legal tie between N and her birth parents) may not have been proportionate to the aim of protecting N's best interests, which appeared to include maintaining contact with her birth parents. Here, it would have been appropriate for the Court to have considered less restrictive measures that would still have had the effect of protecting N's best interests, such as long-term foster care with a contact order in place

[186] C Simmonds, 'Paramountcy and the ECHR: A Conflict Resolved?' (2012) 71 *CLJ* 448, 500.
[187] ibid at 501.
[188] *Johansen v Norway* (n 134).

enabling N to maintain a relationship with her birth parents and siblings. This case is an acute demonstration of the Court's tendency to shy away from considering whether adoption itself is proportionate, seemingly regarding it as falling within the wide margin of appreciation afforded to domestic authorities in cases of this nature. It also demonstrates that despite stressing the importance of post-adoption contact (which social services had managed to arrange in this case), the Court did not assert that the child had the right to post-adoption contact, despite the benefits that can be derived from this arrangement. These benefits can include the contribution that post-adoption contact may have to the child's identity development, and the atmosphere of trust and openness that may be created with the adoptive parents due to the open lines of communication with birth parents.[189]

B. *YC v UK*

This was the first case to be heard by the ECtHR involving a non-consensual adoption in England made under the ACA 2002.[190] YC was the mother of K, a boy, and PC was her partner. The three of them had lived together until reports of domestic violence and social services' intervention led to K's removal (then aged 7) by way of emergency protection under the CA 1989. In foster care, K seemed stable and content, and the local authority (on the basis of recommendations by a psychologist) proposed that K's best interests would be best served by adoption. YC sought to address the local authority's concerns, namely, that her relationship with PC was abusive, that witnessing and intervening in domestic violence had been traumatic for K, and that YC's own behaviour was affected adversely by drinking, thereby impacting on K. She gave up drinking alcohol, ended the relationship with PC and found a new property in which to live. She sought to be the sole carer of K in the light of these new circumstances, but the UK courts refused to perform a fresh parenting assessment to see if K could be safely placed with her, because it had been decided that it was in K's best interests to be placed for adoption.

By the time that the facts had reached the ECtHR, the applicant had accepted that the passage of time rendered adoption the best option for her son. She nonetheless alleged that her Article 8 ECHR right to respect for private and family life had been violated for two main reasons. The first was that the UK courts had not assessed her as a sole carer for K. The second was that the UK courts had failed to take into account all of the relevant considerations when making the placement order preceding the adoption, which meant that no reasoned argument had been provided for making the adoption order that permanently severed the links between YC and K.

[189] E Neil et al, 'Supporting post adoption contact in complex cases – briefing paper' at http://www.adoptionresearchinitiative.org.uk/briefs/DFE-RBX-10-04.pdf.

[190] Specifically, under s 52(1)(b) of the Act.

The ECtHR was satisfied that YC's Article 8 right was engaged in respect of both her arguments. The Court agreed that refusal of the assessment did constitute an interference with Article 8, but the decisive issue was one of the 'necessity and proportionality of the measure'.[191] The Court had to consider whether the measures were 'relevant and sufficient'[192] (the substantive aspect of Article 8), and whether the decision-making process was fair and afforded due respect to the applicant's rights (the procedural aspect of Article 8).[193] The best interests of the child were regarded as paramount in cases concerning the permanent severance of ties between parent and child. Identifying the child's best interests and performing the proportionality assessment depended on considering many non-exhaustive factors, including those contained in the welfare checklists found in CA 1989, section 1(3) and the ACA 2002, section 1(4).

The first argument on the assessment of YC as a sole carer was interwoven with the second argument concerning lack of procedural safeguards. The first argument was dismissed, because it was in K's best interests to ensure the existence of a stable and secure environment for him to live in. The Court took the view that another assessment would not have been in K's best interests because it would threaten the stability of his existing arrangements. The ECtHR accepted the national authorities' conclusion that any assessment made would not have had an impact on the decision to make a care order, which would have been made in any event.

The second argument involved a close examination of the procedure that led to the placement order's being made. The domestic court (the Family Proceedings Court) had to consider an application for a care order and a placement order for K. The court made an interim care order with a direction for a further assessment. In doing so, no specific reference was made to the CA 1989, section 1(3), although reference was made to the making of a care order under CA 1989, section 31(2), with an indication that the 'threshold' criteria were met. The local authority and K's guardian appealed against the court's direction ordering that the assessment take place, and sought a final care order and a placement order. The County Court held that the Family Proceedings Court was mistaken in not making a final care order, but the County Court made no reference to the welfare checklist under the ACA 2002, section 1(4). There was also no reference to Article 8 ECHR, or to the rights of the parents and children. The judge stated that the conditions needed for making a care order existed, and therefore approved the placement order. Despite the fact that the County Court judge had made no reference to the section 1(4) welfare checklist, the appeal courts in the UK accepted that it was a finely balanced case and that the County Court judge had applied his mind to the checklist.[194]

[191] *YC v UK* (n 31) para 131.
[192] ibid para 144.
[193] *Neulinger and Shuruk v Switzerland* (n 55).
[194] See *YC v UK* (n 31) para 5 for the dissenting judgment of Judge De Gaetano, which refers to the Court of Appeal judgment.

The ECtHR asserted that the lack of direct reference to or consideration of section 1(4) of the 2002 Act could have been remedied by YC's requesting clarification from the judge. She was invited to do so by the County Court judge,[195] but it is unclear from the facts of the case why she did not seek further clarification of his reasons for making the placement order. Furthermore, the ECtHR was satisfied that as the threshold for making a care order had been met, it was satisfactory to make a placement order without a care order in place, on the basis that the UK had a margin of appreciation to do so. The approach of the ECtHR was to hold that it was irrelevant that the usual procedure had not been followed, given that the outcome would have been the same in any event: a care order would have been made. The ECtHR concluded that there had been no violation of Article 8 ECHR. The Court also held that the welfare checklist under section 1(4) of the ACA 2002 broadly reflected elements in assessing necessity under Article 8(2).

Ifezu and Rajabali have argued that the decision in *YC v UK* shows that the ECtHR approves of the approach in English law, reflecting a substantial shift in its attitude towards children, particularly in cases of adoption.[196] However, it can be argued that certain aspects of the judgment are unsatisfactory. Thus, for example, the Court did not consider the lack of procedural safeguards for the parents in this case.

YC v UK has been subject to approval by the UK Supreme Court, which regarded it as providing some clearer guidance. See, for example, *ANS and another v ML (AP) (Scotland)*[197] (a non-consensual adoption case discussed in chapter 4), where the Supreme Court opined that *YC v UK* made it clear that the factors laid down in the welfare checklist in the ACA 2002 were factors considered when determining the proportionality of making an order. In *ANS*, Lord Carnwath stressed the importance of both *YC* and the earlier *Neulinger* decision, and stated that there is 'currently a broad consensus – including in international law – in support of the idea that in all decisions concerning children, their best interests must be paramount'.[198] The two-limb test that was first articulated in *Neulinger*[199] was referred to in *YC v UK*[200] but, as Lord Carnwath pointed out, there is some inconsistency within the ECtHR jurisprudence.[201] In other words, *YC* seemed to demonstrate that these two limbs were to be considerations borne in mind rather

[195] ibid para 82.

[196] G Ifezu and M Rajabali, 'Protecting the interests of the child' [2013] *Cambridge Journal of International Comparative Law* 81.

[197] *ANS and another v ML (AP) (Scotland)* [2012] UKSC 30.

[198] ibid [68].

[199] Family ties ought to be severed only in exceptional circumstances, and if and when appropriate the state must help to 'rebuild' the family. See *Neulinger and Shuruk v Switzerland* (n 55).

[200] *YC v UK* (n 31), para 134 referring to *Neulinger and Shuruk v Switzerland* (n 55) para 136: (i) 'the child's ties with its family must be maintained, except in cases where the family has proved particularly unfit', (ii) 'it is clearly also in the child's interest to ensure its development in a sound environment, and a parent cannot be entitled under Article 8 to have such measures taken as would harm the child's health and development'.

[201] *ANS and another v ML (AP) (Scotland)* (n 197) paras 75–76.

than fixed tests to be applied in each case.[202] The approaches in these cases therefore differ with the approach in *YC v UK* indicating that there was flexibility as to whether or not the test should be applied whereas *Neulinger* seemed to suggest that these two limbs must be applied in cases concerning the rights and best interests of children. In *Neulinger*, the ECtHR has arguably and potentially given itself the power to look more closely at the substance of decisions made in adoption proceedings.

The problem is that adoption may be regarded by the ECtHR as quite a different factual context from that of *Neulinger*, which was a case involving international child abduction and which may be fact-specific. The above interpretation of *Neulinger* and the approach taken in adoption cases is supported by Simmonds, who argues that, despite the approach taken in *Neulinger*, the Court had nonetheless been moving towards a 'paramountcy' approach in the context of adoption proceedings, whereby children's best interests take precedence over those of their parents.[203] It is argued that although the ECtHR must defer to national authorities and respect their greater knowledge and possession of the facts in any given case, performing its own best interests assessment in adoption cases would have the benefit of encouraging courts at all levels to provide a more detailed analysis of the child's best interests and rights in such cases. In doing so, the Court ought to have regard to the UNCRC.

With respect to the facts in *YC v UK*, the UK courts placed a great deal of emphasis on the stability that K was offered via adoption. However, this was not weighed against other considerations, such as K's close relationship with his mother. When analysing the decision of the County Court, the ECtHR did not examine the extent to which K's rights were considered by that court, or the lack of weight that was placed on K's apparent bond with his mother and suggestions that the child had expressed a desire to return home to her. Although his wish to return home should not necessarily have been treated as determinative, more weight ought to have been placed on his wishes and feelings by the national courts and the ECtHR. The decision shows that the ECtHR adopts a rather deferential approach to the national courts, without the detailed scrutiny that might be considered to be appropriate in cases where the consequences flowing from this alleged rights violation are so severe, namely the permanent severance of the legal tie between a boy and his birth parents.

As Sloan has observed, in *YC v UK* the ECtHR 'saw no incompatibility between assertions'[204] that the child's best interests are paramount and that 'family ties may only be severed in very exceptional circumstances and … everything must be done to preserve personal relations and, where appropriate, to "rebuild" the family'.[205] In the light of these important principles, it is arguable that the ECtHR should

[202] ibid para 75.
[203] Simmonds (n 186) 500.
[204] Sloan (n 16).
[205] *YC v UK* (n 31) para 134.

have conducted a more thorough analysis of the facts and of K's best interests and rights. Judge De Gaetano gave a dissenting judgment in which he emphasised that the consequences of adoption warranted a greater protection of rights, and that safeguards were needed to prevent improper interference with rights:

> [T]here can be no more draconian measure in the context of the relationship between parent and child than an order which permanently severs family ties. The need for safeguards against arbitrary, or even merely unjustified or unnecessary interference, is compelling ...[206]

He was of the view that Article 8 ECHR had been violated because the UK courts had failed to take into account relevant considerations (such as the child's age and his attachment to his mother) and had not provided a reasoned judgment. He described the placement order as being made in a very 'unorthodox' way, and he expressed his distaste for the 'cavalier' way in which the Court of Appeal had refused to give the mother permission to appeal. He was highly dissatisfied with the analysis of the UK courts and the fact that no reference had been made either to the Article 8 rights of the child and parents, or to the principle of proportionality.[207] He also disapproved of the ECtHR's decision to concede to the UK's margin of appreciation in this matter. He referred to *Saviny v Ukraine*[208] in order to emphasise the draconian nature of severing family ties, despite states' enjoying a margin of appreciation:

> [N]otwithstanding a margin of appreciation enjoyed by domestic authorities in deciding on placing a child into public care, severing family ties means cutting a child off from its roots, which can only be justified in very exceptional circumstances ...[209]

He also suggested that there insufficient consideration had been given to K's age, in light of the fact that K was not a newborn or a young child but an 8-year-old boy who had lived with his parents from birth. The age of the child in this case seems particularly relevant, as most cases concerning adoption tend to involve younger children who will have little or no memory of their birth parents (as seen in *R and H v UK* and most of the cases referred to in chapters 3, 4 and 5). Although the best interests of K were considered by the domestic courts and by the ECtHR, it seems that the analysis was narrowly confined to factors proposed by the UK (ie his stability and security) rather than overt reference being made to the bonds that existed between K and his mother (who were described as having a good relationship), the possibility of the grief that K might suffer as a consequence of the adoption, and considerations of identity and relationships with his wider birth family.

Fenton-Glynn argues that the decision in *YC v UK* demonstrates that paramountcy is no longer so 'alien' to the ECtHR.[210] She argues that the decision in

[206] ibid. See Judge De Gaetano's dissenting judgment, ibid para 6.
[207] ibid. See dissenting judgment of Judge De Gaetano, ibid para 4.
[208] *Saviny v Ukraine* (n 104).
[209] ibid.
[210] Simmonds (n 186) 499–500.

that case demonstrates that greater weight has been given to children's rights in the area of child protection and adoption as there is no longer a strict balancing process[211] or a vigorous analysis of the proportionality of a measure (such as adoption), and that there is no substantive analysis of the content or weight of the best interests by the ECtHR.[212] The author respectfully disagrees with Fenton-Glynn's argument that greater weight has been given to children's rights, on the basis that the ECtHR failed to consider K's relationship rights with YC under Article 8 ECHR or other potentially applicable rights under the UNCRC (such as Articles 7, 8 and 9) in the light of his attachment to his mother and expressed wishes to maintain contact with her. Furthermore, K's adoption was arguably not a necessary measure to protect his rights under Articles 6 and 19 UNCRC; and under Article 21 UNCRC it could be said that, considering the gravity of the measure, greater analysis was required than the bare welfare test applied by the domestic courts (see also chapter 2).

However, Fenton-Glynn has rightly argued that the same is not true in respect of the views of the child. She claims that, in this area, children have not been helped by the 'conservative jurisprudence' of the ECtHR. She has further observed that in Europe there is no clear consensus on the age at which children should (if at all) be able to consent to adoption, of the weight to be given to their views in the context of adoption proceedings, or if they should be given any weight at all.[213] The importance of the voice of the child in court proceedings (see chapter 2) is emphasised in Article 12 UNCRC (the child's right to be heard), but at the domestic level in the UK and in the ECtHR there was very little discussion of K's wishes. The ECtHR simply affirmed the English court's best interests assessments, without considering the child's wishes, even though a child's wishes may form part of an assessment of best interests under the law in England and Wales.[214]

In general, whereas society and the courts are increasingly placing more emphasis on ascertaining the wishes of the child,[215] *YC v UK* shows that there is insufficient consideration of the voice of the child at ECtHR level in the context of adoption proceedings.[216] Considering the age of K, even though there was no legal requirement to listen to his opinion, it is suggested that his thoughts and feelings should have been an important consideration in determining his future, because of his likely ability to understand the consequences of his adoption. Although it has been acknowledged by Gilmore and Herring that the greater the weight that is attached to children's perceptions, the greater the likelihood that children may be manipulated into saying what adults want them to say, they

[211] ibid.

[212] ibid 500.

[213] C Fenton-Glynn, 'The Child's Voice in Adoption Proceedings: A European Perspective' (2014) 22 *International Journal of Children's Rights* 135.

[214] Under English law, see the CA 1989, s 1(3) of which refers to the wishes and feelings of the child as a consideration for the judiciary when deciding whether or not to make a court order. The ACA 2002, s 1(4) also refers to the wishes and feelings of the child as a consideration to which the court can have regard when deciding whether to make an adoption order.

[215] See discussion in *Family Justice Review* (November 2011).

[216] Fenton-Glynn (n 213).

have argued that the benefits of listening to children may outweigh potential fears that they may be manipulated.[217] Daly goes as far to suggest that a child's wishes and feelings ought to be determinative unless harmful to the child.[218] Although K's wishes should not necessarily have been the determining factor in this case, greater emphasis on his Article 12 UNCRC right – which is also emphasised in the UN Guidelines for the Alternative Care of Children – may have led to a different outcome in this case. Indeed, Article 3 UNCRC requires the interpretation of all UNCRC rights in accordance with the child's best interests. It is clear that insufficient regard was given to K's rights in this case, in any of the courts that considered the adoption.

Furthermore, it is argued that the Court ought to have undertaken a more thorough analysis of less restrictive alternatives to non-consensual adoption, as it did in cases such as *Pontes v Portugal*,[219] *RMS v Spain*,[220] *Zhou v Italy*[221] and *SH v Italy*.[222] While none of these cases involved a child's witnessing domestic violence, *SH v Italy* did involve a mother who faced difficulty in parenting her children due to mental illness. In this case, the Court held that the state ought to have continued to offer state assistance, a less restrictive alternative to removal for adoption. With respect to *YC v UK*, it is argued that the potential detriment to K in being adopted might have outweighed the benefits that he would have obtained from the arrangement.

It is also argued that the ECtHR in *YC v UK* should have taken more cognisance of the fact that K was aged 8 and was likely to have a strong sense of identity vis-à-vis his birth family, an important right that is protected by Article 8 UNCRC and relevant in the context of this right, since the adoption resulted in the legal severance of the ties between K and his mother, as well as the loss of his de facto relationship with her. Furthermore, his strong attachment to his mother meant that it would be potentially more difficult for him to adjust to an adoption placement than it would be for a younger child or a child of the same age with a weaker attachment to a parent.

Therefore, in the light of these considerations it could be argued, for example, that the state should have made more concerted efforts to see whether K could have been safely placed with his mother, who had separated from her partner and wanted to be considered as a sole carer. It is possible that with state assistance, for example in the form of therapeutic support and visits from social workers, such a placement might have worked. Alternatively, a special guardianship order could have been considered, as it was envisaged by the Government in England and Wales as a less restrictive alternative to adoption for older children, for whom

[217] S Gilmore and J Herring, 'Listening to Children … whatever' (2014) 130 *LQR* 531.

[218] This is the central argument here: A Daly, *Children, Autonomy and the Courts: Beyond the Right to be Heard* (Leiden, Brill, 2018).

[219] *Pontes v Portugal* (n 104).

[220] *RMS v Spain* (n 91).

[221] *Zhou v Italy* (n 98).

[222] *SH v Italy* (n 99).

it would be desirable to maintain legal ties with their birth family.[223] A special guardianship order would have allowed YC to retain her status as the legal parent of K and respected the bond between YC and K, while ensuring certainty for K. Thus it is argued that less restrictive (and potentially equally effective) measures could have been undertaken to protect K's rights under Articles 6 and 19 UNCRC, and his right to freedom from torture or inhuman or degrading treatment under Article 3 ECHR.

VII. Conclusion

The ECtHR has an important role to play in upholding Convention rights and in assessing the proportionality of state measures when children are removed from their parents and placed for adoption. The most relevant Convention rights in the context of adoption proceedings are Article 2 (the right to life), Article 3 (the right to freedom from torture or inhuman or degrading treatment), Article 6 (the right to a fair hearing) and Article 8 (the right to respect for private and family life).

It is apparent from ECtHR case law that the separation of children and parents is warranted only in exceptional circumstances, and that national authorities must take reasonable steps to reunite children with their parents. If states fail to do so then these are circumstances in which adoption may violate the Article 8 ECHR rights of parents and children. However, the state's positive obligation to reunite children with their parents is counterbalanced by jurisprudence that justifies limiting the parents' and the child's right to respect for private and family life in the name of the child's own best interests. Thus, in cases where neglect or abuse has occurred, or where a child has been settled with other carers for years, it may not be in the child's best interests to be reunited with his or her parents.

It is also apparent that where the neglect or abuse is serious enough to engage the child's rights under Article 2 or Article 3 of the ECHR, a non-consensual adoption may not only be in child's best interests but will also be the most effective way of protecting the child's rights under the ECHR and the UNCRC. However, while a non-consensual adoption is, in some cases, the least restrictive measure available, there are cases where equally effective less restrictive alternatives are available, which would be less likely to violate children's and parents' rights under Article 8 ECHR and children's rights under the UNCRC.

The mere fact that a child could be placed in a more beneficial environment is insufficient to justify removal from the family home, let alone non-consensual adoption. This chapter has also shown that there is a substantial body of case law suggesting that the scope of the state's obligation under Article 8 ECHR to assist families prior to removal of the child from the family home or even non-consensual

[223] See discussion in Department of Health and Social Care, *Adoption: A New Approach* (Cm 5017, 2000). Also see J Nelson, 'Special Guardianship Orders – an Introduction' [2005] *Family Law* 573.

adoption may be widening. Another important issue, which has been highlighted in this chapter, is the lack of consideration of children's rights in adoption cases. Thus, the alleged violations of Convention rights, in adoption cases, are typically brought by the parents. Children's rights are more frequently argued, however, in the context of cases where states have failed to satisfy a positive obligation to intervene to protect children (as demonstrated by the discussion of Articles 2 and 3). When cases are brought by parents, rather than considering the rights of children, the ECtHR focuses on whether the best interests of the child can justify a violation of parental rights. While the Court is not compelled to consider children's rights, it is suggested that some of these cases (especially those discussed in the context of Articles 6 and 8) demonstrate a missed opportunity for the development of children's rights, and that focusing solely on children's best interests may serve to replicate some of the problems that exist in the law of adoption in England and Wales (see chapter 2).

Because of the importance of the rights at stake and the permanent and irreversible nature of adoption, it has been argued that the Court could apply its existing case law in a more methodical way when determining whether or not a non-consensual adoption is a proportionate measure. In performing this analysis, it has been argued that UNCRC rights (eg Articles 3, 5, 6, 7, 8, 9, 18, 19, 20 and 21) are all relevant.

Having outlined the approach applied by the ECtHR in care and adoption proceedings, the next chapter considers the relevant legislative frameworks in England and Wales, and adoption cases heard in the High Court and the Court of Appeal in England and Wales and the Supreme Court in the UK.

4

Adoption Cases in the Courts in England and Wales

I. Introduction: Adoption – First Port of Call or Last Resort?

Should adoption be the first port of call, so to speak, when judges are trying to protect the best interests of a child, or the last resort? Proportionality is an important legal and methodological tool that judges can apply in their decision-making processes. Chapter 3 showed that the European Court of Human Rights (ECtHR) makes much use of that tool. Chapter 4 is underpinned by three important questions. First, to what extent is the legislation on non-consensual adoption proportionate? Second, how do senior judges in England and Wales interpret and apply the proportionality principle in non-consensual adoption cases? Third, what steps might need to be taken prior to a non-consensual adoption to ensure its proportionality?

This chapter tries to answer these questions by examining the main legal framework for non-consensual adoption, the Adoption and Children Act 2002 (ACA 2002). The chapter also considers the gloss on the ACA 2002 rendered by the Children and Families Act 2014 (CFA 2014), which also provides for post-adoption contact and fostering for adoption. It is essential to describe and evaluate these legal frameworks to assess whether further legal reform is required to protect the rights of children and their parents. In addition, chapter 4 discusses notable Court of Appeal and Supreme Court decisions. These cases have interpreted fundamental provisions of the ACA 2002 and have provided guidance on concepts such as proportionality and rights under the European Convention on Human Rights (ECHR),[1] and their relationship with non-consensual adoption in England and Wales.

The United Nations Convention on the Rights of the Child (UNCRC)[2] is both an important instrument and another legal and methodological tool that can be

[1] European Convention for the Protection of Human Rights and Fundamental Freedoms, as amended by Protocols nos 11 and 14, 4 November 1950 (European Convention on Human Rights (ECHR)), ETS 5, available at https://www.refworld.org/docid/3ae6b3b04.html.

[2] United Nations Convention on the Rights of the Child, 20 November 1989, 1577 UNTS 3, available at https://www.refworld.org/docid/3ae6b38f0.html.

applied by the judiciary (see discussion in chapter 2). This chapter considers the application of the UNCRC in judicial decision-making, alongside the use of the proportionality principle. The analysis examines the UNCRC articles referred to in chapter 2, and whether routine consideration of these articles would provide greater protection for children's and parents' rights under the ECHR.

The chapter considers whether the legislation and courts' decisions on non-consensual adoption have managed to strike the appropriate balance in protecting the rights and best interests of children, on the one hand, and the rights of their parents, on the other. This discussion does so by exploring whether the ACA 2002 (in particular, section 52(1)(b)) can be reconciled with the state's obligations to children and parents under the ECHR and the state's positive obligation to make efforts to reunite children with their parents where possible under Article 8 of that Convention.[3]

Legal academics have argued that the current adoption law in England and Wales insufficiently considers parents' interests, and in particular their right to respect for a private and family life under Article 8 ECHR.[4] Harris-Short described adoption as the 'most drastic' and 'devastating' order that a family law court can make.[5] She also worried that the policy of encouraging adoption as quickly as possible can run counter to the attempt to reunite parents and children for the purposes of complying with Article 8.[6] Due to the gravity and irrevocability of adoption, there is understandable concern that in some cases non-consensual adoption may not be a proportionate measure. It is important, therefore, to consider whether the legislation and case law in England and Wales does provides sufficient protection for the rights of children and their parents, under the ECHR and the UNCRC, in non-consensual adoption cases.

II. The Adoption Legislation

A. The Adoption and Children Act 2002: An Overview

The ACA 2002 came fully into force on 30 December 2005.[7] It was introduced primarily to bring the law on adoption into line with the Children Act 1989 (CA 1989), section 1(1) and Article 21 UNCRC (the right to adoption), by making

[3] See, eg, *Hokkanen v Finland* [1996] 1 FLR 289; *K and T v Finland* App no 25702/94 (ECHR, 12 July 2001).

[4] S Harris-Short, 'Making and Breaking Family Life: Adoption, the State and Human Rights' (2008) 35 *Journal of Law and Society* 28, 30; S Choudhry and J Herring, *European Human Rights and Family Law* (Oxford, Hart Publishing, 2010); B Sloan, 'Conflicting Rights: English Adoption Law and the Implementation of the UN Convention on the Rights of the Child' (2013) 25 *Child and Family Law Quarterly* 40.

[5] Harris-Short (n 4) 30.

[6] ibid 35.

[7] It repealed and replaced the Adoption Act 1976.

the child's welfare the paramount consideration in the adoption process[8] and by introducing a welfare checklist (see the ACA 2002, section 1(4)) like that in the CA 1989. The Act was also intended to encourage practitioners to engage in permanency planning and to increase the number of adoptions of children in care, by tackling delays in the adoption process caused by the shortage of adopters, delays in matching children to prospective adopters and delays in the court system.[9] The reforms further sought to improve the support available to prospective adopters, as increasing post-adoption support was regarded as a means of increasing the number of prospective adopters.[10] Another aim of the Act was 'to put the child's rights more to the fore'[11] (despite the fact that there is no explicit reference to children's rights or to the UNCRC itself within the ACA 2002).

The new law under the ACA 2002 replaced the old system of freeing orders (under the Adoption Act 1976) with placement orders, and amended the grounds under which a non-consensual adoption could be ordered by the courts. Furthermore, special guardianship orders were created by the ACA 2002 and inserted into the CA 1989, sections 14A–14G, to offer an alternative to adoption and to provide legal security for older children in foster care or those living with relatives, while enabling such children to maintain legal ties with their birth parents (see further in chapter 5).[12]

The New Labour Government viewed adoption as the solution for the problems relating to children in care that had been highlighted by the Waterhouse Report.[13] The Waterhouse Inquiry investigated the abuse of children in care and the deficiencies in the care provided in children's homes in Wales. Although, as Allen has noted, there is no immediate connection between the abuse that these children suffered in children's homes and the intention to reform adoption law,[14] there is a clear rationale behind the legal reform. Thomas has observed that the Report stimulated further discussion on how to address other issues,[15] such as poor educational and social outcomes for children in care. Dey has suggested that

[8] House of Lords Select Committee on Adoption Legislation, *Second Report of Session 2012–13 Adoption: Post-Legislative Scrutiny* (TSO, 2013) 17.

[9] The House of Commons Library Research Paper 01/78: The Adoption and Children Bill, 26 October 2001, 13 and 33–34. On average, an adoption would take two years and nine months: see Special Standing Committee Discussion on the Adoption and Children Bill, 29 November 2001. See also C Thomas, *Adoption for looked after children: messages from research – An overview of the adoption research initiative* (London, BAAF, 2013) 3–4.

[10] Thomas (n 9) 3.

[11] Quoted from the Special Standing Committee discussion on the Adoption and Children Bill on 19 November 2001.

[12] For further discussion, see A Hall, 'Special Guardianship: A Missed Opportunity – Findings from Research' [2008] *Family Law* 148; D Cullen, 'Adoption – a (fairly) new approach' (2005) 17 *Child and Family Law Quarterly* 475.

[13] Department of Health, *Lost in Care: Report of the Tribunal of Inquiry into the Abuse of Children in the Former County Council Areas of Gwynedd and Clwyd since 1974* (London, TSO, 2000) ('the Waterhouse Report').

[14] N Allen, *Making Sense of the New Adoption Law* (Lyme Regis, Russell House Publishing Ltd, 2003).

[15] Thomas (n 9) 3.

the Waterhouse Report put pressure on the Government to improve outcomes for children in care via legal reform,[16] and the Government identified adoption of children in care as a potential method of reform.[17]

Tony Blair, the Prime Minister at the time, announced that adoption reform would be a priority and that he would lead a major review of adoption law.[18] He stated that adoption was 'less about providing homes for relinquished babies and more concerned with providing secure, permanent relationships for some of society's most vulnerable children'.[19] The Labour Government aimed to increase the number of adoption orders by at least 40 per cent by 2005, with an ultimate target of a 50 per cent increase in adoption.[20]

Having outlined the motivations for and purpose behind the ACA 2002, the following section compares the existing law on adoption with the previous law under the Adoption Act 1976, to determine whether or not the new law strikes the appropriate balance in protecting children's best interests and rights, on the one hand, and parents' rights, on the other, in the context of non-consensual adoption.

B. The 'Old' Law and the 'New' Law

Under the Adoption Act 1976, section 18, children were 'freed' for consensual or non-consensual adoption via a 'freeing order'[21] before a final adoption order was made. Once a freeing order was made, a child no longer retained legal ties with his or her birth family.[22] The child became a statutory orphan, in that he or she was left in a temporary legal limbo before an adoption order was made,[23] although once freed for adoption, there was no guarantee of his or her being adopted. After a freeing order, an adoption order could be made with parental consent under section 16(b)(i), or alternatively parental consent could be dispensed with and an adoption order made under section 16(b)(ii) if one of the grounds listed in section 16(2) was proved, namely, that the child's parent(s) could not be found or was (were) incapable of giving agreement; was (were) withholding agreement unreasonably; had persistently failed without reasonable cause to discharge parental responsibility for the child; had abandoned or neglected the child; had persistently ill-treated the child or had seriously ill-treated the child.

[16] I Dey, 'Adapting Adoption: A case of Closet Politics?' (2005) 19 *International Journal of Law, Policy and the Family* 293.

[17] Waterhouse Report (n 13).

[18] Department of Health and Social Care, *Adoption Procedure: A New Approach* (Cm 5017, 2000).

[19] C Bridge and H Swindells, *Adoption: The Modern Law* (Bristol, Jordan Publishing Limited, 2003) 30.

[20] C Barton 'Adoption Strategy' [2001] *Family Law* 89.

[21] For a more detailed explanation of freeing orders, see *Down Lisburn Health and Social Services Trust and another (AP) v H (AP) and another (AP)* [2006] UKHL 36.

[22] N Lowe and G Douglas, *Bromley's Family Law*, 11th edn (Oxford, OUP, 2015) 699.

[23] M Murch et al, *Pathways to Adoption* (London, HMSO, 1993).

Under the ACA 2002, children are no longer 'freed' for adoption. Instead, a placement order under the ACA 2002, section 18 precedes an adoption order, placing a child with prospective adoptive parents. When a placement order is in force, parental responsibility is shared between the local authority, the prospective adopters and the birth parents, but will vest fully in the adopters once an adoption order is made. Under the ACA 2002, section 21(2), a placement order cannot be made unless one of the following applies:

(a) the child is subject to a care order;
(b) the conditions for making a care order are satisfied;[24] or
(c) the child has no parent or guardian.

If one of these conditions is satisfied, a placement order can be made under section 21(3) if the parents consent to the adoption[25] or parental consent has been dispensed with under section 52(1)(b) because the child's welfare requires it.[26] A placement order remains in place until it is revoked, a final adoption order is made, or if the child marries or reaches 18 years of age and has not been adopted.[27] According to Bridge and Swindells, the creation of placement orders sounded the 'death knell'[28] of the old adoption system, addressing the 'legal limbo'[29] that children previously faced with freeing orders.

Under the new law (the ACA 2002), once a placement order is in force, the birth parents can apply for leave to oppose an adoption order under section 47(5) of the Act. If parents do not oppose adoption or leave to oppose adoption is not granted, the court then considers the grounds for making an adoption order. The ACA 2002, section 52 amended the grounds for making an adoption order. One of the grounds from the Adoption Act 1976 was retained under section 52(1)(a).[30] However, the other grounds were removed and replaced with section 52(1)(b), which provides that 'the welfare of the child requires consent to be dispensed with'. In *Re P*, Wall LJ explained the meaning of the word 'requires' in section 52(1)(b):

> [Requires] is a word which was plainly chosen as best conveying … the essence of the Strasbourg jurisprudence. And viewed from that perspective 'requires' does indeed have the connotation of the imperative, what is demanded rather than what is merely optional or reasonable or desirable.[31]

[24] Threshold criteria under the CA 1989, s 31(2).
[25] ACA 2002, s 21(3)(a).
[26] ibid, s 21(3)(b).
[27] ibid, s 21(4).
[28] Bridge and Swindells (n 19) 160.
[29] C Ball, 'The Adoption and Children Act 2002 A Critical Examination' (2005) 29 *Adoption and Fostering* 6.
[30] The ground is based on the parent's capacity to care for the child. Note that 'cannot be found' is generally interpreted to mean that there is no practical means of communicating with the person whose consent is required. See *Re R (Adoption)* [1976] 1 WLR 34.
[31] *Re P (Placement Orders: Parental Consent)* [2008] EWCA Civ 535 [125], *per* Wall LJ.

Wall LJ also stated it has to be shown that 'the child's welfare "requires" adoption as opposed to something short of adoption',[32] and that even where the child's welfare might require statutory intervention or indefinite removal of the child from his or her family, 'the same circumstances will not necessarily "require" that the child be adopted'.[33] The Adoption Act 1976, section 6 had focused on the 'welfare of the child throughout his childhood', but section 1(2) of the ACA 2002 provides that 'The paramount consideration of the court or adoption agency must be the child's welfare, throughout his life.' Wall LJ has described this as a 'vital'[34] difference. It is argued that basing non-consensual adoption on the child's welfare under the ACA 2002, section 52(1)(b) and making the child's welfare the paramount consideration, minimises the rights of birth parents in adoption proceedings. It is also preferable for child's interests to be primary and not paramount, so that parents' interests are not disregarded. Indeed, Archard has highlighted the difficulty of making children's interests paramount:

> We should allow that the interests of parents and other adults within the child's society may sometimes outweigh those of the child. The implausibility of thinking that a child's interests are paramount extends to what amounts to a disguised discounting of a parent's interests …[35]

It can be argued that the 1976 Act provided more protection to parents' interests than does the ACA 2002. For example, it was uncommon under the Adoption Act 1976 for judges to make adoption orders without parental consent.[36] A review of the case law on non-consensual adoption led Henricson and Bainham to conclude that when the 1976 Act was in force, there were many cases where a birth parent's objection to non-consensual adoption was upheld on the basis that consent was not unreasonably withheld. This was the case, they argued, even where social workers were in favour of adoption due to the need to promote the child's welfare.[37] Thus, it can be argued that the ACA 2002 has had the effect of removing the protection of parental interests, as the sole focus of the Act, when non-consensual adoption takes place, is the child's welfare not the parent's interests.[38] Parents' rights are, in fact, referred to explicitly within the UNCRC (see chapter 2), which implies that they ought to be given ample thought when children's rights are at stake. Thus, if one views the adoption process through the lens of the UNCRC, consideration of

[32] ibid [126].
[33] ibid.
[34] ibid [127].
[35] D Archard, 'Children, adults, best interests and rights' (2013) 13 *Medical Law International* 55, 60.
[36] Bridge and Swindells (n 19) 15.
[37] For further discussion on this point, see C Henricson and A Bainham, *The child and family policy divide: Tensions, convergence and rights* (York, Joseph Rowntree Foundation, 2005). They cite the following cases as examples: *Re M (Adoption and Residence Order)* [1998] 1 FLR 570 and *Re B (Adoption Order)* [2001] 2 FLR 26.
[38] Henricson and Bainham (n 37).

parents' rights should be a crucial part of the analysis carried out by social workers, the judiciary and other practitioners in the field.

In fact, the introduction of non-consensual adoption based solely upon the paramountcy of the child's welfare has been and continues to be controversial. Prior to the changes that the Labour Government sought for adoption law, the Conservative Government had also, in the early 1990s, considered similar reforms.[39] Thus, in 1992, the Adoption Review[40] recommended that children's welfare should be the court's paramount consideration, *except* in cases where adoption was taking place without parental consent. In the Review it was stated that only where adoption would 'be marginally better than another option' should the court 'allow the fact that a parent does not agree to adoption to tip the balance in favour of the other option'.[41]

The appropriateness of making the child's welfare paramount in non-consensual adoption cases has been questioned.[42] Sloan has observed that '[a] strict application of the welfare principle could preclude a court from considering the interests of parents when making an adoption-related decision'.[43] This paramountcy of children's welfare in the adoption process, and the provision permitting non-consensual adoption solely on the basis of welfare, has been controversial because adoption orders are permanent and irrevocable. It has been pointed out, for example, by Herring et al that it is 'too low a hurdle',[44] because it might not be difficult to show that a child would be better off being raised by someone other than his or her birth parents.

Another change introduced by the ACA 2002 was the introduction of a welfare checklist. The Adoption Act 1976, section 6, had provided that the court had a general duty to consider the welfare of the child, but the ACA 2002, section 1(4) includes a welfare checklist similar to that under the CA 1989, section 1(3). The factors in the adoption welfare checklist, however, differ from those in the 1989 one. Of particular importance is section 1(4)(c) of the ACA 2002, which provides that the court can consider 'the likely effect on the child (throughout his life) of having ceased to be a member of the original family and become an adopted person'. No such provision existed under the 1976 Act. The effect of this change is that the judiciary have the discretion to consider much further ahead in the course of their decision-making. However, despite the introduction of this practice, it does not appear to have made a significant difference.

[39] For discussion on adoption reform generally, and in particular discussion before the enactment of the ACA 2002, see Allen (n 14).

[40] Performance and Innovation Unit, *The Prime Minister's Review of Adoption* (London, Cabinet Office, 2000).

[41] ibid, para 12.8.

[42] The House of Commons Library Research Paper 01/78: The Adoption and Children Bill (26 October 2001) 37.

[43] B Sloan, '*Re C (A Child) (Adoption: Duty of Local Authority)* – Welfare and the Rights of the Birth Family in 'Fast Track' Adoption Cases' (2009) 21 *Child and Family Law Quarterly* 87.

[44] J Herring, R Probert and S Gilmore, *Great Debates in Family Law* (London, Palgrave, 2015) 144.

Section 1(4)(f) provides that the court must take into account 'the wishes and feelings of any of the child's relatives, or of any such person regarding the child'. The Select Committee on Adoption has stated that this provision secures the fair balancing of 'the rights and interests of the birth parents in maintaining their existing family life on the one hand and the conflicting rights and interests of the child in favour of adoption on the other'.[45] Under section 1(4)(f), the courts may consider a range of different rights, such as, for instance, those of the parents, siblings, grandparents or other family members. The Children and Social Work Act 2017, section 9 recently amended this provision to place a duty on courts to also have regard to children's relationships with prospective adopters.

Sloan has argued that the 'extended meaning' of welfare may guard against precluding the interests of parents from adoption matters.[46] However, it is clear that this provision falls short of making explicit reference to the rights of either children or their parents. Adoption legislation that makes explicit reference to the UNCRC or specific UNCRC provisions would improve the protection of children's and parents' rights through improvement of the quality and detail of judicial reasoning in the lower courts, because judges would be required to apply it. This would therefore increase the likelihood that non-consensual adoption would only take place when equally effective and less restrictive alternatives are unavailable.

Nonetheless, there may be problems arising from not considering parents' interests independently from those of their children. This approach may lead to the permanent severance of relationships between children and their parents, as well as those with other relatives such as grandparents. Reflecting on *Re C (A Child) (Adoption: Duty of Local Authority)*,[47] for example, Sloan has observed that the Court of Appeal 'took a very individualistic view of child welfare, at the expense of a child's links with her biological father … and with her grandparents'.[48] An important issue, then, is the extent to which the ACA 2002 is compatible with the requirements of Article 8 ECHR (the right to respect for private and family life).[49] Wall LJ has stated that adoption under the 2002 Act must be necessary (defined as somewhere between indispensable, on the one hand, and useful, reasonable and desirable on the other)[50] and must also 'be proportionate to the legitimate aim of protecting the welfare and interests of the child'.[51]

Although the ACA 2002, section 1(4)(f) indicates that children's relationships with their parents is a relevant factor under the welfare checklist, it may be argued

[45] HL Select Committee on Adoption Legislation (n 8) 17–18.

[46] Sloan (n 43). See also P Parkinson, 'Child Protection, Permanency Planning and Children's Right to Family Life' (2003) 17 *International Journal of Law, Policy and the Family* 147.

[47] *Re C (A Child) (Adoption: Duty of Local Authority)* [2007] EWCA Civ 1206.

[48] Sloan (n 43).

[49] For discussion, see Choudhry and Herring (n 4) ch 10.

[50] *Re P (Placement Orders: Parental Consent)* (n 31) [120], *per* Wall LJ.

[51] ibid [119].

that this subsection does not provide sufficient protection to parental rights in the process of non-consensual adoption. It can be argued that the operation of the welfare checklist[52] should have been reviewed to ensure respect for other people's Article 8 rights, especially those of parents.[53] Harris-Short, for example, has stated that section 1(4)(f) is not sufficient to meet the requirements of Article 8 because it does not require independent weight to be given to parents' rights.[54] The rights that should be considered are the rights children and parents have to develop and maintain relationships with one another (by children's being raised by their parents or via direct contact) and for parents to be able to make decisions in relation to their children. These are rights that are, arguably, also protected via the UNCRC.

In practice, when a court decides whether to make an adoption order, parental rights are not balanced equally with the child's rights. Relevant parental rights (such as those under Article 8 ECHR) are considered purely in the context of the child's welfare. When the court performs its analysis, the approach to adoption is similar to that taken in other cases where orders are made in respect of children. The approach, which was endorsed by Wall LJ in *Re P*,[55] can be highlighted by reference to *J v C*,[56] in which Lord McDermott said:

> [T]he child's welfare is to be treated as the top item in a list of items relevant to the matter in question … [Although] all the relevant facts, relationships, claims and wishes of parents, risks, choices and other circumstances are taken into account and weighed, the course to be followed will be that which is most in the interests of the child.[57]

The Court of Appeal decision in *The Matter of Q (A Child)*[58] has also emphasised that there is no enhanced welfare test in the context of non-consensual adoption cases, even though the consequences are permanent and more serious when compared with orders that may be made based on a child's welfare under the CA 1989. This is despite the fact that, as considered in chapter 2, it can be argued that an enhanced welfare test ought to be applied in the context of adoption proceedings. In other words, the courts ought to go beyond the bare welfare analysis that takes place when the courts make other types of order (eg care and supervision orders), due to the severity and permanence of making an adoption order.

This section has considered the reforms to the law made under the ACA 2002, which are relevant to the subject matter of this book. The following section considers relevant reforms implemented by the CFA 2014.

[52] See ch 2 for discussion of the new welfare checklist under the ACA 2002.

[53] J Mitchell, *Adoption and Special Guardianship: A Permanency Handbook* (Bristol, Jordan Publishing Ltd, 2009) 6.

[54] S Harris-Short, 'Adoption and Children Bill – A Fast Track to Failure?' (2001) 13 *Child and Family Law Quarterly* 405.

[55] *Re P (Placement Orders: Parental Consent)* (n 31) [114], *per* Wall LJ.

[56] *J v C* [1970] AC 668.

[57] ibid 710–11.

[58] *The Matter of Q (A Child)* [2011] EWCA Civ 1610 [58].

C. The Children and Families Act 2014

The CFA 2014 came into force on 22 April 2014.[59] It has been described by Gilmore and Bainham as 'deeply ideological legislation',[60] which seeks to address various policy objectives, including the reduction of delays in care and adoption proceedings.[61] It aims to address these delays by imposing a 26-week limit on care proceedings under section 14(2)(ii) of the Act, and by widening the scope of the 'early permanence' principle, whereby children are placed for adoption as early as possible. It brings forward the point at which local authorities will have a duty to consider fostering for adoption under section 22(9)(A), which consequently brings forward the point at which adoption will be considered.

This duty may exist in the first week a child is in care, or even before the child has been born.[62] The Act also contains a statutory provision explicitly allowing local authorities to stop contact between children in care and their parents under section 8, and a provision allowing for post-adoption contact between children and parents under section 9. The reforms are wide-ranging and have been criticised for their lack of coherence. Gilmore and Bainham have described the legislation as a 'ragbag of apparently disconnected adoption provisions'.[63] Furthermore, Sloan has argued that these provisions on post-adoption contact may, in fact, jeopardise English law's compliance with the ECHR and the UNCRC (for further discussion see chapter 5).[64]

Section 7 of the CFA 2014 enables prospective adopters to register their details and inspect a register to find a child 'for whom they could be appropriate adopters'.[65] The Action Plan[66] observed that, despite the reforms enacted by the ACA 2002, prospective adopters still received insufficient practical and financial support[67] during the adoption process and after the final adoption order.[68]

[59] Note that most provisions of the Children and Families Act 2014 came into force on 22 April 2014. However, s 7 did not come into force until 13 May 2014, and pt 1 did not come into force until 25 July 2014 (pt 1 only applied to England).

[60] A Bainham and S Gilmore, 'The English Children and Families Act 2014' (2015) 46 *Victoria University of Wellington Law Review* 627, 628.

[61] See discussion in Joint Committee on Human Rights, *Legislative Scrutiny: Children and Families Bill; Energy Bill, Third Report of Session 2013–14*, 9. See also Department for Education, *Further action on adoption: finding more loving homes* (London, Department for Education, 2013); T Ross and J Bingham, 'Speed up adoption process, David Cameron urges councils' *The Telegraph* (9 March 2012) at http://www.telegraph.co.uk/news/politics/9132407/Speed-up-adoption-process-David-Cameron-urges-councils.html#.

[62] See discussion in Joint Committee on Human Rights (n 61) 10.

[63] Bainham and Gilmore (n 60) 637.

[64] B Sloan, 'Post-Adoption Contact Reform: Compounding the State-Ordered Termination of Parenthood?' (2014) 73 *CLJ* 378. Also see Bainham and Gilmore (n 60) 647.

[65] This register is referred to as the 'National Gateway'.

[66] Department for Education, *An Action Plan for Adoption: Tackling Delay* (London, Department for Education, 2012).

[67] See HL Select Committee on Adoption Legislation (n 8) para 207.

[68] Department for Education (n 66) 4. Also see: Children and Families Bill: Written Evidence from the British Association for Adoption and Fostering.

Thus, the CFA 2014 has increased the funding and practical support for prospective adoptive parents. Section 5 provides financial support for adopters after the adoption process has taken place. Under section 6, local authorities have a duty to provide information on assessment and post-adoption support to prospective adopters. Sections 5–7 not only speed up the process for prospective adopters, but the provision of increased support is also intended to encourage more prospective adopters to come forward. However, support is not typically provided to birth parents post-adoption, despite the fact that non-consensual adoption is traumatic for them, as well as constituting an interference with their rights under Article 8 ECHR.

Having looked throughout this section at the legislation relating to non-consensual adoption, section III discusses the relevant case law and academic commentary related to the subject.

III. The Controversy of *Webster and Norfolk County Council and Others*

A. *Webster v Norfolk County Council and Others*

There has been public debate and emphasis of the need for transparency in the Family Courts[69] to avoid injustice in non-consensual adoption cases. The best example of such an injustice is *Webster v Norfolk County Council and others*,[70] an important case that merits in-depth discussion because of the media attention and academic discussion it generated. This case demonstrates the injustice that may occur when a non-consensual order is made under the section 52(1)(b) of the ACA 2002. The appellants, Mr and Mrs Webster, alleged that wrongful adoptions of three of their children had taken place, and that in the process their rights under Article 8(1) ECHR had been violated.

In 2003, the Websters took their 2-year-old son (Child 'B') to hospital because he had a swollen ankle. They visited two different hospitals, which discharged him. They were still concerned and returned to the first hospital, where B was x-rayed; six bone fractures were discovered. The consultant radiologist suspected non-accidental injury (NAI) and informed social services, who subsequently applied for a care order under the CA 1989. The court was satisfied, on the balance of probabilities, that the child had sustained non-accidental injuries, and care orders were made in respect of all three of the couple's children.[71] The children were

[69] For general discussion on transparency in the context of non-consensual adoption, see C Fenton-Glynn, *Adoption without Parental Consent: Study for the Peti Committee* (Strasbourg, European Parliament, 2015) 42–45. See also *Re J (A Child)* [2013] EWHC 2694 (Fam), esp [29] *per* Munby LJ, which refers to *Webster* and miscarriages of justice.

[70] *Webster v Norfolk County Council and others* [2009] EWCA Civ 59.

[71] The three children were born between 2000 and 2003.

subsequently freed for adoption under the old legislation (the Adoption Act 1976) and were subsequently adopted under the ACA 2002, section 52(1)(b), the court dispensing with the Websters' consent on the basis of the children's welfare.

In 2006, when Mrs Webster became pregnant again, she and her husband fled to Ireland for the child's birth as they feared that the finding in respect of Child B and the removal of all three of their children into care meant that social services would remove their fourth child and seek to place him or her for adoption. The child, Brandon, was born on 27 June 2007, by which time the Websters had put forward testimony from a medical expert that proved that they had not harmed B. The report stated that B's injuries were caused not by NAI but by iron deficiency and a rare condition known as scurvy,[72] caused by the child's unusual diet, which consisted solely of soya milk. This evidence, coupled with a positive residential assessment[73] with Brandon, led Holman J to agree that care proceedings against them ought to be discontinued.[74]

After this decision, the Websters appealed against the making of care and freeing orders in relation to their other three children, alleging that the adoptions amounted to a violation of their right to respect for private and family life that was not justified by Article 8(2) ECHR.[75] They challenged several findings made by the judge at first instance, Judge Barham. In particular, they challenged the finding that the threshold criteria under the CA 1989, section 31(2) had been satisfied on the basis of 'clinical and emotional harm',[76] thereby enabling the judge to make care orders. They also argued that the judge had been wrong not to consider the lack of reference to reunification of the children with their parents in the care plan. They argued that the freeing orders would not have been made if the medical evidence had been available at that time. Although an adoption order is generally regarded as irrevocable, in rare cases of procedural irregularity an adoption order may be set aside.[77] The Websters' counsel argued that the facts of the case amounted to exceptional circumstances',[78] which thus justified overturning the adoption orders and returning the children to their parents.

The judgment was delivered by the Court of Appeal in 2009. Despite acknowledging the potential for a violation of Article 8(1) and the evident injustice that had occurred, the Court refused to allow the appeal and revoke the adoption order for two reasons. First, on a public policy basis, the Court did not want to undermine the social importance of adoption. Second, the Court determined that it was in the children's best interests to remain with their adoptive parents because of the

[72] A deficiency of Vitamin C.

[73] Residential assessments under the CA 1989, s 38(6) are where, for example, a mother and newborn baby may live together and be observed by authorities in a specialised unit.

[74] *Re Brandon Webster (A Minor)* [2007] EWHC 549 (Fam).

[75] *Webster v Norfolk CC* (n 70) [65].

[76] ibid [133].

[77] *Re K (Adoption and Wardship)* [1997] 2 FLR 221; *ZH v HS and Others (Application to Revoke Adoption Order)* [2019] EWHC 2190 (Fam).

[78] *Webster v Norfolk CC* (n 70) [64].

number of years that they had been separated from their parents and because of the emotional attachments they had formed, in the meantime, with their adoptive parents. The leading judgment was delivered by Wall LJ. In determining whether or not the adoption orders could be revoked, the Court of Appeal considered Swinton LJ's judgment in *Re B (Adoption: Jurisdiction to Set Aside)*,[79] where he drew attention to the irrevocability and finality of adoption orders:

> There is no case in which it has been held that the court has the inherent power to set aside an adoption order by reason of misapprehension or mistake. To invalidate an otherwise properly made order would undermine the whole basis on which these orders are made, namely they are final and for life as regards to adopters.[80]

Although the Websters initially sought to have the adoptions set aside and have their children returned to them, they later had a change of heart due to the passage of time. Wall LJ asserted that if the parents had sought to have the adoption orders set aside, they would not have obtained this remedy, on the basis that reversing the adoption orders would run counter to the children's welfare. He asserted that, after four years with their adoptive parents, it would be disruptive to remove the children. While Wall LJ and Wilson LJ acknowledged that adoption orders could be reversed in rare cases where procedural irregularity had occurred, particularly where there had been a breach of natural justice, they would not revoke the adoption orders in this case, and they took a public policy approach emphasising the social importance of adoption as well as its permanence.

Wilson LJ observed that it was too late for the Websters to appeal, emphasising that the three children had been settled in new homes for four years and had not seen their parents. He also emphasised the 'vast social importance of not undermining the irrevocability of adoption orders'.[81] Wall LJ acknowledged that the parents had been wrongfully accused of abusing one of their children, and as a result three of their children had been wrongfully and permanently removed from the family home. Furthermore, he stated that the three children who had been placed for adoption and their brother Brandon (whom the Websters had been allowed to keep) had missed the opportunity of growing up together as a family. He said that this was 'deeply worrying, and, on the face of it, a clear breach of their rights to respect for their family life under Article 8(1) of the European Convention on Human Rights'.[82]

Although Wall LJ referred to cases decided by the ECtHR,[83] he concluded that 'the European authorities [did] not assist Mr and Mrs Webster'.[84] The following

[79] *Re B (Adoption: Jurisdiction to Set Aside)* [1995] Fam 239.
[80] ibid, 245–49.
[81] *Webster v Norfolk CC* (n 70) [204], *per* Wall LJ.
[82] ibid [2]–[3], *per* Wall LJ.
[83] *Görgülü v Germany* [2004] 1 FLR 894; *Kearns v France* [2008] 1 FLR 888; *Odièvre v France* [2003] 1 FCR 621; *Evans v UK* [2007] 2 FCR 5.
[84] *Webster v Norfolk CC* (n 70) [175].

section explores Wall LJ's judgment further and in more detail, to see whether or not the decision can be regarded as proportionate.

B. A Critical Analysis of *Webster v Norfolk County Council*

The segment of Wall LJ's judgment on the applicability of the ECHR is, with respect, open to criticism. Although Wall LJ refers to the Convention, the analysis of its applicability is insufficient. There is no explanation or reasoning with regard to his conclusion about the relevance of the ECHR.[85] Despite reference to the relevant Convention rights, there is no analysis of European cases and how they might apply to the facts in *Webster*. This author agrees with Herring, who has observed that while the result in *Webster* might have been the correct one, 'the reasoning is not such that would convince the person in the street'.[86] Diver has also been critical of the decision, and has observed that there was no attempt to weigh or balance the conflicting familial rights of the children and parents.[87] Thus, without a proper application of the European jurisprudence to the facts of the case, or an explanation as to why the authorities did not assist the Websters, it is difficult to agree with Wall LJ's conclusion.

In fact, although Wall LJ referred to *Görgülü v Germany*,[88] which cited *P, C and S v UK*,[89] he did not consider the relevance of the facts and principles from *P, C and S* and whether they could be of assistance to the Websters. In *P, C and S*, the ECtHR held that the close alliance between the care and freeing orders decreased the likelihood that the mother would be reunited with her child, and consequently her right to respect for private and family life under Article 8(1) ECHR had been violated. Similarly in *Webster*, the children were taken into care in December 2003 and were freed for adoption less than a year later (in November 2004). Although a key distinction between *P, C and S v UK* and *Webster* is that in the former case the mother lacked legal representation, it can be argued that it was nonetheless a relevant decision for the Court of Appeal to have discussed in the context of the Article 8 issues raised in *Webster*. Wall LJ's judgment in *Webster* may be contrasted with his later judgment in *Re P*,[90] in which he more thoroughly considered Article 8 ECHR and *P, C and S*, while emphasising that the facts of the case were unusual, and stated that the 'juxtaposition'[91] of the care and placement orders warranted examining the cases with 'particular care'.[92]

[85] J Herring, 'Revoking Adoptions' (2009) 159 *NLJ* 377.
[86] ibid.
[87] A Diver, *A Law of Blood-Ties – The 'Right' To Access Genetic Ancestry* (London, Springer, 2014) 276.
[88] *Görgülü v Germany* (n 83).
[89] *P, C and S v UK* [2002] 2 FLR 631.
[90] *Re P* (n 50).
[91] ibid [132].
[92] ibid.

In *Webster*, it was understandable that the Court refused to reverse the adoption order due to the length of time the children had been with their adoptive parents. However, it could be argued that the apparent 'vast social importance' of adoption orders is not a strong enough justification for not revoking adoption orders in an exceptional case like *Webster*, and that adoption of the children was not necessarily a proportionate outcome. This case also provides a stark contrast to the Court's willingness to revoke adoptions in rare cases where procedural errors have occurred.[93] DeBlasio has expressed concern about the ruling in *Webster*:

> There is something about this case and others like it that lack a missing component of justice. It thus raises the question as to whether mistakes which concern the separation of children from their parents are simply justified at law in this way; and that [local authorities] and the courts can 'hide behind the law' in the ACA rather than admit mistakes.[94]

Herring has argued that because approximately 5,000 adoptions take place each year,[95] it is questionable whether adoption orders have such huge social importance that they ought not to be set aside in exceptional cases like *Webster*. The Council of Europe has expressed concern about the potential for injustice where children have been adopted without parental consent, particularly in England and Wales. The Council of Europe said the fact that an adoption order made in England and Wales could not be reversed in any circumstances was 'a misunderstanding of the "best interests of the child" who actually has a right to return to his/her birth family'.[96] The emphasis on maintaining the relationship between children and parents is further emphasised by various provisions of the UNCRC, considered throughout this book. Therefore it could be said that in some circumstances a child's welfare may be best served by the reversal of an adoption order.

A decade later, a case that bore similarities to *Webster* and led to litigation spanning six years[97] was the subject of considerable media attention. The *Re X* litigation seemed to emphasise everything that was wrong about non-consensual adoption. It appeared to demonstrate that the social importance of the permanence of adoption would not outweigh an apparent injustice.[98] The six-week-old baby of Karissa Cox and Richard Carter was taken into care by social services in Surrey, due to

[93] See, eg, *Re M (A Minor) (Adoption)* [1991] 1 FLR 458; and *Re K (Adoption and Wardship)* [1997] 2 FLR 221. Also see Herring, Probert and Gilmore (n 44) 151–52.

[94] L DeBlasio, 'Hiding Behind the Law? A Critique of the Law and Practice under the Adoption and Children Act 2002' [2014] 1 *Plymouth Law and Criminal Justice Review* 148, 164. Also see T Buck, *International Child Law* (New York, Routledge, 2011) 19.

[95] Herring (n 85).

[96] O Borzova, *Social services in Europe: legislation and practice of the removal of children from their families in Council of Europe member states* (Strasbourg, Council of Europe, 2015) para 74.

[97] *Re X (A Child)* [2016] EWHC 1342 (Fam); *Re X (A Child) (No 2) (reporting restriction orders: guidance)* [2016] All ER (D) 47; *Re X (A Child) (No 3)* [2016] EWHC 2755 (Fam); *Re X (A Child) (No 4)* [2018] EWHC 1815 (Fam).

[98] I Johnston and E Dugan, 'Couple wrongly accused of abuse unlikely to see their child again' *The Independent* (8 October 2015) at http://www.independent.co.uk/news/uk/crime/couple-who-were-wrongly-accused-of-abuse-unlikely-to-see-their-child-again-a6685471.html.

a finding of fact of non-accidental injuries to the child. Subsequently, the baby was placed for adoption without parental consent under the ACA 2002, section 52(1)(b). The parents were prosecuted for child abuse, but the case against them collapsed because of the contradictory findings of two medical experts. The judge directed the jury to acquit.

It was discovered that the child had a rare blood disorder (Von Willebrands II), which the parents argued made the child more susceptible to injury. The parents argued that they had not abused their child and that a miscarriage of justice had occurred. They challenged the original finding of fact with a view to seeking revocation of the adoption order itself, depending on the court's fresh findings. Once the fresh medical evidence was obtained, the parents sought to withdraw from court proceedings, but the child's guardian and adoptive parents argued that the child had the right to know the truth about whether his parents had abused him. In *Re X (A Child) (No 4)*,[99] the findings were not favourable to the parents, and Munby LJ held that the birth parents had caused non-accidental injuries to their baby.

The *Webster* case and the *Re X* litigation demonstrate the difficult dilemma social services and the courts face in protecting children's rights under Article 2 ECHR (the right to life) and Article 3 ECHR (the right to freedom from torture or inhuman or degrading treatment), while balancing these rights against the rights of children and their parents to have a family life under Article 8 ECHR. As considered in chapter 2, a welfare test applied in adoption cases arguably ought to include a routine consideration of a wide range of children's rights (including but not limited to UNCRC Articles 5, 6, 7, 8, 9, 12 and 18). While the removal of the children into care in the above cases was proportionate, it is questionable whether the adoption in *Webster* was proportionate. The necessity of removing children from parental care should not be equated with the necessity of placement for adoption without direct contact.

Many adoption cases heard in the lower courts are unreported, which makes it difficult for researchers to assess how many non-consensual adoptions are made when less restrictive but equally effective alternatives may have been available. The lack of transparency of the family court system, particularly in non-consensual adoption proceedings, increases the likelihood of one-sided, inaccurate media reports. This can be seen, for example, in the *X* litigation, where the media portrayal of the case bore little relation to the facts until the case reached the Court of Appeal and was heard by Munby LJ. John Hemming MP has claimed that cases like *Webster* are not uncommon and more than 1,000 'wrongful' adoptions take place every year.[100] It is essential to improve the reporting of inferior court judgments to determine whether cases like *Webster* occur more regularly than we

[99] *Re X (A Child) (No 4)* (n 97).

[100] 'MP claims 1,000 children "wrongfully" adopted every year' (13 December 2011) at http://www.bbc.co.uk/news/uk-politics-16157124.

would like to think, or whether many of these cases are like *Re X* – cases that appear to be miscarriages of justice but which turn out not to be when subjected to fresh scrutiny. At present, reliance must be placed on scant cases that are reported by the inferior courts, or cases that reach the superior courts.[101]

Despite the extensive media reports on *Webster* and the *Re X* litigation, it has been difficult to gain reliable evidence and form a clear picture of the scale of the problem. Access to all adoption judgments in the lower courts is crucial to provide a clearer indication of the number of cases in which adoption orders are a disproportionate measure. Evidence of a significant problem would provide a compelling justification for policy reform and even law reform to take place. Such reform could even include legislation that requires the courts to consider provisions of the UNCRC during the adoption process, to ensure that viable alternatives to adoption (such as state assistance or kinship care) have been adequately taken into account.

The Council of Europe has also attempted to investigate the number of justified or unwarranted decisions, and has concluded that it is not possible to provide an accurate estimate of the numbers.[102] It can be argued, however, that although it may be difficult to make an accurate estimation, this is far from impossible to achieve. Considering the serious consequences of adoption and the potential for injustice, more research needs to be undertaken to determine whether other cases like *Webster* may not have reached the superior courts and have consequently gone unreported.

Regardless of whether *Webster* can be regarded as an unusual case or indicates a systemic problem,[103] the Websters' rights under Article 8 ECHR did not receive sufficient protection. In other countries, their rights might have been better protected and, as Diver has argued, a case like *Webster* might have been treated differently in another jurisdiction:

> Had such a case [like *Webster*] perhaps occurred in a jurisdiction where the duty to preserve genetic ties was enshrined in statute, either on the basis of parental rights, paramountcy or constitutional protection of the family unit, the Webster children might well have been returned to their birth parents, or at least permitted to engage in

[101] *London Borough of Islington v Al Alas and Wray* [2012] EWHC 865 (Fam). For a detailed summary of this case, see J Delahunty and K Purkiss, 'The vitamin D and rickets case: *LB Islington v Al Alas and Wray*' [2012] *Family Law* 659. Also see Johnston and Dugan (n 98). Another commonly cited example of a miscarriage of justice is *Sutton London Borough Council v Gray and Butler* [2012] EWHC 2673 (Fam). For further discussion, see J Delahunty and W Tyler, 'A "miscarriage of justice" corrected: the difference expert evidence and a full re-hearing can make to the outcome: *Sutton LBC v Gray and Butler*' [2012] *Family Law* 1344. One difficulty that plagues these types of cases is that it can be very difficult to establish whether or not non-accidental injury is attributable to parents. Ultimately, *Gray and Butler* was a sad case, because some years after the judgment the father was charged with the murder of his daughter: A Anglesey, 'Murder accused Ben Butler represents himself in court' *Sutton Guardian* (2 June 2015) at http://www.suttonguardian.co.uk/news/13219787.Murder_accused_Ben_Butler_represents_himself_in_court/.

[102] Borzova (n 96) para 38.

[103] F Moss, 'Dangerous Consensus' *NLJ* (6 August 2009) at https://www.newlawjournal.co.uk/content/dangerous-consensus.

> some meaningful level of contact with them, perhaps on the basis of fresh, exonerating evidence subsequently arising over the issue of the alleged child abuse.[104]

In *Webster*, the issue of proportionality was not considered by the Court of Appeal in the way that it has been in subsequent judgments, such as in *Re B-S Children*.[105] It is argued that an issue that should have underpinned the Court of Appeal's decision-making is the extent to which the non-consensual adoption was a proportionate measure, and whether or not the Webster children could have been protected from harm through less restrictive measures. *Webster* also raises important questions about whether non-consensual adoption is proportionate when it results in a loss of contact between children and their parents (see further in chapter 3).

In some cases, an adoption order may be justified but termination of contact might not. Thus, while state intervention and removal from the family home may have been justified to protect the children from harm, terminating contact between the Websters and their children was not. It is unclear why there could be no provision for open adoption, on the facts of this case. Herring has expressed similar reservations, and has argued that the termination of the contact while the children were in care was a potential violation of the Article 8(1) rights of both the children and their parents.[106] Despite the clear potential for a breach of the children's and parents' Article 8 rights, the lack of contact while the children were in care and lack of post-adoption contact were not analysed by the Court of Appeal. This is unsatisfactory, as termination of contact will make it difficult to reunite children and their parents, and may even lead to a non-consensual adoption's being regarded as appropriate in the circumstances, as the bond between parent and child will have been broken.[107]

Diver has been critical of the Court of Appeal's lack of reference to contact between members of the Webster family, observing that it was unclear whether two of the siblings who had been adopted were in contact with their other sibling, who had been adopted separately.[108] Contact between children and parents is an important component of children's and parents' rights under Article 8 ECHR, and ought to have been considered and analysed by the Court of Appeal in this case, even if the Court would have decided that contact was not in the children's best interests. It has also been emphasised throughout that the UNCRC has the potential to be a valuable tool in assessing the proportionality of non-consensual adoption.

Another important issue raised by the *Webster* case that applies to other cases on non-consensual adoption is that adoption was arguably not the least restrictive

[104] Diver (n 87) 276.
[105] *Re B-S Children* [2013] EWCA Civ 1146.
[106] Herring (n 85).
[107] See, eg, *Görgülü v Germany* [2004] ECHR 74969/01 para 46. Also see *K and T v Finland* App no 25702/94 (ECHR, 12 July 2001).
[108] Diver (n 87) 275.

measure available. One aspect in this case, which has not been the subject of academic comment, relates to the issue of whether the grandparents would have been suitable alternative carers instead of placing the children for adoption. However, although the grandparents were assessed as carers, placement with them was not permitted because they found it difficult to accept that the Websters had neglected their children. Social services believed that the grandparents would be unable to meet the children's needs and that the arrangement would be 'confusing' for the children. It is not clear why this arrangement was confusing, or why it would not have been possible for sufficient safeguards to have been put in place. Although this might have been true and the grandparents might not have been suitable kinship carers, there ought to have been a more thorough analysis of this possibility, as placement with the grandparents would have been a less restrictive alternative to non-consensual adoption. In fact, Bainham has also criticised the *Webster* decision, as it demonstrates the dangers of making adoption orders too readily without first exploring alternative options.[109] It is clear that the children could have been placed with their grandparents or in long-term foster care.

Cases such as *Webster* raise questions about the proportionality of non-consensual adoption. Bainham has argued that in the light of the *Webster* case, 'there should be urgent reconsideration of the doubtful official policy which prefers public law adoption as the best long-term option for "looked after" children'.[110] Delahunty and Tyler have stated that there may be cases where parents cannot accept a finding of fact that they have abused their children and may challenge a judgment, despite having neglected and/or abused their children. However, the authors have proposed that there is a need to 'weed out' cases where 'no realistic argument' exists but to welcome reconsideration of cases like *Webster* where 'there is a real possibility the system has previously got it wrong. No other approach will safeguard the affected children's interests'.[111] This can be seen in the *Re X* litigation already discussed, for example, where contradictory medical evidence warranted a further examination of the facts.

In other words, in order to ensure that a non-consensual adoption order is a proportionate measure, it is necessary to conduct a more thorough scrutiny of cases of this nature.[112] This could be achieved by reference to principles from the ECtHR (considered in chapter 3) and also by reference to children's UNCRC rights. Consideration and application of these factors in adoption cases would provide greater protection not only for parents' rights under Article 8 ECHR, but also for children's rights under both the ECHR and the UNCRC (in particular, Articles 7, 8 and 9 of the latter instrument).

[109] A Bainham, 'The Peculiar Finality of Adoption' (2009) 68 *CLJ* 283.
[110] ibid.
[111] J Delahunty and W Tyler, 'Re-litigation in family cases: the emerging law and practice' [2013] *Family Law* 40.
[112] For example, see *London Borough of Islington v Al Alas and Wray* (n 101). For a detailed summary of this case, see Delahunty and Purkiss (n 101). Also see *London Borough of Sutton v Gray and Butler* (n 101). For a detailed summary of the case, see Delahunty and Tyler (n 101).

Having considered the issues raised by the *Webster* case, it is important to examine how the law on non-consensual adoption and proportionality has been addressed by the Court of Appeal in England and Wales, and by the UK Supreme Court in subsequent cases.

IV. The Proportionality of Non-Consensual Adoption: Legal Challenges in the Supreme Court

A. *ANS and Another v ML (AP) (Scotland)*

ANS and another v ML (AP) (Scotland)[113] is a UK Supreme Court decision that considers the proportionality of the Scottish equivalent of the ACA 2002. While Scotland is not governed by the same law of adoption as England and Wales, the legislation is based on and similar to English law. Furthermore, the final appeal court in the land for Scottish cases is the Supreme Court of England and Wales. Consequently, this judgment is relevant to all courts in the UK,[114] and is significant because it considered whether the legislation on non-consensual adoption itself was proportionate. A finding that the Scottish legislation was not proportionate would impact on the proportionality of the ACA 2002. Specifically, whether or not non-consensual adoptions under section 52(1)(b) of the Act – where parental consent can be dispensed with on the basis of a child's welfare – could be regarded as proportionate.

In *ANS*, the appellant was a mother whose child had been placed for adoption without her consent. Here, the Supreme Court was invited to assess the compatibility of the Adoption and Children (Scotland) Act 2007, section 31(3)(d), which was similar to and in fact based on the ACA 2002, section 52(1), with Article 8 ECHR. Section 31(3)(d) stated that 'where neither of … subsections [(4) or (5)] applies,[115] the welfare of the child otherwise requires the consent to be dispensed with'. In contrast to *Webster*, where the parents challenged the reasons behind the making of the adoption orders, *ANS* involved a challenge to the adoption legislation itself. In *ANS*, the mother claimed that the effect of section 31(3)(d) was that there could be permanent severance of the parent–child bond. She argued that as this severance was based solely on the child's welfare, the non-consensual adoption violated her own right under Article 8 ECHR. The key issue was whether or not section 31(3)(d) itself represented a proportionate interference with parents' rights under Article 8 of the Convention.

[113] *ANS and another v ML (AP) (Scotland)* [2012] UKSC 30.

[114] M Donnelly, 'The Supreme Court and the welfare ground for dispensing with parental consent to adoption: *ANS and another v ML (Scotland)*' [2014] *International Family Law Journal* 110. For further information on the Scottish approach to children's rights generally, see K Tisdall, 'Children's Wellbeing and Children's Rights in Tension?' (2015) 23 *International Journal of Children's Rights* 769.

[115] Section 31(4) and (5) of the Adoption and Children (Scotland) Act 2007 provide for adoption without parental consent on the basis of the child's welfare.

The Court's analysis rested on the presumption that the 2007 Act would not have been enacted to put the UK in breach of international obligations, and that it was in keeping with international obligations[116] that the child's welfare was the paramount consideration.[117] The Court held that the statutory provision was compatible with the ECHR and wider international obligations (under the UNCRC, Article 21, which concerns the child's welfare when he or she has been adopted, for example).

In *ANS*, Lord Reed referred to the ECtHR in *YC v UK*,[118] which had approved similar adoption legislation in England and Wales. In the Strasbourg Court's judgment, it had indicated that there were several factors laid down in the checklist under section 1(4) of the ACA 2002 that reflected the various elements taken into account in assessing proportionality, such as the age, maturity and wishes of the child, the likely effect on the child of ceasing to be a member of his original family, and the relationship the child has with his or her relatives.

Lord Reed opined that the ECtHR had deemed the application of section 1(4), in conjunction with section 52(1)(b), to be in accordance with law. Thus, the reasoning of the Supreme Court appeared to be that since the Strasbourg Court had accepted that section 1(4) of the ACA 2002 was in accordance with law, and broadly reflected the elements required for proportionality, then so too was section 31(3)(d) of the Scottish statute. It is submitted that *YC v UK* ought not to have been used to support the lawfulness and the proportionality of section 31(3)(d) of the 2007 Act, since this provision was not equivalent to section 1(4) and, more importantly, in *YC v UK*, the ECtHR was not invited to question either whether section 52(1)(b) was in accordance with law,[119] or whether the non-consensual adoption in that case was in accordance with law. The issues of the case focused on the necessity for and proportionality of the state's actions.

In *ANS*, the Supreme Court reflected on *Keegan v Ireland*,[120] where the ECtHR had previously made it clear that adoption could only take place in 'exceptional circumstances'. Similarly, *YC v UK* emphasised that familial ties could not be severed unless there were 'exceptional circumstances' to justify permanent separation and quoted from the decision in *Neulinger*:

> [F]amily ties may only be severed in exceptional circumstances and that everything must be done to preserve personal relations and, if and when appropriate, to 'rebuild' the family …[121]

However, despite repeated reference to the need for 'exceptional circumstances' where familial ties are to be severed, such as in the case of adoption, Lord Reed did not emphasise this important principle stemming from the European

[116] Such as the UNCRC.
[117] *ANS v ML (AP) (Scotland)* (n 113) [37].
[118] *YC v UK* App no 4547/10 (ECHR, 13 March 2012).
[119] ibid para 131.
[120] *Keegan v Ireland* App no 16969/90 (ECHR, 26 May 1994).
[121] *Neulinger and Shuruk v Switzerland* App no 41615/07 (ECHR, 6 July 2010) para 136.

jurisprudence (see chapter 3). Lord Reed asserted that 'exceptional circumstances' was not a 'legal test but an observation about the rarity of the circumstances in which the compulsory severing of family ties will be in accordance with article 8'.[122] With the greatest possible respect, it is argued that this is a misinterpretation of Strasbourg jurisprudence. Fenton-Glynn, for example, is of the view that 'exceptional circumstances' is very clearly a test, even though it may be one which it is easy to satisfy on the basis of the child's best interests.[123] This can also be seen from the discussion in chapter 3.

An important part of the Court's analysis in *ANS* rested upon its interpretation of what was meant by 'requires' in the context of dispensing with parental consent to adoption under section 31(3)(d) of the Scottish adoption legislation. The leading judgment was delivered by Lord Reed, who referred to the notion of proportionality and dispensing with consent to adoption:

> The court must be satisfied that the interference with the rights of the parents is proportionate: in other words, that nothing less than adoption will suffice. If the child's welfare can be equally well secured by a less drastic intervention, then it cannot be said that the child's welfare 'requires' that consent to adoption should be dispensed with.[124]

The Supreme Court observed that the word 'requires' used in the Scottish legislation is in the ACA 2002, section 52(1)(b), and that it also reflected the language used by the ECtHR.[125] Furthermore, Lord Reed stated that when the Scottish Act was drafted, the wording was based on the ACA 2002, section 52(1)(b), but it was amended to reflect the fact that it ought to be subject to a necessity test equivalent to that in Article 8 ECHR.[126] The Supreme Court further observed that Wall LJ, in a Court of Appeal decision,[127] had previously held that the ACA 2002, section 52(1)(b) was compatible with the ECHR. Lord Reed opined that the 2007 Act conveyed 'the essence of the Strasbourg jurisprudence',[128] and as the less detailed provision in section 52(1)(b) had been regarded by Wall LJ as compatible with Article 8, the Supreme Court held that section 31(3)(d) of the 2007 Act was also compatible with Article 8 ECHR.[129]

It can be argued that the *ANS* decision provides some protection for parents' interests[130] for two main reasons. First of all, because it acknowledges that a court ought to start with a less interventionist approach and, secondly, because it places some emphasis on the Strasbourg Court's decision in *YC v UK*.[131] However, closer

[122] *ANS v ML (AP) (Scotland)* (n 113) [44].
[123] C Fenton-Glynn 'Adoption in a European Perspective' in JM Sharpe (ed), *Research Handbook on European Family Law* (Cheltenham, Edward Elgar Publishing, 2016).
[124] *ANS v ML (AP) (Scotland)* (n 113) [34].
[125] ibid [35].
[126] ibid [19]–[21].
[127] See *Re P (Placement Orders: Parental Consent)* (n 31) [125].
[128] *ANS v ML (AP) (Scotland)* (n 113) [35].
[129] ibid [43].
[130] G Ifezue and M Rajabali, 'Protecting the interests of the child' [2013] *Cambridge Journal of International Child Law* 81, 81–83.
[131] *YC v UK* (n 118).

scrutiny of the decision reveals that, not unlike the *Webster* decision, there is a lack of the in-depth analysis of the rights of children and parents that one might expect, considering the seriousness of the issue at stake. Thus, Ifezue and Rajabali, for example, have pointed out that while the Supreme Court in *ANS* takes into account parental interests, 'this is only done on a superficial basis'.[132] This is demonstrated by its analysis of the decision of *YC v UK*, in which the ECtHR stated that the factors to be considered in adoption cases included the wishes of the child, the likely effect of ceasing to be a member of the original family and the child's existing relationships with family members. Despite this emphasis in *YC v UK*, the paramountcy of the child's welfare in the adoption process, and how this could justify overriding the interests of the parents, was emphasised in *ANS*, thereby reducing the significance of parental rights. UNCRC-based analysis would have improved the analysis, and would have provided greater clarity in respect of the scope of children's and parents' rights.

In *ANS*, the Supreme Court focused primarily on analysing whether or not the legislation justified non-consensual adoption, rather than on whether or not the mother's Article 8 right had been violated. While one might not disagree with the Court's interpretation of the legislation itself, and the Court may not have been compelled to provide further analysis of ECHR rights, the decision provided the Supreme Court with a perfect opportunity to explore the circumstances in which non-consensual adoption may or may not be a proportionate interference with parental rights, and also to consider the role of children's rights in non-consensual adoption cases.

As was argued in chapter 2, compliance with the best interests principle under Article 3 UNCRC, applied in the context of adoption under Article 21 UNCRC, may require a more detailed analysis of factors that are relevant in a decision about whether or not a child should be adopted. *ANS* was an important case, since it affirmed that the ACA 2002 was in fact Convention-compliant. Subsequent case law in the Supreme Court and the Court of Appeal has started to consider what type of analysis needs to be undertaken and what measures ought to be taken for a non-consensual adoption to be regarded as a proportionate measure. In the case discussed in section III.B, the UK Supreme Court had to consider whether or not the rights of the child and the parents had been violated under Article 8 ECHR in relation to a non-consensual adoption.

B. *In the Matter of B (A Child)*

In the Matter of B (A Child)[133] is an important case because it is the first time the UK Supreme Court has provided a detailed assessment of the significance

[132] Ifezue and Rajabali (n 131) 83.
[133] *In the Matter of B (A Child)* [2013] UKSC 33.

of Article 8(1) ECHR and the principle of proportionality in a non-consensual adoption case. In this case, the Court considered whether the parents' and child's Article 8(1) rights to respect for private and family life were relevant at the threshold stage of care proceedings under the CA 1989, section 31(2). The Court also considered the applicability of section 6 of the Human Rights Act 1998 (HRA 1998) (under which public authorities are duty-bound to act compatibly with Convention rights). The Supreme Court had to decide whether it was required to carry out a fresh determination of the issues at stake, rather than a secondary review, in order to assess whether the non-consensual adoption had been a proportionate interference with the rights of a newborn baby (Amelia) and her parents under Article 8 ECHR.

Primarily because of the mother's factitious disorder,[134] but also because of the father's drug use, social services argued that Amelia was at risk of emotional harm and she was removed into care under the CA 1989, section 31. While she was in care, both parents visited Amelia regularly and sought to be reunited with her. Social services considered that it would be in her best interests to be adopted, and the High Court granted an adoption order under the ACA 2002, section 52(1)(b). The parents appealed to the Court of Appeal, which affirmed the trial judge's decision. They subsequently appealed to the Supreme Court, which was invited to consider whether Article 8(1) ECHR was relevant at the threshold stage of care proceedings and whether, under the HRA 1998, section 6, an appellate court needed to conduct a fresh determination instead of a secondary review when a violation of a Convention right has been alleged.

The Supreme Court dismissed the appeal by a majority[135] of 4:1 (with Lady Hale dissenting). The Court held that the grounds for the care order had been made out and that, due to the mother's disorder and the risk of emotional harm to her child, Amelia should be placed for adoption. However, it was held that a high degree of justification would be needed under Article 8 for a child to be placed for adoption against the birth parents' wishes. In order for the adoption to take place, the child's interests must render this necessary. The Supreme Court held that Article 8 did not apply at the first stage when determining whether the section 31 threshold for making a care order has been crossed, because it is simply a hurdle that must be cleared before the court can go on to consider whether or not to make an order. However, analysis of Convention rights would apply at the second stage, when a court was conducting the welfare assessment and deciding whether to make a substantive order.[136]

The Supreme Court thus considered whether or not the parents' Article 8 rights had been violated in the course of the welfare assessment. Lord Neuberger opined that 'no substantive order is made without all Convention rights being taken into account'.[137] Lord Neuberger cited English case law, drawing attention

[134] This is where people fabricate false symptoms of illness and their medical history.
[135] Lords Neuberger, Wilson, Clarke and Kerr.
[136] *In the Matter of B (A Child)* (n 133) [29], *per* Lord Wilson.
[137] ibid [62], *per* Lord Neuberger.

to the fact that it is recognised that it is best for children to be raised by their birth parents (see chapter 2).[138] Despite the existence of this principle, the facts in this case justified departing from this presumption. Lord Neuberger concluded that the risk of the harm to the child amounted to defective parenting, which satisfied the threshold under the CA 1989, section 31(2). The Supreme Court thus held that the making of the care order did not violate Amelia's or her parents' rights under Article 8 ECHR.

In terms of whether the non-consensual adoption violated the Article 8 rights of Amelia and her parents, Lord Wilson discussed *YC v UK*.[139] He considered how this case had a bearing on the proportionality assessment in non-consensual adoption cases. He observed that paragraph 134 of the judgment in *YC v UK* 'demonstrates the high degree of justification which article 8 demands of a determination that a child should be adopted or placed in care with a view to adoption'.[140] Lord Wilson opined that European jurisprudence was 'parallel'[141] to domestic law, which emphasises that it must be necessary to make an adoption order. In terms of the proportionality principle, Lord Wilson[142] considered *Kutzner v Germany*,[143] where it was stated by the ECtHR that the authorities had violated Article 8(1) where they had not 'given sufficient consideration to additional measures of support as an alternative'[144] to adoption. Lord Wilson stated that a three-month adjournment to explore the possibility of reuniting Amelia with her parents might have been a proportionate response, but accepted Cryan J's view that Amelia could not be reunited with her parents because further exploration would have been unsuccessful due to the 'barriers erected by the parents'.[145] In other words, the judge had concluded that the parents would be unwilling to cooperate with the relevant authorities (ie social services).

Lord Neuberger reached a similar conclusion, but in the course of his reasoning referred to the UNCRC[146] and emphasised that 'before making an adoption order in such a case, the court must be satisfied that there is no practical way of the authorities (or others) providing the requisite assistance and support'.[147] Despite the fact that the judgment was not favourable to Amelia's parents, Lord Neuberger's obiter dicta may constitute persuasive precedent in future cases. In fact, this judgment, along with relevant UNCRC provisions and ECtHR jurisprudence, could be used to argue that authorities in England and Wales have a positive obligation under both the ECHR and the UNCRC to provide state assistance to keep families together.

[138] ibid [67]–[69], *per* Lord Neuberger.
[139] *YC v UK* [2012] 2 FLR 332.
[140] *In the Matter of B (A Child)* (n 133) [34], *per* Lord Wilson.
[141] ibid.
[142] ibid [48], *per* Lord Wilson.
[143] *Kutzner v Germany* App no 46544/99 (ECHR, 26 February 2002) para 75.
[144] ibid.
[145] *In the Matter of B (A Child)* (n 133) [48].
[146] ibid [103]–[105].
[147] ibid [105].

Furthermore, the Supreme Court also held that the HRA 1998, section 6 did not require the appellate courts to consider afresh issues that related to ECHR rights. Appellate courts were only required to review the lower court's decision. The majority of the Supreme Court held that while the Court had a duty under section 6 of the HRA 1998 to ensure that there was no violation of Article 8 ECHR, the appropriate test was to consider simply whether the lower court exceeded its discretion, and to determine whether the lower court was 'wrong' in its decision.[148] Lord Neuberger stated:

> [T]he fact that a Convention right is involved does not require an appellate domestic court to consider again the issue of proportionality for itself … [T]he court system as a whole must fairly determine for itself whether the requirement of proportionality is met, but that does not mean that each court up the appeal chain does so.[149]

Although Lord Kerr was in the majority and dismissed the appeal, he disagreed with the majority on the second argument in relation to the need for appellate courts to consider issues afresh. He argued that under the HRA 1998, section 6, appellate courts might be required to perform their own assessment of proportionality. He opined that

> an appellate court cannot avoid the imperative of section 6 of HRA by viewing the matter of proportionality through the prism of the defensibility of the trial judge's decision. An appeal in an adoption case requires the appellate court to confront the possibility that its decision could involve the infringement of a Convention right. The duty not to act in a way which is incompatible with such a right gives rise to an inevitable, concomitant duty to inquire whether the order that the court makes would have that consequence. That is an inquiry which cannot be satisfactorily answered by the conclusion that another agency has so decided. The inquiry must require the appellate court to decide for itself if the freeing order is proportionate/necessary.[150]

Lady Hale provided the sole voice of dissent, with an opinion that was in striking contrast to that of the majority.[151] Lady Hale agreed with the majority that the threshold for taking Amelia into care had been crossed. Nonetheless, she held that this did not mean that nothing else but adoption would do for the child, as from her perspective, 'nothing else'[152] had been tried. She held that an adoption order was not a proportionate measure on the facts of the case; and that the potential for social workers to take other measures to protect Amelia, which would have enabled her to have been returned to her parents, had not been properly examined.[153] In other words, in her Ladyship's opinion, it would have been possible for a less restrictive measure to have been chosen instead of non-consensual adoption. Lady Hale accepted the threshold had been crossed in

[148] ibid [47], [91]–[92], [139].
[149] ibid [85].
[150] ibid [121].
[151] J Doughty, 'Re B (A Child) (Care Order) [2013] UKSC 33' (2013) 35 *Journal of Social Welfare and Family Law* 491.
[152] *In the Matter of B (A Child)* (n 133) [223].
[153] ibid.

this case, but she stated that an adoption order was not justified. She disagreed with the majority of the Supreme Court and, like Lord Kerr, indicated that the Court had the jurisdiction to do more than merely review the decision of the lower court when performing a proportionality analysis. According to Lady Hale, the Court had the discretion to reconsider the issue based on the material put before it.

Despite referring to Amelia's Article 8 rights and a 'relatively rare'[154] reference to the UNCRC, there was no analysis of what these rights were (except for a brief reference to Article 21 and its emphasis on paramountcy[155]). Furthermore, there was no reference to how such rights could be weighed and whether the rights were relevant considerations in the welfare assessment under section 31, which preceded the adoption. For instance, Amelia's right under Article 7 UNCRC (to know and be cared for by her parents) and her right under Article 9 UNCRC (not to be separated from her parents) are rights that could have been referred to in the Court's analysis of the case. Amelia lost the opportunity to be raised by or at least maintain contact with her parents, even though contact had taken place since her birth and had been positive.

In contrast to *ANS*, the UK Supreme Court in the case of *In the Matter of B (A Child)* gave a more detailed analysis of proportionality and of non-consensual adoption, and a more in-depth discussion of relevant ECHR rights. However, one aspect of the decision that is disappointing is that the Supreme Court gave limited attention to the child's rights (despite the fact that the parents argued that not only had their Article 8 right been violated, but so had the Article 8 right of their daughter). Overall, though, this case can be used to support arguments made in both chapter 2 and chapter 3 that have emphasised that the state has a positive obligation not only to respect and protect the rights of children and parents in adoption cases, but also to consider, and where appropriate apply, less restrictive alternatives before making an adoption order.

Having outlined the significance of the Supreme Court jurisprudence on non-consensual adoption, the following section considers the guidance on non-consensual adoption that has been provided by the Court of Appeal in England and Wales.

V. Court of Appeal Guidance on Non-Consensual Adoption: *Re B-S (Children)*

A. The *B-S (Children)* Guidance

Re B-S (Children)[156] is an important case for three reasons. First, it provides guidance on the circumstances in which a non-consensual adoption may or may not be

[154] B Sloan, 'Adoption decisions in England: Re B (A Child) (Care Proceedings: Appeal) and beyond' [2015] *Journal of Social Welfare and Family Law* (online: 27 December 2015).

[155] *In the Matter of B (A Child)* (n 133) 104.

[156] *Re B-S (Children)* [2013] EWCA Civ 1146.

regarded as proportionate. Second, it provides explanation and application of the 'balance sheet' approach advocated by Munby LJ in such cases. Third, it provides helpful guidance for parents on when it will be possible to oppose the making of an adoption order based on a change in their circumstances.

This case concerned an appeal by a mother whose two children had been removed into care in 2011 and in respect of whom care and placement orders were made. The mother's consent to adoption was dispensed with and she applied under the ACA 2002, section 45(7) for leave to oppose the adoptions, arguing that her circumstances had changed. At first instance, her claim was refused by Parker J, on the basis that even though her circumstances had changed, her application to oppose the adoption would not have succeeded because of the bonds that the children had formed with their prospective adopters.

The mother appealed to the Court of Appeal on seven different grounds, which included arguments based on Article 6 ECHR (the right to a fair hearing) and Article 8 ECHR (the right to respect for private and family life). Munby LJ rejected the mother's appeal on all seven grounds but laid down important guidelines for adoption proceedings in the lower court. At a NAGALRO[157] Conference held in Birmingham in March 2015, Munby LJ described the case as one of the most 'important' in terms of practice. In *Re B-S (Children)*, Munby LJ acknowledged his 'misgivings'[158] about how lower courts had been addressing non-consensual adoptions and criticised them for their 'lack of attention'[159] to previous judgments, and provided guidance on the matter.

Munby LJ stated that where there had been no welfare analysis considering realistic options and no evaluation of the proportionality of the adoption, the decision-making would be 'flawed'[160] because an interference with Article 8 ECHR would not be justified. Munby LJ referred to the importance of ECtHR jurisprudence and the need to ensure that the state satisfied its obligation under Article 8, so as to ensure that legal ties between children and parents were severed only in exceptional circumstances and reasonable efforts were made to rebuild these relationships.[161] Munby LJ's judgment was highly critical of the lower courts with reference to four cases where failures to provide leave to challenge adoption without parental consent had been based on what he regarded to be inadequate judicial analysis. Furthermore, he was critical of the courts' tendency to place too much reliance on the evidence of social services, which is often insufficient and which he described as 'sloppy practice'.[162]

In *Re B-S*, the Court held that a high threshold would need to be reached before it could be determined that the child's welfare 'requires' parental consent to be dispensed with. In *Re B-S*, reference was made to Lady Hale in *Re B (A Child)*

[157] National Association of Guardians Ad Litem and Reporting Officers.
[158] *Re B-S (Children)* (n 156) [15].
[159] ibid [17].
[160] ibid [21].
[161] The Court referred to *K and T v Finland* (n 3) and *YC v UK* (n 118).
[162] *Re B-S (Children)* (n 156) [40].

(Care Proceedings: Threshold Criteria),[163] where she stressed that application of the ACA 2002 and Article 8 ECHR requires dispensing with parental consent only if 'nothing else will do'. Reference was also made to *Re P (Placement Orders: Parental Consent)*,[164] where Wall LJ stressed that to 'require' intervention or even long-term removal of a child did not necessarily mean that an adoption order would be required. In other words, just because a care order was necessary, it would not mean that a non-consensual adoption would be necessary and proportionate.

In sum, the decision in *Re B-S* has provided very important guidance on how the courts should exercise their powers and conduct their reasoning when deciding whether or not to make an adoption order. Munby LJ said that, first of all, it would be necessary for the courts to conduct a proper weighing up of the pros and cons of each potential option for a child in what is known as a 'balance sheet'[165] approach (see chapter 2). Second, the courts should provide a reasoned judgment, which should demonstrate a 'global holistic' approach whereby it considers the different options available to meet the child's needs. The decision in *Re B-S* therefore requires the consideration of at least one alternative less restrictive than adoption, and the balance sheet approach assists in determining whether that alternative is equally effective.

B. Change of Circumstances – A Tall Hurdle to Clear?

Re B-S (Children)[166] has also had an impact on the legal test to be applied when parents seek leave to revoke a placement order and when they oppose the making of a final adoption order. It is important to consider this aspect of the decision as it increases the protection of parents' rights under Article 8 ECHR, in that it provides parents with a meaningful form of legal recourse where their circumstances have changed and they seek to be reunited with their children.[167] The ACA 2002, section 24(2) provides that 'an application may not be made by a person other than the child or local authority' to revoke a placement order unless (i) the court has given leave to apply and (ii) the child is not placed for adoption by the authority. Under the ACA 2002, section 24(3), the court cannot revoke a placement order 'unless satisfied that there has been a change in circumstances since the order was made'. To obtain leave to revoke a placement order, the birth parents must prove that a change of circumstances has occurred within the family.

Where an application for an adoption order has been made, parents can no longer submit an application under section 24 but instead have the opportunity to challenge the making of the adoption order itself. The ACA 2002, section 47 lays

[163] *Re B (A Child) (Care Proceedings: Threshold Criteria)* [2013] UKSC 33.
[164] *Re P (Placement Orders: Parental Consent)* (n 31).
[165] First proposed by Thorpe LJ in *Re A (Male Sterilisation)* [2000] 1 FLR 549, 560.
[166] *Re B-S (Children)* (n 156).
[167] It has been observed that a notable aspect of the decision in *Re B-S* is its emphasis on human rights. See Herring, Probert and Gilmore (n 44) 146.

down the conditions for making an adoption order. Section 47(3) provides that parents (or guardians) may not oppose the making of an adoption order without the court's permission. In determining whether or not to permit parents to oppose the making of an adoption order, the court will consider whether or not there has been a change of circumstances.[168]

In assessing whether or not there has been a change of circumstances, the court has to consider whether the applicant (typically one or both of the birth parents) has a real prospect of success in his or her application. In deciding whether or not to give permission to an application, the welfare of the child must be considered and a two-stage test is applied.[169] First, the court asks if there has been a change in circumstances. If not, this is the end of the court's analysis and the application is dismissed. If there has been a change, the court must ask if leave to oppose the placement order should be given by evaluating 'whether the parent's prospects of success are more than just fanciful, whether they have solidity'.[170] The child's welfare will be the paramount consideration, and in evaluating welfare the court will consider the current state of affairs and what may happen in the future. If the child's welfare will be adversely affected by an application to oppose adoption, permission will not be granted.[171]

In *Re W (Adoption: Set aside and leave to oppose)*,[172] Thorpe LJ stressed that only 'exceptionally rare circumstances'[173] would justify disrupting a placement for adoption. In *Re B-S (Children)*,[174] McFarlane LJ's perspective was that the approach outlined by Thorpe LJ was untenable after the Supreme Court's decision in *Re B*,[175] because the jurisdiction under the ACA 2002, section 47(5) was only triggered when children had been placed for adoption and in such a placement for a minimum of 10 weeks. He viewed section 47(5) as intended to provide parents with a meaningful remedy against the making of an adoption order.

Re B-S shows that a change of circumstances need not be 'significant'[176] for permission to be granted to oppose a placement or an adoption order. This is because permission does not guarantee that parents will succeed in their application and prevent an adoption order from being made; it merely provides them with an opportunity to challenge it. The way in which a 'change of circumstances' may be interpreted by the courts is significant, since a restrictive interpretation of 'change of circumstances' means that few parents would be able to appeal against a non-consensual adoption. The conclusion in *Re B-S*, however, arguably increases

[168] *Re B-S (Children)* (n 156) [72]–[74].
[169] *Re W & Re H* [2013] EWCA Civ 1177.
[170] ibid [20], *per* Munby LJ.
[171] ibid.
[172] *Re W (Adoption: Set aside and leave to oppose)* [2010] EWCA Civ 1535. Also see: *Re C (A Child)* [2013] EWCA Civ 1431, which suggested that circumstances that might justify leave to appeal against adoption would be 'stringent'.
[173] *Re W (Adoption: Set aside and leave to oppose)* (n 172) [17].
[174] *Re B-S (Children)* (n 156).
[175] *In the Matter of B (A Child)* (n 133).
[176] *Re B-S (Adoption: Application of s 47(5))* [2013] EWCA Civ 1146 [8].

the likelihood that parents may be able to successfully argue that their circumstances have changed. The impact of this decision, then, is that it provides more protection to birth parents in cases where parents seek leave to revoke placement orders and to oppose adoption orders.

C. A Change of Approach?

At first glance, the decision in *Re B-S* appears to encourage caution in making adoption orders[177] and to emphasise thorough exploration of alternatives to adoption. Arguably, *Re B-S* also increases the protection of parents' rights in relation to the opposition of adoption orders, since the courts may be more willing to grant permission to oppose such an order.[178] Sloan has suggested, too, that the decisions in *Re B* and *Re B-S* have increased the likelihood of the judiciary's approach in non-consensual adoption cases being compatible with the UNCRC.[179]

The emphasis on legislative provisions (both in the ACA 2002 and the CFA 2014) to decrease delay in the adoption process, along with the current Conservative Government's clear commitment to adoption policy, suggests that adoption is the current Government's preferred choice for permanence for children in care, as it was for its Labour predecessor. In *Re B-S*, the Court has firmly stated that there ought not to be a presumption about what option is in the child's best interests. In fact, the Court in *Re B-S* has emphasised that adoption ought to be a last resort rather than a first consideration. Sloan has thus argued that there may be some conflict between the Government's pro-adoption policy and the courts' approach to adoption.[180]

According to Bainham and Markham, until the decision in *Re B-S* the lower courts often paid only 'lip service' to human rights requirements in adoption cases. They have suggested that this ruling puts pressure on judges to make balanced decisions based on proper evidence, for otherwise their decisions may be appealed by parents.[181] Although the High Court, Court of Appeal and the Supreme Court decisions have also emphasised that adoption ought to be a measure of last resort, the lower courts have not always treated it as such.[182]

Sprinz speculated that a possible result of the guidance in *Re B-S* would be fewer adoptions, with the consequence that more children will remain in long-term

[177] Herring, Probert and Gilmore (n 44)146.

[178] K Holt and N Kelly, 'When adoption without parental consent breaches human rights: implications of Re B-S (Children) [2013] EWCA Civ 963 on decision making and permanency planning for children' (2015) 37 *Journal of Social Welfare and Family Law* 228.

[179] Sloan (n 154).

[180] B Sloan, 'Loving but potentially harmful parents in the Supreme Court' (2014) 73 *CLJ* 28, 30. Also see J Doughty, '"Where nothing else will do": Judicial approaches to adoption in England and Wales' (2015) 39 *Adoption and Fostering* 105.

[181] A Bainham and H Markham, 'Living with Re B-S, Re S and its implications for parents, local authorities and the courts' [2014] *Family Law* 991, 998.

[182] L Sprinz, 'Adoption in 2014' [2014] *Family Law* 335.

foster care in order to ensure that ties with birth parents are not severed and that children remain in direct contact with them.[183] Despite the existence of Court of Appeal guidance, Sprinz has observed that the High Court has re-stated the key principles from *Re B-S* in many cases, because many of the Family Proceedings (Magistrates') Courts and County Courts still have not followed the authority of *Re B-S*.[184] This is cause for concern, as it may mean that some non-consensual adoptions are still taking place when less restrictive alternatives are available. In other words, some adoptions may not be human-rights compliant, in that they are not necessary and proportionate, and some children and parents may have had their legal and family ties unfairly and unnecessarily severed.

Another consequence of *Re B-S* is that there has been a significant increase in litigation by birth parents opposed to the adoption of their children.[185] There have been many subsequent cases where the Court of Appeal has allowed parents' appeals against adoption orders.[186] In *Re E*,[187] for instance, a mother appealed against care and placement orders. The Court of Appeal applied the test enunciated by the Supreme Court in *Re B*[188] and looked at the proportionality of the outcome, based on the evidence in the case. The child had been removed because of a finding of fact that the mother's boyfriend had caused harm to the child. The mother had continued to live with her boyfriend, before finding alternative suitable accommodation. The Court held that the adoption of a young child who was securely attached to the mother (who was seen as loving and capable) was not proportionate.

In another case, *Re J*,[189] the Court of Appeal considered a grandmother's appeal against care and placement orders in respect of a 21-month-old child. The Court stressed that Article 8 ECHR was important in this context, and it had to be shown that the adoption was 'necessary'. The Court allowed the appeal, since on the facts it was not clear why it was necessary for an adoption to take place or why the child could not have been placed with the birth family. These decisions demonstrate that the courts are recognising the requirements of proportionality, a legal principle that has long existed but which has not always been considered by the lower courts.

[183] ibid 336.

[184] ibid. See, eg, *Re V (Long-Term Fostering or Adoption)* [2013] EWCA Civ 913; *K v London Borough of Brent* [2013] EWCA Civ 926; *Re G (Care Proceedings: Welfare Evaluation)* [2013] EWCA Civ 965; *Re P (Care Proceedings: Balancing Exercise)* [2013] EWCA Civ 963; *Re B-S (Adoption: Application of s 47(5))* (n 176). Also see *Re D (A Child)* EWCA 1150. In contrast, see *Local Authority A v N & Ors* [2015] EWHC 1301 (Fam) (2 April 2015), which makes explicit reference to terminology from the decision in *Re B-S*. See also *F (a child) (placement order: proportionality)* [2018] EWCA Civ 2761.

[185] Doughty (n 180).

[186] For example, see *Re W (Children)* [2015] EWCA Civ 403.

[187] *Re E* [2013] EWCA Civ 1614.

[188] *Re B (A Child) (Care Proceedings: Threshold Criteria)* (n 163).

[189] *Re J (A Child)* [2013] EWCA Civ 1100.

In *Re Y (Children)*,[190] Ryder LJ suggested it is unnecessary for the Family Court to undertake a separate human rights proportionality evaluation balancing the effects of the interference on every individual's Article 8 right in private law cases, where there are no public law consequences. This is unlike in adoption cases, where there is public authority involvement, as the HRA 1998, section 6 provides that 'it is unlawful for a public authority to act in a way which is incompatible with a Convention right'. By implication, then, Ryder LJ's judgment has the potential to be used as authority for the proposition that when making adoption orders, which *do* have public law consequences, the courts must consider the rights of children and their parents to determine the proportionality of the order.

The present position of the Court of Appeal, after the decision in *Re B-S*, is that a holistic approach, taking into consideration a range of different options, does not require the courts to consider every possible option but simply those that are 'realistically possible'.[191] However, in *Re R (A Child)*, despite further criticism of social work practice in subsequent cases,[192] Munby LJ addressed 'myths' that might lead to fewer adoptions. These included the idea that there might be a higher threshold to satisfy before a child could be placed for adoption than there had been prior to the decision in *Re B-S*, or that more assessments would be needed before kinship carers could be ruled out. He asserted that despite the importance of his judgment in *Re B-S*, he had not intended to discourage the making of adoption orders. Munby LJ thus emphasised that local authorities 'must not shy away from seeking, nor courts from making'[193] adoption orders where it was necessary to do so.

Despite the welcome clarification that *Re B-S* provided (namely, that adoption should be regarded as a last resort, and that the quality of social work assessments and judicial reasoning needed to improve), concern has been expressed that the judgment in *Re B-S* has been used inappropriately to criticise social workers and local authorities.[194] Thus, for instance, Holt and Kelly have argued that social workers' decisions are under scrutiny in the wake of *B-S*.[195] Furthermore, Masson has pointed out that it is not just local authorities but also judges who are under pressure, because of the additional hearings that now take place after *B-S* and because higher standards of judicial reasoning are now expected.[196] The biggest impact, however, is the fact that 47 per cent fewer children were placed for

[190] *Re Y (Children)* [2014] EWCA Civ 1287.

[191] *Re R (A Child)* [2014] EWCA Civ 1625 [53], *per* Munby LJ.

[192] *Re W (A Child)* [2017] EWHC 829 (Fam).

[193] *Re R (A Child)* (n 191) [44], *per* Munby LJ.

[194] 'Adoption Myths Busted' (2015) 45 *Family Law* 105.

[195] K Holt and N Kelly, 'When is it too late to oppose an adoption order? *A and B v Rotherham Metropolitan Borough Council*' (2015) 45 *Family Law* 349.

[196] J Masson 'Third (or fourth) time lucky for care proceedings reform?' (2015) 27 *Child and Family Law Quarterly* 3. An example of such a judgment is *Re DE (A Child)* [2014] EWFC 6. For commentary, see C Fenton-Glynn, 'The Rise of Strict Scrutiny: Extending Re B-S to changes in care plans' (2015) 37 *Journal of Social Welfare and Family Law* 105.

adoption in the months following the decision.[197] For the first time since 2011, the 2015 annual statistics from the Department for Education demonstrated an overall decline in the number of children being placed for adoption (ie where placement orders had been made).[198] In the year ending 31 March 2017, 2,520 children in care were placed for adoption,[199] which was a decrease of 20 per cent on previous years.[200]

The National Adoption Leadership Board has attributed the decrease in the number of adoptions to the decisions in *Re B* and *Re B-S*.[201] NAGALRO has suggested that pre-*B-S*, special guardianship and kinship carers were ruled out as carers for 'quite spurious reasons'[202] without being afforded the chance to make representations to the court. Now, more special guardianship orders are made (see further discussion in chapter 5). It is apparent, then, that the *Re B-S* decision has had a considerable impact on the number of adoptions that have been made, and challenges existing adoption policy.

This following section considers some specific issues that have been raised by the legislation and the case law on non-consensual adoption.

VI. Adoption Law – More Adoptions, More Quickly

A. Overview

This section considers three issues that impact on the proportionality of non-consensual adoption and that, it is argued, have increased the likelihood that non-consensual adoption orders will take place in circumstances where less restrictive alternatives might have been available. These issues are:

- the potential for social engineering to occur in the context of non-consensual adoption;
- the impact of the 26-week limit in care and adoption proceedings;
- how new provisions that explicitly limit contact between children in care and their parents, both before and after adoption proceedings, may impact on the proportionality of non-consensual adoption.

[197] National Adoption Leadership Board figures for 2014 suggest that 1,830 children were placed for adoption between July and September 2013, and this figure decreased to 960 between April and June 2014.

[198] Department for Education, *Children Looked After in England (including care leavers) year ending 31 March 2015* (Department for Education, 2015).

[199] Department for Education, *Children looked after in England (including adoption), year ending 31 March 2017* (Department for Education, 2017) 9.

[200] ibid.

[201] National Adoption Leadership Board, *Impact of Court Judgments on Adoption, What the judgments do and do not say* (National Adoption Leadership Board, 2014).

[202] NAGALRO, *Nagalro Response to the Government Consultation on Special Guardianship 15 September 2015* (NAGALRO, 2015) 4.

B. Non-Consensual Adoption: A Proportionate Measure or Social Engineering?

Chapter 3 conveyed the importance of European jurisprudence that, under the HRA 1998, section 2, must be considered during court decision-making in England and Wales. In *Pontes v Portugal*,[203] *RMS v Spain*,[204] *Zhou v Italy*[205] and *SH v Italy*,[206] for example, the ECtHR has held that Member States ought to seek less restrictive alternatives to non-consensual adoption. In *Kutzner v Germany*[207] and *Haase v Germany*,[208] the ECtHR emphasised that merely showing that a child could be placed in a 'more beneficial environment for his or her upbringing'[209] would not, in and of itself, justify the compulsory removal of the child, and thus arguably would not justify an even more serious intervention with children's and parents' Article 8 ECHR rights to respect for private and family life, such as a non-consensual adoption. In other words, then, the ECtHR is against social engineering (ie deciding that a child would be better off living away from his or her birth parents). A similar perspective can be found from case law in England and Wales. Lady Hale, for example, has stated that social engineering must not lead to the removal of children from their parents:

> [I]t is not enough that the social workers, the experts or the court think that a child would be better off living with another family. That would be social engineering of a kind which is not permitted in a democratic society. The jurisprudence of the European Court of Human Rights requires that there be a 'pressing social need' for intervention and that the intervention be proportionate to that need …[210]

Of course, poverty and other social problems within families, such as mental illness, drug abuse, alcohol abuse or domestic violence, may, in certain circumstances, lead to the need for state intervention. And once children have been removed into care, non-consensual adoption is one of many possible options that may be proposed to the courts. Thus the concern about social engineering in non-consensual adoption cases is not merely academic. This is an issue that has also been raised in the Court of Appeal[211] and the Supreme Court. It can be seen in *Re A (A Child)*,[212] for example. In this case, a boy was removed into care and was due to be adopted, because the father was considered an unsuitable role model and was unable to raise his child due to his previous convictions.

[203] *Pontes v Portugal* [2012] ECHR 1573.
[204] *RMS v Spain* App no 28775/12 (ECHR, 18 June 2013).
[205] *Zhou v Italy* App no 33773/11 (ECHR, 21 January 2014).
[206] *SH v Italy* App no 52557/14 (ECHR, 13 October 2015).
[207] *Kutzner v Germany* (n 143) para 69.
[208] *Haase v Germany* [2004] 2 FLR 39, para 95.
[209] ibid para 95.
[210] *Re S-B (Children)* [2009] UKSC 17 [7], *per* Lady Hale.
[211] For example, see *N (Children) (Adoption: Jurisdiction)* [2015] EWCA Civ 1112 [10], *per* Munby LJ.
[212] *Re A (A Child)* [2015] EWFC 11.

The Court of Appeal acknowledged that the concerns expressed by social workers were relevant but found that there was a need for a careful analysis of the information. Non-consensual adoption was not regarded to be a proportionate response to the concerns about the father's ability to parent. In *Re A (A Child)*, Munby LJ expressed concern about social engineering and approved of the judgment in *North East Lincolnshire Council v G & L*[213] where Jack J stated:

> [T]he courts are not in the business of social engineering. The courts are not in the business of providing children with perfect homes. If we took into care and placed for adoption every child whose parents had had a domestic spat and every child whose parents on occasion had drunk too much then the care system would be overwhelmed and there would not be enough adoptive parents. So we have to have a degree of realism about prospective carers who come before the courts.[214]

Munby LJ reminded the lower courts of the key principle laid down in *YC v UK*,[215] which is that:

> Family ties may only be severed in very exceptional circumstances and that everything must be done to preserve personal relations and, where appropriate, to 'rebuild' the family. It is not enough to show that a child could be placed in a more beneficial environment for his upbringing. However, where the maintenance of family ties would harm the child's health and development, a parent is not entitled under article 8 to insist that such ties be maintained.

Lady Hale has expressed similar concerns about social engineering in her powerful dissent in the UK Supreme Court decision of *In the Matter of B (A Child)*.[216] An issue in care proceedings, which impacts on adoption proceedings, is that there is a fine line between necessary intervention and social engineering. In *In the Matter of B*, Lady Hale made it plain that parents' negative character traits and behaviour would not always justify removal of their children from the family home:

> We are all frail human beings, with our fair share of unattractive character traits, which sometimes manifest themselves in bad behaviours which may be copied by our children. But the State does not and cannot take away the children of all the people who commit crimes, who abuse alcohol or drugs, who suffer from physical or mental illnesses or disabilities, or who espouse anti-social political or religious beliefs.[217]

Furthermore, Porter has expressed wider concerns that social engineering may have played a role in the increasing number of care proceedings involving children from Eastern Europe,[218] some of whom may be placed for adoption.[219] Eastern European children sometimes come from countries where poverty is endemic,

[213] *North East Lincolnshire Council v G & L* [2014] EWCC B77 (Fam).
[214] ibid, as approved by Munby LJ in *Re A (A Child)* (n 212) 15–16.
[215] *YC v UK* (n 139) para 134.
[216] *In the Matter of B (A Child)* (n 133).
[217] ibid [143].
[218] J Porter, 'Families from Eastern Europe and care proceedings' [2014] *Family Law* 183.
[219] *LA v DG & Ors* [2013] EWHC 734 (Fam); *Kent County Council v IS & Ors* [2013] EWHC 2308 (Fam); *CB (A Child)* [2015] EWCA Civ 888. See also Fenton-Glynn (n 69).

and while these standards of living may be acceptable in those countries, they may not be so regarded in England and Wales. It may be difficult for some parents to reach the standards of living and parenting expected in England and Wales.[220] Porter has argued that there is a perception by countries such as Slovakia[221] that the English authorities are taking into care and holding on to 'white' children who are adoptable.[222] Furthermore, in recent years, there has been increasing media attention given to cases concerning children placed for adoption, born to parents who are not of English origin,[223] and there has also been increased litigation on this subject in England and Wales,[224] with some children being returned to their parents while others have been placed for adoption. The issue of if and when it will be appropriate for children born to parents of different nationalities to be adopted has been raised before the Council of Europe[225] and the European Parliament. Fenton-Glynn has drawn attention to this:

> The English adoption system has caused tension between the government and several other EU Member States, in particular Latvia, Slovakia and Bulgaria. Concerns have also been expressed by Nigeria in this regard.[226]

It is thus argued that social engineering is not merely an academic concern but is a real problem in non-consensual adoption cases, and a problem that may impact on whether the courts decide to choose a less restrictive (but equally effective) alternative to such adoptions. Where there is concern about parents' ability to raise their children due to different perceptions of parenting standards, assistance from the state might be a more appropriate and less restrictive form of intervention. In other words, it would be a more proportionate response. Such situations raise the potential for parents and children to argue that their rights under Article 8 ECHR and under the UNCRC have been violated, particularly in cases where insufficient assistance has been provided by the state (see the discussion in chapter 3).

[220] For example, see *LA v DG & Ors* (n 220); *Kent County Council v IS & Ors* (n 220).

[221] See a case concerning a child from Slovakia, and Munby LJ's discussion about care and adoption proceedings in relation to children from other countries: *Re E (Brussels II Revised: Vienna Convention: Reporting Restrictions)* [2014] EWHC 6 (Fam), [2014] 2 FLR 151, paras 13–15. Also in regard to Latvia, see *Re CB (A Child)* [2015] EWCA Civ 888.

[222] Porter (n 219) See also C Booker, 'Slovaks protest at Britain's "illegal child snatching"' *The Telegraph* (22 September 2012) at http://www.telegraph.co.uk/comment/9559657/Slovaks-protest-atBritains-illegal-child-snatching.html; O Bowcott, 'Latvia complaints to UK parliament over forced adoption' *The Guardian* (9 March 2015) at http://www.theguardian.com/uk-news/2015/mar/09/latvia-complains-to-ukparliament-over-forced-adoptions; F Capon, 'Baltic States say Norway, UK and Finland have stolen their children' *Newsweek* (23 April 2015) at http://europe.newsweek.com/baltic-states-say-norway-uk-andfinland-have-stolen-their-children-324031.

[223] See, eg, *N (Children) (Adoption: Jurisdiction)* (n 212); *Re CB (Adoption and Children Act 2002)* [2015] EWHC 3274 (Fam).

[224] See B Yuksel and K Trimmings, 'Choice of law aspects of non-consensual adoption of Eastern European Children in England and Wales [2017] *International Journal of Family Law* 202.

[225] Borzova (n 96).

[226] Fenton-Glynn (n 69) 25.

C. The 26-Week Limit on Care Proceedings: More Non-Consensual Adoptions?

An important aim of the adoption legislation in England and Wales (ie the ACA 2002 and the CFA 2014) is to reduce delay in the adoption process, so as to reduce the length of time that children remain in care and in a state of uncertainty. The UK Government has engaged in a pro-adoption policy, which aims to speed up the adoption process. This may be well-intentioned and beneficial for some children, but there is a danger that some children will be rushed into adoption without less draconian alternatives being explored and implemented (eg reuniting children with their birth parents or placing them with other birth relatives). Section 14(2)(ii) of the CFA 2014 is worthy of further scrutiny, because the 26-week limit in care proceedings has the potential to decrease delay in adoption proceedings but may lead to children in care being placed for adoption when they could have been returned to their families or placed with birth relatives. In general, academic opinions on the 26-week limit have been mixed.[227] It is argued that the change in the law, while intended to protect children's best interests, may not achieve the intended effect, and may even violate children's and parents' Article 8 ECHR rights.[228]

The CFA 2014, section 14(2)(ii) states that care proceedings must be concluded within 26-weeks of the date of the initial application. Although this time limit relates to care proceedings, not adoption proceedings, it is relevant to the proportionality of non-consensual adoption, because swifter care proceedings means that adoption proceedings are also likely to be concluded at a much earlier stage. Masson has acknowledged that while delays reduce the likelihood of finding and settling children into a new family, in some cases a delay may be 'constructive', as it may provide parents with time to resolve their problems and enable social workers to fully explore different care options that may be available.[229] In other words, this in-built delay allows for potentially equally effective but less restrictive alternatives to non-consensual adoptions to be used, which are less likely to violate parents' and children's Article 8 ECHR rights. Thus, removing delay in care proceedings, and potentially in adoption proceedings, may mean that children are placed for adoption when additional time might have enabled them to be returned to their parents or for birth relatives to have been identified as carers.

Furthermore, Holt and Kelly have argued that working with families might be more beneficial for children than removing delay in care proceedings via statutory reform.[230] They have argued that 'the focus appears to be increasingly upon

[227] See, eg, Holt and Kelly (n 178); Masson (n 196); J Doughty, 'Care proceedings – is there a better way?' (2014) 26 *Child and Family Law Quarterly* 113; J Harwin et al, 'Recurrent care proceedings: Part 2: Young motherhood and the role of the court' (2014) 44 *Journal of Family Law* 1439.

[228] See, eg, Bainham and Gilmore (n 60).

[229] Masson (n 196).

[230] K Holt and N Kelly, 'The emperor has no robes: Is the judiciary in the most complex of child-care cases, abandoning a sinking ship' [2014] *Family Law* 1421.

achieving targets rather than engaging in face-to-face contact with children and their families'.[231] Gilmore and Bainham have argued that care proceedings involve matters that have great importance to parents and ought not be rushed. They have argued that speeding up the process may not give parents sufficient time to come to terms with the fact that their children are being take into care, and this may lead to an increase in contested care proceedings.[232]

Holt and Kelly have also raised concerns that this statutory limit may simply mean that the delay may occur much earlier in the process, and that children could be left with their parents and remain at risk of harm while local authorities build their case.[233] Holt et al have argued that delay in taking a child into care may have the knock-on effect that children then wait longer for a permanent adoptive placement once the proceedings have been concluded.[234] If such consequences were to occur because of the 26-week limit, children might be able to argue that their rights under Article 8 ECHR (the right to respect for private and family life) have been violated.

D. The Relationship between Human Rights, Parental Contact and Non-Consensual Adoption

It is important to consider sections 8–9 of the CFA 2014, and assess the impact that they have had and may continue to have on non-consensual adoption cases. It has been seen from the case law that it is typical for contact between children in care and their parents to dwindle prior to adoption, and it is unusual for post-adoption contact to occur. It is argued that the new statutory provisions on contact in the CFA 2014 may further decrease the likelihood of contact between children and parents both before and after adoption proceedings. This is undesirable, since reducing contact prior to a non-consensual adoption order weakens the bonds between children and their parents, thereby making it easier to justify a non-consensual adoption order. Furthermore, even in circumstances where non-consensual adoption is a necessary and proportionate measure, it can be argued that this does not necessarily mean that terminating contact between the children and their parents will also be a proportionate measure. In fact, it is suggested that in certain cases (such as in *Aune v Norway*,[235] for example), permitting contact between children and their parents increases the likelihood that non-consensual adoption will be a proportionate measure.

[231] ibid.

[232] Bainham and Gilmore (n 60) 639. They also argue for a focus on addressing delay that is caused by incompetence, rather than delay in general.

[233] K Holt and N Kelly, 'Why parents matter: exploring the impact of a hegemonic concern with the timetable for the child' (2016) 21 *Child and Family Social Work Journal* 156.

[234] K Holt et al, 'Access to Justice for families? Legal advocacy for parents where children are on the "edge of care": an English case study' [2013] *Journal of Social Welfare and Family Law* 1.

[235] *Aune v Norway* App no 52502/07 (ECHR, 28 October 2010).

Although section 8 of the CFA 2014 on parental contact with children in care does not overtly refer to adoption, it does have a bearing on the adoption process and amends the CA 1989, section 34. The CFA 2014, section 8 concerns contact between children in care and their birth parents, which may take place prior to the adoption process, and provides that local authorities are 'authorised to refuse to allow contact between the child and a person mentioned' and that local authorities are not required 'to endeavour to promote contact between the child and that person'. This means that it is not necessary for a local authority to promote contact between a child and his or her birth parents. Reduced contact between a child and his or her birth parents means it is likely to weaken the relationship between them. This may, in some cases, make it easier to justify making an adoption order, and raises questions about the proportionality of the legislation.

Interestingly, while section 8 permits explicit limitation of contact between children and parents, it does not elaborate on the types of situations in which it will be appropriate to refuse contact. Furthermore, it is suggested that a requirement that local authorities do not need to 'endeavour to promote contact' is vague in nature, since it is unclear what local authorities' duties are in relation to contact between children and their parents. It can also be argued that section 8 appears to contradict ECtHR jurisprudence on contact between children and parents, which emphasises that restrictions on contact may in some cases violate the Article 8 ECHR rights of children and parents (see chapter 3 for further discussion). The ECtHR has made it apparent that once a child has been removed from his or her parents, reduction or termination of contact may weaken the bond between them and lessen the likelihood of their being reunited, which may constitute a violation of Article 8 of the Convention.[236]

In contrast to section 8 of the CFA 2014, section 9 of the Act explicitly recognises post-adoption contact within English law. It allows for the making of a contact order, which can be enforced against adopters under section 9(2)(a) in favour of the following persons listed under section 9(3), which include: a blood relative; a former guardian; someone who has had parental responsibility for the child; any person entitled to make an order under section 26; or anyone with whom the child has lived for a period of at least one year. Under section 9(2)(b), however, the court can make an order prohibiting any of these persons from having contact with the child.

These provisions do not appear to confer additional powers on the courts, since the courts have long been empowered to make orders in relation to contact or to prohibit contact under the CA 1989, section 8 (via a 'no contact' order or a prohibited steps order, for example). However, the courts have tended not to make contact orders because of concerns about the impact it would have on adoptive parents, who would need to facilitate contact arrangements.[237] Section 9 is thus

[236] *Scozzari and Giunta v Italy* App no 41963/98 (ECHR, 13 July 2000).

[237] See discussion in M Ryburn, *Contested Adoptions: Research, law, policy and practice* (Farnham, Ashgate Publishing, 1994).

seen by Dodgson as a 'symbolic'[238] acknowledgement of the importance of maintaining relationships with the birth family in the wake of adoption.

However, the simultaneous strengthening of local authorities' powers to prevent contact arguably may make this provision on post-adoption contact meaningless, since if contact is stopped between children and parents prior to adoption, it will be more difficult to argue that contact then ought to take place after the adoption order has been made. It will be interesting to see whether the CFA 2014, section 9 will in, in the future, encourage the courts to make more post-adoption contact orders in favour of birth parents, or whether it will make no practical difference to the courts' apparent reluctance to make orders enforcing post-adoption contact. At present, the courts continue to be reluctant to enforce post-adoption contact[239] even where prospective adopters have agreed that it ought to take place.[240]

The House of Lords Select Committee on Adoption Legislation has identified a problematic aspect of section 8 of the CFA 2014. Many children are not adopted with their siblings, and in such cases direct contact may be important to maintain these relationships. The Committee has expressed concern that the new provision has the potential to operate as 'a barrier to maintaining such contacts'.[241] It has identified that under the new provision, parents – and siblings too – would need to seek permission from the court to make a contact application. It has drawn attention to the fact that the ability of children to seek contact with a brother or sister via a court order 'may be constrained in practice'.[242] However, the difficulty is that, in some cases, such contact may be burdensome for adoptive parents, as contact with siblings can make children's behaviour more difficult to manage.[243]

It will be interesting to see whether section 8 will be the subject of future litigation under Article 8 ECHR, since to say that local authorities do not have 'to endeavour to promote contact between the child and that person' appears to contradict the approach taken by the ECtHR, which stresses both the importance of protecting relationships between children and parents and enabling contact to take place (see chapter 3). A report by the Children's Commissioner of England observed that under the current law, post-adoption contact is neither encouraged nor discouraged, which is in line with Article 9 UNCRC, which concerns the separation of children from their parents.[244] The Commissioner has stated that the current law on contact is compliant with both the ECHR and the UNCRC, but has suggested that more emphasis should be placed on taking a 'full account' of children's wishes and feelings about contact,[245] in line with the requirements

[238] L Dodgson, 'Post-Adoption Contact: All Change or More of the Same?' at http://www.familylaw-week.co.uk/site.aspx?i=ed136606.

[239] *B (A Child: Post-Adoption Contact)* [2019] EWCA Civ 29.

[240] See *Re W (A Child – No 4)* [2017] EWHC 1760 (Fam). The father applied for post-adoption contact under s 51A of the ACA 2002 and was unsuccessful in his application.

[241] HL Select Committee on Adoption Legislation (n 8) 64.

[242] ibid.

[243] ibid.

[244] Children's Commissioner, *A Child Rights Impact Assessment of Parts 1–3 of the Children and Families Bill (HC Bill 131)* (27 February 2013) 30.

[245] ibid 13.

under Article 3 UNCRC on the best interests of the child and Article 12 UNCRC on the views of the child.[246] Therefore, in some cases, adoption without parental consent that does not provide for contact between children and their birth parents (and/or their siblings) may not be proportionate. For further discussion of the issue of adoption with parental contact and its infrequent usage, see chapter 5, section VI.

VII. Conclusion

This chapter has outlined and analysed the key legislation on non-consensual adoption and whether or not these provisions strike the appropriate balance in protecting the best interests and rights of children, on the one hand, and the rights of parents, on the other. Analysis of the Adoption Act 1976, the ACA 2002 and the CFA 2014 has shown that there has been a shift away from protecting the rights of parents and towards protection of the best interests of children (rather than their rights). The current adoption legislation has the right aim – namely, to create stability and permanence for children in care, at the earliest possible point in time. However, adoption will not always be in the best interests of children in care. Furthermore, as demonstrated by the preceding discussion, the CFA 2014 has some features that may be subject to future challenges under the ECHR via the HRA 1998, and perhaps even before the ECtHR.

This chapter has also discussed adoption cases heard in the courts in England and Wales, with a focus on cases heard in the Court of Appeal and the Supreme Court. While the birth parents did not always manage to reverse a non-consensual adoption, let alone have their children returned to them, these cases have nonetheless laid down important principles for the lower courts (such as the Family Proceedings Court, the County Court and the High Court) to follow when making an adoption order without parental consent. *Re B-S (Children)*[247] is an important Court of Appeal case that emphasised that non-consensual adoption ought to be a measure of last resort and that a balance sheet approach ought to be applied. It has been observed in this chapter, however, that despite being the persons most affected by adoption proceedings, children's rights are afforded very little direct consideration in the courts' judgments. Even where reference is made to children's rights in adoption cases heard in England and Wales,[248] the courts tend to perform a limited analysis of what these rights are and how they may be balanced against parents' rights, for example, under Article 8 ECHR.

It has been observed that there is a potential clash between government policy, which advocates adoption as the best option for children in care, and recent case

[246] ibid 30.

[247] *Re B-S (Children)* (n 156).

[248] In particular, see the following Supreme Court decisions: *ANS and another v ML (AP) (Scotland)* (n 113); *In the Matter of B (A Child)* (n 133).

law, which seems to emphasise adoption as a measure of last resort.[249] This raises issues of how the potential clash between government policy and judicial principle will be resolved in the future. Despite the issues raised by the ACA 2002 and the CFA 2014, and potential incompatibility of some aspects of the CFA 2014 with Article 8 ECHR (and the UNCRC[250]), the pro-adoption trend appears set to continue. The Education and Adoption Act 2016 made another change under section 15, which requires councils to combine their adoption functions with those of other councils, so as to increase the potential matches between prospective adopter and child.

This is likely to mean that more adoptions would take place, more quickly. This is because, like the other measures enacted under the ACA 2002 and the CFA 2014, the Education and Adoption Act 2016, section 15 is another provision that aims to address delays in the adoption process. Furthermore, the Children and Social Work Act 2017 has amended the ACA 2002, section 1(4)(f) to include 'any person who is a prospective adopter with whom the child is placed' after 'relatives'. This means that when a placement or adoption order is made, explicit consideration needs to be given to the interests of prospective adopters.

The intention behind both the ACA 2002 and the CFA 2014 may have been to create stability and permanence for children in care, who might otherwise face uncertainty and poor prospects in the future. The changes enacted by the CFA 2014, part 1 provide support to prospective adoptive parents, increase the number of prospective adopters and aim to decrease delays in the adoption process. However, it is argued that the UK Government ought to assess whether or not reducing delay and promoting adoption serves the best interests of all children in care. In doing so, the Government could examine whether a different approach considering alternatives to adoption might better serve children's best interests, and protect the rights of children and their birth parents under Article 8 ECHR.

The next chapter will go on to consider less restrictive alternatives to non-consensual adoption, which may, in some circumstances, be equally effective when compared with non-consensual adoption.

[249] Bainham and Markham (n 181). Also see a similar observation from the following: Sloan, 'Loving but potentially harmful parents in the Supreme Court' (n 180) 31; B Sloan, 'Fostering and Adoption as a Means of Securing Article 6 Rights in England' (2015) 26 *Stellenbosch Law Review* 363, 377. More generally, see Bainham and Gilmore (n 60).

[250] Sloan, 'Fostering and Adoption as a Means of Securing Article 6 Rights in England' (n 249) 377–78.

5

Alternatives to Non-Consensual Adoption

I. Introduction: Adoption in Proportion?

Non-consensual adoption should be a measure of last resort. Or so claims Munby LJ, former President of the Family Division of the High Court.[1] For he emphasises the need to consider alternatives to adoption that are 'realistically possible'[2] and has reminded the lower courts that they should consider such alternatives. Also, Lady Hale, the President of the UK Supreme Court, has stressed that any order (including an adoption order) should be proportionate to the needs of the child.[3] The jurisprudence of the European Court of Human Rights (ECtHR) has sent out a similar message, which was considered in chapter 3. The Court has emphasised the state should undertake work to keep families together. After all, the state has a positive obligation under Article 8 of the European Convention on Human Rights (ECHR)[4] to make reasonable efforts to reunite children with their parents.[5] The failure of Member States to use alternatives to adoption led the ECtHR, in *Pontes v Portugal*,[6] *RMS v Spain*[7] and *Zhou v Italy*,[8] to conclude that the adoption orders made in these cases amounted to violations of the parents' rights under Article 8. Despite the lack of consideration of children's rights in these cases, it can be argued that these decisions violated their rights under Article 8 ECHR too.

[1] *Re B-S (Children)* [2013] EWCA Civ 1146.

[2] *Re R (A Child)* [2014] EWCA Civ 1625 [53], *per* Munby LJ.

[3] For example *Re O (Supervision Order)* [2001] 1 FLR 923, 928; *Oxfordshire County Council v L (Care or Supervision Order)* [1998] 1 FLR 70, 74; *In the Matter of B (A Child)* [2013] UKSC 33; *In the Matter of J* [2013] UKSC 9.

[4] European Convention for the Protection of Human Rights and Fundamental Freedoms, as amended by Protocols nos 11 and 14, 4 November 1950 (European Convention on Human Rights (ECHR)), ETS 5, available at https://www.refworld.org/docid/3ae6b3b04.html.

[5] *Johansen v Norway* App no 17383/90) 7 August 1996; *Hokkanen v. Finland* [1996] 1 FLR 289; *Görgülü v. Germany* [2004] ECHR 74969/01; *Neulinger and Shuruk v. Switzerland* (App no 41615/07) 6 July 2010; *Pini and Others v. Romania* App no 78028/01 (ECHR, 22 June 2014).

[6] *Pontes v Portugal* [2012] ECHR 1573.

[7] *RMS v Spain* App no 28775/12 (ECHR, 18 June 2013).

[8] *Zhou v Italy* App no 33773/11 (ECHR, 21 January 2014).

It is a premise of this book that a proportionality analysis undertaken by the domestic courts in England and Wales (and by the ECtHR) should consider whether less restrictive but equally effective alternatives to non-consensual adoption are available. If so, it may be concluded that non-consensual adoption cannot be a necessary and proportionate measure. Thus, this chapter considers less restrictive alternatives to non-consensual adoption. Those alternatives seek to achieve the same objective of ensuring stability and permanence for children in care, thereby protecting their best interests and reducing the likelihood of violating the rights of children and parents. The chapter will consider the different long-term alternatives to adoption, such as state assistance, kinship care, special guardianship orders or adoption with direct contact. In doing so, it will analyse whether these less restrictive alternatives are in fact equally effective when compared with non-consensual adoption and, if so, in what types of cases or situations these alternatives might be effective.

This chapter argues that these alternatives to non-consensual adoption may, in some circumstances, be equally effective and less restrictive, and thus be less likely to violate children's and parents' Article 8 ECHR rights. Furthermore, this chapter will also consider and assess the potential resource implications of using less restrictive alternatives to non-consensual adoption. This discussion will assess whether or not these alternatives are cost-effective and less expensive than non-consensual adoption, since even if these measures may be regarded as more proportionate, resource limitations may mean that the state is reluctant to use these alternatives.

II. State Assistance in England and Wales

A. Overview of State Assistance: When to Assist and When to Adopt?

It is important to consider state assistance (ie social care services enabling children to remain in their parents' care) as an alternative to adoption, because there may be cases where early intervention reduces the likelihood of children's being taken into care in the first place. Bainham has argued that although child protection and family autonomy appear to be conflicting ideas, they are not necessarily so, as public involvement of a supportive nature may assist children and parents.[9] In fact, intervention (which is less restrictive than adoption) may protect children and parents from potential violations of their Article 8 ECHR rights. State assistance, which may be temporary or permanent and financial or practical, has the benefit of protecting family groups who are likely to be affected by the law on

[9] A Bainham, *Children, Parents and the State* (London, Sweet & Maxwell, 1988) 77.

non-consensual adoption. In particular, it can help vulnerable groups of persons, such as those living in poverty, and individuals with a learning disability, physical disability, mental illness or some other type of impairment that may impact on their ability to raise their children.[10]

Financial and practical assistance from the state may also help kinship carers in situations where birth parents are unable to raise their children (see section IV.C and section VII). This assistance could be delivered with or without a less intrusive court order, such as a supervision order under section 35 of the Children Act 1989 (CA 1989) (enabling individuals such as social workers to 'advise, assist and befriend the supervised child') or a family assistance order (FAO) under section 16 of the Act. An FAO has a similar aim to section 35, in that it also provides that individuals can 'advise, assist and befriend' the child. However, an FAO differs, in that it cannot be the subject of a standalone application. It is necessary to apply for it in an application for another type of order, and it is usually recommended as a result of a CA 1989, section 7 welfare report in private law proceedings, despite its potential use in public law proceedings.

Regardless of the specific form that state assistance may take, it offers benefits to children and parents alike, and offers a less restrictive alternative to non-consensual adoption. It is clear from the Strasbourg jurisprudence on Article 8 ECHR that there may be cases where the state is under a positive obligation to make reasonable efforts to reunite children with their parents, which may include the need to provide state assistance.[11] There is, however, a need to ensure that assistance to the family unit is not at the expense of the child's welfare. The House of Lords Select Committee on Adoption has acknowledged that there is a tension between the time spent helping parents address their problems (such as drug or alcohol addiction) and the negative impact on the child of delay in a final decision about whether he or she can be raised safely by his or her parents or should be placed for adoption.[12]

Certainly, if the state does not make reasonable efforts to attempt to reunite children with their parents then it may fail to satisfy its positive obligation under Article 8 ECHR. However, if the state invests too much time in trying to reunite children and parents in order to avoid adoption, it may breach the child's rights under Articles 2, 3 and 8 of the Convention. Thus, in some cases, leaving a child with or returning a child to abusive or neglectful parents may not be appropriate at all, and may potentially violate the child's rights under Articles 2 and 3 ECHR. Furthermore, the state faces other challenges in providing assistance, such as reduction in support to vulnerable families due to cuts to local authorities' budgets.[13]

[10] *Working Together to Safeguard Children: A guide to inter-agency working to safeguard and promote the welfare of children* (HM Government, March 2013).

[11] See, eg, *RMS v Spain* (n 7); *Zhou v Italy* (n 8).

[12] House of Lords Select Committee on Adoption Legislation, *Second Report of Session 2012–13 Adoption: Post-Legislative Scrutiny* (London, TSO, 2013).

[13] P Alston, *Visit to the United Kingdom of Great Britain and Northern Ireland: Report of the Special Rapporteur on extreme poverty and human rights* (New York, UN General Assembly, 2019).

B. Types of State Assistance: Law, Practice and Innovation

The CA 1989 aims to protect the rights of both parents and children in England and Wales. Part III of the Act recognises the importance of support services for children and families so that court intervention will be a last resort. Such support could, for instance, include home-based assistance, day care,[14] placement with a child-minder,[15] kinship care or payments to the family.[16] Provision of assistance from the state is potentially a less restrictive alternative to non-consensual adoption, and there is considerable support in favour of promoting measures that help families stay together. Munro, for example, has stated that

> with good practice and trying to help families you can reach a quicker decision about whether they can use help, whereas if you are not actively trying to engage them in change, then you cannot work out whether they can change or not.[17]

In other words, early state intervention may avoid the need for children to be taken into care and adopted without parental consent. This is particularly relevant for mothers of newborn babies, as research by Broadhurst et al demonstrates that there has been a significant rise in the number of newborns subject to care proceedings in England.[18] The current trend is towards an increase in the use of care proceedings for newborns. In 2007/08, 1,039 babies were subject to care proceedings within a week of birth. In 2017/18 there was a 136 per cent increase, and 2,447 newborns were subject to care proceedings.[19] While it is unknown what percentage of these babies were adopted, Broadhurst et al identified that adoption was one of the options available to the state, and that if a mother had previously had a child placed for adoption, this increased the likelihood that any subsequent children she had would also be adopted. Cox has argued that the recurrent removal

[14] UN General Assembly, Resolution 64/142 of 24 February 2010 (reissued 13 April 2010), Guidelines for the Alternative Care of Children 2010, IV A38; R Hodgkin and P Newell, *Implementation Handbook for the Convention on the Rights of the Child*, 3rd edn (Geneva, United Nations Publications, 2007) 237; G Lansdown and P Newell, *UK Agenda for Children* (London, Child Rights Development Unit, 1994) 25.

[15] Department of Health, *Framework for the Assessment of Children in Need and their Families* (London, TSO, 2000) 8–9.

[16] P Selman and K Mason, *Alternatives to Adoption for Looked After Children* (Edinburgh, Scottish Executive, 2005). Also, more generally for the role in the effect of income on family well-being, see F Ssewamala, L Stark and M Canavera, 'Economic dimensions of child protection and well-being' (2014) 47 *Children and Youth Services Review* 103.

[17] ibid. Also see E Munro, *The Munro Review of Child Protection (Final Report May 2011)* (Cm 8062, 2011).

[18] K Broadhurst et al, 'Connecting Events in Time to Identify a Hidden Population: Birth Mothers and Their Children in Recurrent Care Proceedings in England' (2015) 45 *British Journal of Social Work* 2241.

[19] K Broadhurst et al, *Born into Care: newborn babies subject to care proceedings in England* (London, The Nuffield Family Justice Observatory: Nuffield Foundation, 2018).

and subsequent adoption of children from 'highly marginalized mothers'[20] has a 'disproportionate impact'[21] on the child protection system, and has emphasised the importance of early intervention to prevent the cycle of recurrent care and adoption proceedings.

Newborns are vulnerable and in most need of the state's protection,[22] so the state must intervene, and may need to remove children from their parents to protect their rights under Articles 2 and 3 ECHR. However, early state intervention that is less restrictive than non-consensual adoption decreases the likelihood of their being subject to neglect and abuse in the first place.[23] State intervention, even prior to the child's birth, in the form of practical assistance from social services, such as parenting classes or other forms of therapeutic intervention (such as counselling or psychotherapy), could increase the likelihood that a parent or parents will develop the parenting skills required for raising the child. This type of intervention could have enabled Amelia, in the case of *In the Matter of B (A Child)*[24] (see chapter 4), to have been raised by her birth parents.

The difficulty is that while the scope of the state's positive obligation to provide assistance under Article 8 ECHR is widening, it is unclear what assistance would need to be provided in individual cases so as to satisfy this obligation. It seems likely, however, that the positive obligation only exists towards children who have already been born. Social services may advise that a child ought to be removed at birth, but arguably the state has no legal obligation to intervene to assist pregnant women in becoming better parents to their unborn children when they do not, in the eyes of the law, have children in need of protection.[25]

Cox et al[26] monitored two pioneering services in Suffolk – Positive Choices and MPower – that offered support packages to parents whose children had been removed into care. It was found that these services reduced immediate future unplanned pregnancies (ie within next one to two years) and improved the emotional well-being of many of the parents. The programmes aimed to improve parents' reflection on their own behaviour, thereby increasing the likelihood that such parents would be able to address the factors that led to care and adoption proceedings (such as poor mental health, domestic abuse, addiction).

Despite the pro-adoption policy for children in care, there are many programmes in England and Wales to assist parents whose children are at risk of

[20] P Cox, 'Marginalized Mothers, Reproductive Autonomy and Repeated Losses to Care' (2012) 39 *Journal of Law and Society* 541, 547.

[21] ibid.

[22] C Cuthbert, G Rayns and K Stanley, *All Babies Count: Protection and prevention for vulnerable babies* (London, NSPCC, November 2011).

[23] R Chandiramani, 'Bang for the buck' [2012] *Children and Young People Now* 25.

[24] *In the Matter of B (A Child)* [2013] UKSC 33.

[25] *Vo v France* App no 53924/00 (ECHR, 8 July 2004).

[26] P Cox et al, *Reducing Recurrent Care Proceedings Service Evaluation: Positive Choices and MPower* (unpublished report, University of Essex, 2015); P Cox et al, 'Reducing recurrent care proceedings: initial evidence from new interventions' [2017] *Journal of Social Welfare and Family Law* 332.

being taken into care and, in some circumstances, may potentially be placed for adoption without parental consent.[27] For example, the Family Nurse Partnership programme, established in 2007, provides specially trained nurses to help families from early pregnancy until the child is 2 years old.[28] Research has shown that where professionals work with parents and assist them via education, training or therapeutic intervention (eg counselling), children are more likely to be returned home to their parents. Even in cases where this is not possible, subsequent siblings born to the same parents are less likely to be abused.[29] This is significant in circumstances where mothers have repeat pregnancies. In such cases, then, concurrent planning (see section II.C) might be a way of protecting the best interests of children who cannot be returned to their parents, while giving parents another opportunity to parent effectively in the future, thereby providing protection to those parents' Article 8 ECHR rights.

There is evidence that shows that state assistance helps families stay together. For example, a project undertaken by Barnados found that in 78 per cent of the cases they looked at, children could be reunited with their birth parents if the parents were given adequate support in maintaining themselves (eg via housing, education, residential units, child-minding, benefits, support networks and/or a social worker).[30] This project suggests that, with support from local authorities, it is more likely that children can continue to live with their birth parents, which protects children's and parents' Article 8 ECHR rights and the child's rights under the United Nations Convention on the Rights of the Child (UNCRC),[31] namely, under Article 7 (to know and be cared for by his or her parents), Article 8 (to know his or her identity) and Article 9 (not to be unnecessarily separated from his or her parents).

However, despite the apparent benefits of the above-mentioned programmes, limited state resources may affect the number of such schemes available to parents. Doughty has observed that government funding is used to support the pro-adoption policy instead of helping vulnerable families.[32] In fact, the Adoption Reform Grant resulted in £150 million of funding being taken away from the Early Intervention Grant, which was aimed at keeping children and parents together.[33]

[27] See, eg, Salford City Council's 'Strengthening Families' project (Warrington, Gardner & Garraway, 2014) at https://www.salford.gov.uk/familyintervention.htm; and Suffolk County Council's 'Positive Choices' (Suffolk Children and Young People's Service, 2010) at https://www.suffolk.gov.uk/council-and-democracy/council-news/show/programme-to-support-suffolks-vulnerable-recurrent-mothers-shows-real-success.

[28] HL Select Committee on Adoption Legislation (n 12). Also see at http://www.dh.gov.uk/en/Publicationsandstatistics/Publications/PublicationsPolicyAndGuidance/DH_118530.

[29] HL Select Committee on Adoption Legislation (n 12).

[30] L Charlton et al, *Still Screaming: Birth parents compulsorily separated from their children* (Manchester, After Adoption, 2008) 114.

[31] United Nations Convention on the Rights of the Child, 20 November 1989, 1577 UNTS 3, available at https://www.refworld.org/docid/3ae6b38f0.html.

[32] J Doughty, 'Care proceedings – is there a better way?' (2014) 26 Child *and Family Law Quarterly* 113.

[33] HL Select Committee on Adoption Legislation (n 12).

The Select Committee on Adoption has warned that investment in adoption should not be at the expense of the financial resources used to help children remain with their birth families. The Committee has stated that where there is evidence of a parental capacity to change, financial investment in reuniting children with their parents reduces the number of children in care and the numbers of children waiting for an alternative placement.

The Committee emphasised the need to strike the appropriate balance between providing parents with enough time to address their problems and respecting the child's need for a secure attachment. According to the Committee, this balance could be achieved if social workers conducted a 'robust assessment of parental capacity to change'.[34] In written evidence presented to the Committee, TACT[35] and Action for Children[36] both recommended more wide-ranging legal reforms to permanency for children in care. Action for Children argued in favour of a system whereby adoption is not regarded as being the preferred care option but instead as 'a system which has at its heart a drive to find the right placement for each individual child, rather than creating a false hierarchy of care – where adoption is interpreted as being the preferred care option'.[37]

The Select Committee on Adoption has expressed concern that focusing solely on adoption may mean there is 'a real risk of overlooking the needs of the vast majority of children in care for whom adoption [is] not appropriate'.[38] This can be seen in respect of older children (eg children aged between 10 and 15), who are less likely to be placed for adoption anyway and for whom options such as counselling, therapeutic family support or foster care will be more effective alternatives.[39] Therefore, it is clear that adoption is not the only route to permanence for children in care and that other equally effective options (such as long-term fostering, kinship care or special guardianship) are available for children who cannot be raised by their parents. Thus, less restrictive alternatives to non-consensual adoption, which may be equally effective, ought to be considered and implemented, where appropriate.

In fact, the Government ought to invest more financial resources in supporting families than in placing children for adoption, since doing so may prevent children from going into care in the first place.[40] The Select Committee on Adoption, for example, strongly recommended that adoption and all of its viable alternatives should be given equal attention and appropriate financial investment.[41] Similarly,

[34] ibid 73.

[35] ibid 16. Written evidence of TACT (The Adolescent and Children's Trust), a fostering and adoption charity.

[36] ibid. Written evidence of Action for Children, a charity for vulnerable and neglected children.

[37] ibid.

[38] ibid.

[39] J Boddy et al, *Working at the 'Edge' of Care? – European Models of Support for Young People and Families* (London, Department for Schools and Families, 2009).

[40] Selman and Mason (n 16).

[41] HL Select Committee on Adoption Legislation (n 12) 16.

Sloan has argued that applying state resources more widely instead of focusing solely on adoption could lead to better outcomes for the best interests and rights of children and the rights of their birth parents.[42] Larizadeh has also advocated that more support ought to be available for parents, on the basis that 'miracles do happen' where parents are provided with the tools to care for their children.[43] Arguably, too, under Article 20 UNCRC (considered in chapter 2), the state ought to assist families and provide the least restrictive alternative available to non-consensual adoption, where it is possible to do so.

The question, then, is what level of effort is needed by the state in order to satisfy its positive obligation under Article 8 ECHR? Lord Scott said in *Re G*[44] that 'there was no article 8 right to be made a better parent at public expense'. Yet it is arguable that section 20 of the CA 1989, under which local authorities have a duty to provide accommodation for specific children in need, has relevance in this context. This provision could potentially be read in conjunction with Article 8 ECHR, to require such state assistance as to help children in need under section 17 of the CA 1989.[45] Although *Re G* still amounts to good law, cases can be found where an emphasis has been placed on providing parents with assistance so as to help their children, even if the existence of or scope of such a right has not been fully considered. For example, the Court of Appeal in *EH v London Borough of Greenwich*[46] allowed the parents' appeal against a care and placement order because they were given insufficient help with their child, despite evidence of good parenting.[47] Although the Court did not state that the parents had a right to assistance under Article 8 ECHR, it opined that non-abusive parents ought to receive proper support at the earliest possible stage, provided they had 'sufficient qualities'[48] to be good parents. However, the Court did not refer to what sorts of qualities were 'sufficient' for parents to receive such support and assistance.

Larizadeh has persuasively argued that the decision in *EH* suggests that, even if the state does not have a positive obligation under Article 8 ECHR to help improve parenting, there is a 'social responsibility at public expense to support parents to improve'.[49] This is supported by the discussion in chapter 3 of this book. It was argued that recent case law of the ECtHR shows that the national authorities'

[42] B Sloan, 'Conflicting Rights: English Adoption Law and the Implementation of the UN Convention on the Rights of the Child' (2013) 25 *Child and Family Law Quarterly* 40. Also see K O'Halloran, *The Politics of Adoption: International Perspectives on Law Policy and Practice*, 3rd edn (Brisbane, Springer, 2015).

[43] C Larizadeh, 'Keep Calm and Read *B-S*' paper presented at *Between a Rock and a Hard Place. 26 weeks and Re B-S: conflicting pressures for family courts*, NAGALRO Conference (16 March 2015).

[44] *Re G (Interim Care Order: Residential Assessment)* [2006] 1 FLR 601.

[45] H Fenwick, G Phillipson and R Masterman, *Judicial Reasoning under the UK Human Rights Act* (Cambridge, CUP, 2007) 327–28.

[46] *EH v London Borough of Greenwich* [2010] EWCA Civ 344.

[47] ibid [13].

[48] ibid [16].

[49] C Larizadeh, 'Section 38(6) Assessments: The Good, the Bad and the Ugly' (2011) at http://www.familylawweek.co.uk/site.aspx?i=ed79118.

positive obligation under Article 8 ECHR to reunite families (which may in some cases include the need to provide state assistance) is widening.[50] Furthermore, in *Re B-S (Children)*[51] (see chapter 4), the Court of Appeal held that local authorities must treat adoption as a last resort and use measures other than adoption to protect a child's welfare, where possible. It can be argued that the need to use less restrictive alternatives to non-consensual adoption, where possible, is becoming an important part of the proportionality process (see chapter 3).

It can be argued that state assistance increases the likelihood that local authorities will have satisfied their positive obligation under Article 8 to undertake reasonable steps to reunite families.[52] If reasonable steps have been taken to keep a family together but this has failed to improve children's well-being, it may be necessary and proportionate for children to be placed for adoption without parental consent. For example, there may be cases where, despite the efforts of the state to intervene, the neglect or abuse suffered by children has reached a stage at which Article 2 ECHR (the right to life) or Article 3 ECHR (the right to freedom from torture or inhuman or degrading treatment) is engaged, and the state may violate these rights if the children are not removed from their parents.

An example where it is suggested that reasonable steps were taken by the state to keep a family together can be seen in *LA v DG & Ors*.[53] In this case, six children were taken into care, three of whom were placed for adoption because of neglect. In the care of their parents, the children suffered from emotional and intellectual delay and health problems, because their parents did not always seek the medical treatment required. Their living conditions were deemed inadequate by social services, and the parents suffered with financial problems. The parents challenged the adoption orders but failed, because, despite 10 months of state assistance (including financial assistance and housing), the children still had delayed emotional and intellectual development. In the circumstances, it was held to be in the children's best interests to be permanently removed from their parents and placed for adoption. In this case, the parents themselves had stopped attending contact sessions with their children and left the country. Only one of the children appeared to express sentiments suggesting that she missed her parents; the others were described as not being 'unduly concerned'[54] by their absence.

Although the Family Division of the High Court did not refer to the ECHR in this case, it is arguable that the concrete steps that the state took to keep the family together, in the form of financial and housing assistance, amounted to reasonable efforts within the meaning of the state's positive obligation under Article 8 ECHR. If the local authority had spent more time trying to keep the family together, the

[50] See, eg, *RMS v Spain* (n 7); *Zhou v Italy* (n 8); and *SH v Italy* App no 52557/14 (13 October 2015).
[51] *Re B-S (Children)* [2013] EWCA Civ 1146.
[52] See the discussion in ch 2.
[53] *LA v DG & Ors* [2013] EWHC 734 (Fam).
[54] ibid [53].

children could have argued that their own rights under Article 3 ECHR had been violated (see chapter 3 for further discussion).[55] Therefore, in this case, it can be concluded that the state had first attempted to explore less restrictive alternatives to non-consensual adoption and had made concerted efforts to keep the family together.

Although continued state assistance might not be appropriate in every case (as already seen), it may keep families together. The benefits of a greater emphasis on preventative work and putting resources into assisting birth families are also evidenced by the approach utilised by European countries that favour state assistance and preventative measures over adoption, including non-consensual adoption. Thus, a comparative international study by Warman shows that other European countries, such as France and the Netherlands, devote more financial resources to family support and reunification in comparison to England and Wales.[56] However, France's preference for long-term fostering can be criticised, as it is favoured even in circumstances where serious neglect and abuse have occurred.[57] In some circumstances, it might be in the best interests of some children if the authorities in France were more inclined to consider adoption, and even non-consensual adoption, where children cannot be reunited with their parents or placed with birth relatives.

In Nordic countries, one reason why non-consensual adoption is less prevalent is that their preventative services are much more advanced than elsewhere in Europe.[58] For instance, in Sweden,[59] Norway[60] and Denmark,[61] the adoption of children in care is virtually unheard of,[62] and resources tend to be set aside to help birth parents keep their children and maintain the family unit.[63] In Norway, only 80–100 children are adopted annually, and most of these are infants born to drug-abusing parents.[64] In Norway, the state has a guaranteed minimum standard of income, livelihood and housing accommodation for families,[65] all of which are

[55] See, eg, *Z and others v UK* App no 29392/95 (ECHR, 10 May 2001).

[56] A Warman and C Roberts, *Adoption and Looked After Children: International Comparisons* (Oxford, OUP, 2002); Selman and Mason (n 16).

[57] O'Halloran (n 42) 534 and 543. On France's approach towards adoption generally, see ibid ch 13. Also see K O'Halloran, *Adoption Law and Human Rights: International Perspectives* (Abingdon, Routledge, 2018).

[58] O'Halloran (n 42).

[59] M Cocozza and S Hort, 'The Dark Side of the Universal Welfare State? Child Abuse and Protection in Sweden' in N Gilbert, N Parton and M Skivenes (eds), *Child Protection Systems: International Trends and Orientations* (Oxford, Oxford University Press, 2011) 89.

[60] M Skivenes, 'Norway: Toward A Child-Centric Perspective' in Gilbert, Parton and Skivenes (eds) (n 59) 154.

[61] A-D Hestbaek, 'Denmark: A Child Welfare System Under Reframing' in Gilbert, Parton and Skivenes (eds), (n 59) 131.

[62] A Warman and C Roberts, *Adoption and Looked After Children: International Comparisons* (Oxford, OUP, 2002); Selman and Mason (n 16).

[63] C Bridge and H Swindells, *Adoption: The Modern Law* (Bristol, Jordan Publishing Limited, 2003) 33.

[64] Selman and Mason (n 16).

[65] Skivenes (n 60) 155.

likely to improve the standard of living of families, prevent children from being harmed and may be regarded as less restrictive forms of intervention into family life when compared with non-consensual adoption.

In Sweden, a key difference between its care system and the care system in England and Wales is not only that there is greater availability of preventative services, but also very few children are taken into care via the coercive intervention of the state. Most children in care are there with the consent of their parents,[66] and while children may be placed away from home without parental consent under the Social Services Act 1980, the Swedish Board of Social Welfare has emphasised the importance of reunion between children and parents, where possible.[67] However, the approach towards child protection in Sweden is not without criticism. For example, the Nordic Committee for Human Rights has expressed concern about the high numbers of children removed into care, in potential violation of children's right to respect for private and family life under Article 8 ECHR.[68]

Furthermore, the Czech Republic and Lithuania have voiced similar criticisms about the Norwegian child protection system's taking children into care rather than providing support to parents.[69] It can be argued that these complaints are similar to those of Eastern European countries who have challenged the use of non-consensual adoptions in England and Wales. Thus, while other countries may favour less restrictive alternatives to non-consensual adoption and place an emphasis on state assistance, this does not mean that children's and parents' rights under Article 8 ECHR or the UNCRC have received sufficient protection. This will depend on the effectiveness and the length of the measures of assistance provided by the state. Regardless of any criticism that may be made about state intervention in other European countries, this intervention is not as draconian as non-consensual adoption.

While every European country has a mechanism for enabling non-consensual adoption, Fenton-Glynn has pointed out that other European countries do not exercise this power to the same extent as the courts in England and Wales.[70]

[66] O'Halloran (n 42) 505. To see Sweden's approach towards adoption generally, see ibid ch 12.

[67] Selman and Mason (n 16).

[68] Secretary General of the Council of Europe, *Child Removal Cases in Sweden and the neighbouring countries* (Nordic Committee for Human Rights, 2012). Also see the Swedish cases discussed in ch 3, for example. Also, for further information on controversy in Swedish cases, see RA Gardner, SR Sauber and D Lorandos, *The International Handbook of Parental Alienation Syndrome* (Springfield, IL, Charles C Thomas Publisher Ltd, 2006).

[69] C Fenton-Glynn, *Adoption without Parental Consent: Study for the Peti Committee* (Brussels, European Parliament, 2015) 26; B Yuksel and K Trimmings, 'Choice of law aspects of non-consensual adoption of Eastern European Children in England and Wales [2017] *International Family Law Journal* 202; '"Similar to Nazi foster care": Czech president slams Norwegian child welfare' *RT* (10 February 2015) at http://rt.com/news/230951-czech-president-norway-nazi/; F Capon, 'Baltic States say Norway, UK and Finland have stolen their children' *Newsweek* (23 April 2015) at http://europe.newsweek.com/baltic-states-say-norway-uk-and-finland-have-stolen-their-children-324031.

[70] Fenton-Glynn (n 69) 27.

It can be concluded from the discussion above that countries in Europe manage to protect children without resorting to non-consensual adoption. However, the examples of France and Sweden highlight that other European countries may face their own challenges in deciding how best to protect the welfare of children. The examples considered demonstrate that it is not just England and Wales that struggles to ensure that children are protected from harm (and to protect their rights under Articles 2 and 3 ECHR) while protecting children and parents' rights under Article 8 ECHR. A method of state assistance known as concurrent planning has increased in popularity in England and Wales. This practice has the potential to strike the balance between protecting children's best interests and rights, on the one hand, and parental rights, on the other. Concurrent planning is considered in section II.C.

C. Concurrent Planning: Twin-track or Foregone Conclusion?

One way in which the state can provide assistance to parents and protect their rights under Article 8 ECHR, while avoiding the potential pitfalls of violating the child's rights under Articles 2, 3 or 6(1) ECHR, is through concurrent planning. Concurrent planning is where a local authority simultaneously plans two possible options for the child. This could, for example, involve working towards returning children in care to their birth parents, while at the same time establishing an alternative plan such as non-consensual adoption.[71] Concurrent planning has been used by local authorities for many years and was endorsed by the Government in *An Action Plan for Adoption: Tackling Delay*.[72]

An important case concerning concurrent planning was the Court of Appeal decision of *Re P (A Child)*,[73] in which the local authority considered two different options: non-consensual adoption and long-term foster care. In this case, the mother argued that dual planning was inconsistent with the framework of the ACA 2002 under section 52(1)(b) and section 22(1)(d). Wall LJ, however, confirmed the appropriateness of dual planning, since it shortens the time period a child remains in limbo. He also confirmed that this approach is compatible with birth parents' Article 8 rights and Strasbourg jurisprudence generally. There are clear benefits in using concurrent planning, in particular that it enables different options to be explored early on and local authorities are likely to act more

[71] See *Re D and K (Care Plan: Twin-Track Planning)* [1999] 2 FLR 872, where the court considered return to the parents and adoption.

[72] Department for Education, *An Action Plan for Adoption: Tackling Delay* (London, Department for Education, 2012).

[73] *Re P (A Child)* [2008] EWCA Civ 535.

expeditiously in ensuring that a child's needs are met.[74] The House of Lords Select Committee on Adoption Legislation approved of concurrent planning, suggesting that it 'provides significant benefits in terms of enabling early attachments, minimising disruption, and reducing delay'.[75]

It is helpful to consider the benefits of concurrent planning by referring to a concurrent planning project led by the charity Coram. Under the scheme, children in care were placed with prospective adoptive parents but had frequent contact with their birth parents. This scheme was used by parents with mental health problems and drug addictions. The parents were provided with assistance in developing parenting skills, and if they managed to turn their lives around within a year, the children were returned to them. Extended family members potentially able to care for the child were identified early on. If the parents were unable to improve their parenting skills or no alternative carers within the family were available, the children were placed for adoption.

Between 2000 and 2011, Coram arranged 59 placements of which 57 were successful.[76] Three of the 57 children were returned to their birth parents, and the other 54 remained with their prospective adopters and were adopted by them.[77] Compared with the usual delays in the adoption process, this scheme meant that an adoption was finalised, on average, when a child was aged 17 months, not at the national average of 3 years, 7 months.[78] The findings from the Coram study suggest that concurrent planning leads to more efficient adoption outcomes. This is in line with the Government's pro-adoption policy, which emphasises minimising delay in the process of adoption (see chapter 4), which, however, may not be an appropriate way of protecting the best interests of children in care.

At first glance, concurrent planning seems to provide respect for birth parents' and wider birth family's rights under Article 8 ECHR. It appears to do so by ensuring that birth parents and the extended family have an ongoing relationship with their children prior to adoption, as well as a chance of being reunited with their children.[79] Furthermore, the exploration of viable kinship care options enables children to have the potential opportunity to have blood ties acknowledged and respected, thereby protecting children's right to know and be cared for by their family and their right to know their identity under Articles 7 and 8 UNCRC respectively. Concurrent planning also acknowledges children's best interests under the welfare checklist in ACA 2002, section 1(4), such as a child's

[74] R Langsdale and J Weston, 'Guidance on the Adoption and Children Act 2002; Re P' [2008] *Family Law* 769.

[75] HL Select Committee on Adoption Legislation (n 12) 27.

[76] S Laws, R Wilson and S Rabindrakumar, *Coram Concurrent Planning Study: Interim Report* (Coram Policy and Research Team, July 2012) 2.

[77] ibid 5.

[78] ibid 3.

[79] *Note*: it is not stated within the study whether the adoptions that took place were without consent via the ACA 2002, s 52(1)(b), or with the consent of the birth parents.

need under section 1(4)(b) to be provided with a stable and permanent home, as soon as possible, without delay (as is required by the ACA 2002, section 1(3)).

Concurrent planning ensures that a child is protected from neglect and abuse, and is able to form a secure attachment to a carer should a parent be unable to care for him or her.[80] Concurrent planning also respects the rights of the child and birth parents to have a relationship (eg under Articles 7, 8 and 9 UNCRC), and increases the likelihood that the state will satisfy its positive obligation under Article 8 ECHR to make reasonable efforts to reunite children with their parents. However, in cases where a non-consensual adoption is determined to be in the child's best interests, the child's right to know his or her identity under Article 8 UNCRC will not be protected, since adoptive parents are not obliged to inform the child that he or she is adopted, and the adoption results in the loss of legal ties with the child's parents, which is, it is submitted, an important part of his or her identity.

Concern has been expressed, however, that concurrent planning is not necessarily Convention-compliant. O'Halloran has argued that by allowing attachments to form with prospective adopters, this may prejudice the welfare principle and make it less likely that children will be returned to their birth parents, and may even pre-empt the court's decision-making process, thereby violating parents' rights under Articles 6 and 8 ECHR.[81] Furthermore, a potential disadvantage of concurrent planning, which the Coram project demonstrated, was that there was no guarantee a child would have post-adoption contact with his or her parents, even where contact was positive. Contact itself, prior to the non-consensual adoption, has also been controversial. Kenrick has argued that contact may, in the context of concurrent planning, be distressing to babies and young children, but that it is difficult to assess the long-term impact that such contact has on children.[82]

Another issue with the Coram project is the way in which it was funded. Moss has suggested that Coram received a £35,000 payment for each adoption.[83] In other words, if Coram's support package failed to reunite children with their parents, they would not receive money from the Government.[84] This observation raises questions about the potential for a conflict of interest. In addition, it

[80] Laws, Wilson and Rabindrakumar (n 76) 7.

[81] O'Halloran (n 42) 67.

[82] J Kenrick, 'Concurrent planning: A retrospective study of the continuities and discontinuities of care, and their impact on the development of infants and young children placed for adoption by the Coram Concurrent Planning Project' (2009) 33 *Adoption & Fostering* 5.

[83] F Moss, 'Treading Carefully' (2011) *Solicitor's Journal* (1 February 2011). Also, for general information on the cost of adoptions, see J Selwyn et al, *Adoption and the Inter-agency Fee*, Research Report no DCSF-RR149 (London, Department for Education, 2009).

[84] Moss (n 83). See also 'Coram's instant adoption plan helps to keep babies out of care system' *National Literacy Trust* (7 November 2009) at http://www.literacytrust.org.uk/news/748_coram_s_instant_adoption_plan_helps_to_keep_babies_out_of_care_system.

is important to observe that the rates of reunification of child and birth parent in this particular concurrent planning were low;[85] only three children were returned to their parents. While the scheme clearly provided parents with a second chance, the low success rate raises questions about its effectiveness, and about whether this scheme provided sufficient protection for children's and parents' rights under Article 8 ECHR.

The criticism of concurrent planning in general, and specifically of the Coram project, is relevant because there has been growth in its use. Since the success of the pilot study,[86] the Government decided to provide funding to Coram so that it become a National Centre for Excellence in Early Permanence,[87] which means that the charity's role in achieving permanence for children in care via concurrent planning and, where appropriate, adoption has grown and continues to grow.[88] In order to reach firm conclusions on the effectiveness of this project for protecting the rights of children and parents, or the cost-effectiveness of this type of project, it would be helpful to have more detail about the specific methods Coram used to help parents improve their skills, the frequency of these classes and whether the parents found the classes helpful.

It can be argued that offering parents the chance to take parenting classes and providing assistance to attend classes (eg financing travel costs, where required) would enable them to continue to develop relationships with their children. This could mean, for example, that any assistance provided would need to consider impediments or aspects of daily life that may affect parents' ability to attend classes, such as work commitments, specific disabilities, physical or mental illness, drug or alcohol addiction.

Parents who take these classes but who are still regarded as unfit to raise a child may improve their parenting skills sufficiently to be able to parent any children born in the future. An important part of a concurrent planning project, then, ought

[85] J Kenrick, 'Concurrent planning: A retrospective study of the continuities and discontinuities of care, and their impact on the development of infants and young children placed for adoption by the Coram Concurrent Planning Project' (2009) 33 *Adoption & Fostering* 5; and J Kenrick, 'Concurrent planning "The rollercoaster of uncertainty"' (2010) 34 *Adoption and Fostering* 38.

[86] See, eg, Cambridgeshire Concurrent Planning Scheme at http://www.coramcambridgeshireadoption.org.uk/how-our-adoption-works/find-out-about-our-concurrent-planning-scheme; and also East Sussex and Hampshire. See 'Coram to become a National Centre of Excellence in Early Permanence' at http://www.familylawweek.co.uk/site.aspx?i=ed98944.

[87] Cambridgeshire Concurrent Planning Scheme at http://www.coramcambridgeshireadoption.org.uk/how-our-adoption-works/find-out-about-our-concurrent-planning-scheme; and also East Sussex and Hampshire. See 'Coram to become a National Centre of Excellence in Early Permanence' at http://www.familylawweek.co.uk/site.aspx?i=ed98944. Also see Department for Education, *Proposals for placing children with their potential adopters earlier* (London, Department for Education, 2012).

[88] Education and Adoption Bill (session 2015 – 16) Written evidence submitted by Coram (EAB 33) at http://www.publications.parliament.uk/pa/cm201516/cmpublic/educationadoption/memo/educ33.htm; 'Adoption Service gets boost with new Thurrock and Coram Partnership' (9 July 2015) at https://www.thurrock.gov.uk/news/adoption/adoption-service-gets-boost-with-new-thurrock-and-coram-partnership.

to be whether parents who have had children adopted are able to keep subsequent children because of the new skills they have learned in parenting classes.[89]

In conclusion, it can be argued that a concurrent planning scheme that provides effective parenting classes increases the likelihood that the state will satisfy its positive obligation under Article 8 ECHR to attempt to reunite children with their parents. While concurrent planning may speed up the adoption process and raise issues about potential breaches of parental rights, if effective parenting classes are delivered and post-adoption contact is a possibility, concurrent planning is an option that provides better protection to both parents' and children's Article 8 rights than non-consensual adoption without this form of state assistance. There are, however, cases where, despite the provision of state assistance, children cannot be safely reunited with their parents, and thus it is essential to consider other, less restrictive alternatives to non-consensual adoption, such as foster care, kinship care and special guardianship. These are considered in the following sections.

III. Foster Care: Short-Term Stepping Stone or in for the Long Haul?

Foster care refers to people taking children into their homes and looking after them permanently or temporarily. Children enter foster care via care orders under section 31 of the CA 1989, or voluntary accommodation under section 20 of the Act. Children are placed in foster care due to one or more of the following factors: abuse or neglect, the child's disability, parental illness or disability, the family's being in acute distress, familial dysfunction, socially unacceptable behaviour, low income and absent parenting.[90] Typically, children in foster care are placed with unrelated carers, but they may, alternatively, be placed with other family members (eg grandparents) or with friends of the family.[91]

Foster care gives rise to four potential pathways: as an interim measure pending the return of the child to his or her birth parents; performing a dual role, whereby those who foster act as both foster parents and prospective parents; as an important stage prior to adoption with unknown prospective adoptive parents; or as a viable long-term alternative to non-consensual adoption. These options will be considered in detail below.

[89] State assistance and intervention to help with parenting skills in mothers who have repeat pregnancies, for example, has been advocated by Broadhurst and Mason. See K Broadhurst and C Mason, 'Maternal Outcasts: Raising the profile of women who are vulnerable to successive, compulsory removals of their children – a plea for preventative action' (2013) 14 *Journal of Social Welfare and Family Law* 291.

[90] Department for Education, *Fostering Better Outcomes* (London, Department for Education, 2018) 15.

[91] See Department for Education, *The Fostering System in England: Evidence review* (London, Department for Education, 2017).

Foster care can be a short-lived interim measure prior to a child's return to his or her birth family or the making of an adoption order. Foster care is an intermediate measure for the majority, if not all, of children who are adopted without parental consent under section 52(1) of the ACA 2002. Under section 2(3) of the Children and Families Act 2014 (CFA 2014), local authorities have a duty to consider fostering for adoption. A fostering for adoption placement enables foster parents to obtain a placement order under section 21 of the ACA 2002, and subsequently become children's legally recognised parents via an adoption order under section 52 of the Act. In some respects, fostering for adoption resembles concurrent planning[92] (considered in section II.C), in that parents may, in some cases, be able to demonstrate a change of circumstances sufficient to warrant return of a child into their care. Fostering for adoption has the added benefit of reducing the number of placements the child experiences, enabling him or her to form secure attachments at an earlier stage.

In some cases, children may be fostered prior to being placed with different prospective adopters. In such circumstances, foster care can, nonetheless, provide a pivotal role in improving children's ability to form attachments prior to being placed for adoption, since many children who have suffered from severe neglect and abuse may have difficulties in forming healthy new attachments. The formation of such an attachment prior to the making of an adoption order, may improve children's ability to form healthy attachments with primary carers.

In other circumstances, foster care is a long-term measure of intervention, with children remaining in care until they reach adulthood. However, foster care has many perceived disadvantages, so adoption is often seen as preferable. On 31 March 2017, there were 53,420 children in foster care, with 35,570 of these children in public fostering placements and 17,850 in independent fostering placements.[93] Foster care is associated with lower educational and social outcomes, since care leavers are less likely to achieve GCSE pass grades compared to the general population,[94] are less likely to attend university,[95] more likely to suffer from mental illness[96] and are more likely to commit criminal offences.[97] Comparatively, research spanning decades demonstrates that children who are adopted tend to fare better than those who remain in care.[98]

[92] E Dibben and V Howorth, *The Role of Fostering for Adoption in Achieving Early Permanence* (London, Coram, 2017) 5–7.

[93] Department for Education, *Looked After Children in Foster Care: Analysis* (London, Department for Education, 2018) 7.

[94] See Department for Education, *Foster Care in England: A Review for the Department for Education* (London, Department for Education, 2018).

[95] Approximately 6%. See ibid 9.

[96] Department for Education, *The impacts of abuse and neglect on children; and comparison of different placement options: Evidence review* (London, Department for Education, 2017) 36–38.

[97] R Blades et al, *Care – A Stepping Stone to Custody?* (London, Prison Reform Trust, 2011).

[98] Department of Health and Social Care, *Adoption Procedure: A New Approach* (Cm 5017, 2000). For example, see J Castle, C Beckett and C Groothues, 'Infant Adoption in England: Policy and Practice

However, many children in foster care have faced severe neglect and abuse at the hands of their birth parents, and may have been subject to multiple foster care placements,[99] thereby impairing their ability to form healthy attachments and flourish.[100] In such situations, it may be that the children's circumstances mean they are not regarded as viable candidates for adoption. Therefore, the success of adoption compared with foster care may be in part due to external factors over which foster carers have limited control. Thus the probable success of an adoptive placement may depend more on the background and the characteristics of the children rather than upon the fact of adoption. In other words, children who are recommended for adoption may be those who are most likely to thrive in any circumstances.

Foster parents' misunderstanding of their roles is also another problem with foster care. Some foster carers view themselves as professional carers on a wage from the state. This emphasis on the professional nature of foster care (referred to as 'corporate parenting'[101]) may mean less emphasis on the need for emotional support and nurturing of children in their care. Research has shown, for example, that some foster carers may be reluctant to show affection towards foster children due to misunderstanding the nature of their role, as well as concerns about false allegations of abuse.[102] It seems probable that this lack of affection could have a corresponding effect on children's emotional development,[103] thereby affecting their outcomes once they leave foster care. The problem has been acknowledged in a recent Department for Education report, *Fostering Better Outcomes*,[104] and work is being undertaken to address these misconceptions.[105]

While research has emphasised the value of the adoption, a core aspect of adoption that makes it an effective measure of permanence is the stability that it provides.[106] Foster carers do not have parental responsibility for the children in their care, which can create difficulties in day-to-day decision-making (ie which school the child ought to attend). Parental responsibility is shared between the local authority and parents under a care order,[107] unless a subsequent court order is made. The perceived lack of stability of foster care could be cured by a court order providing parental responsibility via residence under a child arrangements order under section 8 of the CA 1989, which automatically provides parental

at Placement' (2000) 24 *Adoption and Fostering* 26. See also subsequent research that confirms the benefits of adoption: J Triseliotis, 'Long-term foster care or adoption? The evidence examined' (2002) 7 *Child and Family Social Work* 23; D Quinton and J Selwyn, 'Adoption: Research, Policy and Practice' (2006) *Child and Family Law Quarterly* 459.

[99] Department for Education (n 91) 163.

[100] ibid.

[101] See the Children and Social Work Act 2017, s 1.

[102] Department for Education (n 94) 31.

[103] G Trasler, *In Place of Parents* (London, Routledge, 1998).

[104] Department for Education (n 90) 32.

[105] ibid.

[106] Department for Education (n 96).

[107] This is made under s 31(a) of the CA 1989.

responsibility, or via a special guardianship order[108] under section 14A of the Act, which also has the effect of providing parental responsibility. The difficulty here is the financial implications of the change of status that comes with a court order. Foster parents can go from receiving a generous foster care allowance to a means-tested allowance that may provide less income.[109] This ought to be remedied so that children and carers alike can benefit from the increased legal recognition of their relationship, without consequent loss of income. Conversely, it cannot be assumed that adoptive placements are always stable, since there are reported cases where adoptions of children in care have been disrupted and the placements have failed, with such children returning to the care system.[110] It may be the case that adoption is not always a more stable option than long-term foster care or other measures of intervention considered in this chapter.

Despite the concerns that exist about foster care, it has been shown that its defects may be addressed by court orders to create stability for children and their foster carers. Furthermore, it has been argued that outcomes for foster care compared with adoption may rest upon the individual children's characteristics and history rather than the type of placement itself. Although each case must be determined on its facts, it is argued that long-term foster care may be more compatible with the UNCRC and UN Guidelines for the Alternative Care of Children,[111] especially where foster care is coupled with kinship care. This is due to the increased likelihood of maintaining relationships with birth parents and other relatives, such as siblings and grandparents, since many children in foster care enjoy direct contact with their birth family. However, there are circumstances in which parents can be alienated from their children via reduced contact, not having been provided with information (eg the address of the foster carer or school[112]). Therefore, great care must be taken to ensure that such measures are taken only if in the best interests of the child, in accordance with Article 3 UNCRC.

It is argued that foster care can potentially strike an effective balance between protection of children's and parents' relationship rights under the Article 8 ECHR, the right to respect for private and family life, and children's rights under the UNCRC. This is because children can be protected from harm (under Article 3 ECHR and Article 19 UNCRC), but they are also able to continue to maintain and develop relationships with their birth parents under Article 8 ECHR and Articles 7, 8 and 9 UNCRC, where it is safe for them to do so.

A potential benefit of foster care is that contact arrangements may also extend to sibling relationships. In circumstances where siblings do not share the same

[108] See the following discussion: Department for Education (n 90) 21.

[109] S Nandy et al, *Spotlight on kinship care using census microdata to examine the extent and nature of kinship care in the UK at the turn of the twentieth century* (London, TSO, 2013) 5.

[110] Department for Education, *Beyond the Adoption Order: Challenges, interventions and adoption disruption* (London, Department for Education, 2014).

[111] Guidelines for the Alternative Care of Children (n 14).

[112] V George, *Foster Care: Theory and Practice* (London, Routledge & Kegan Paul, 1970) 176.

foster placements, they may be unable to develop and maintain relations with one another via direct contact. This is of particular importance, as children, particularly those over the age of 11, have voiced their wishes to maintain sibling contact.[113] Furthermore, research shows that positive relationships with siblings improve the mental health of many children in foster care.[114] Typically, it is unusual for direct contact to take place between children placed for adoption and their birth parents and wider birth family, including siblings.[115] Therefore, it is argued that in some cases, long-term foster care may be equally effective as non-consensual adoption, thereby providing more effective protection of children's and parents' relationship rights under the ECHR and the UNCRC.

IV. Kinship Care: Keeping Extended Family Units Together

A. An Overview of Kinship Care: What is a 'Relative'?

Kinship care may be an alternative to non-consensual adoption where the child has relatives available and willing to care for him or her. Kinship care occurs where a relative cares for the child, when the child's birth parents are unwilling or unable to do so. Under English law, a 'relative' is a step-parent, an aunt or uncle related by blood, a sibling or grandparent. Cousins and aunts and uncles who are not related by blood are not included within this definition of 'relative' under English law. When carers are relatives of the child, there is no requirement to notify the local authority. It is thought that most kinship arrangements are informal.[116]

The use of formal kinship placements is a relatively recent phenomenon[117] and there are many ways it can be formally recognised: via a private fostering arrangement, where a looked-after child is placed in kinship foster care, through a child arrangements order,[118] a special guardianship order[119] or even an

[113] Department for Education (n 94) 87.

[114] M Tarren-Sweeney and P Hazell, 'The mental health and socialisation of siblings in care' [2005] *Children and Youth Services Review* 821.

[115] S Meakings, A Coffey and K Shelton, 'The Influence of Adoption on Sibling Relationships: Experiences and Support Needs of Newly Formed Adoptive Families' [2017] *British Journal of Social Work* 1781.

[116] Nandy et al (n 109) 2; J Selwyn et al, *The Poor Relations? Children and Informal Kinship Carers Speak Out: A Summary Research Report* (London, Buttle UK, 2013).

[117] R Hegar and M Scannapieco, 'Kinship Care' in G Mallon and P McCartt (eds), *Child Welfare for the 21st Century* (New York, Columbia University Press, 2005) 522; J Mitchell, *Adoption and Special Guardianship: A Permanency Handbook* (Bristol, Jordan Publishing Ltd, 2009) 520; K Brisebois, 'Caseworker attitudes on Kinship Care in Ontario' (2013) 12 *Qualitative Social Work* 289.

[118] Formerly known as a residence order under the CA 1989, s 8. Under the CFA 2014, s 12, contact and residence orders are both referred to as 'child arrangement' orders.

[119] *Northampton County Council v AS and Others* [2015] EWHC 199 (Fam). See also the CA 1989, ss 14A–14G.

adoption order.[120] Changes to policy and legislation have given a clear message to social workers that wherever possible, children should be placed in the care of their birth family or friends of the family.[121] The White Paper *Care Matters: Time for Change* emphasised the 'gateway approach',[122] which involved looking at family and friends first, where children were in care. It can be argued, however, that further legal developments like the CFA 2014 suggest otherwise.

It may be argued that kinship placements are as effective as placement with unrelated foster carers, if not more so, in terms of both behavioural development and mental health functioning, and that this is supported by research.[123] Kinship care is associated with greater continuity, stability and security than non-kinship care.[124] If children are placed with the wider family, research suggests these placements last longer than other types of placement, such as placement in foster care with families previously unknown to them.[125] Statistically, where local authorities opt for kinship care in a child's care plan, these care plans have the highest likelihood of being fulfilled (78 per cent).[126] Kinship care also prevents a loss of roots and connection with the birth family.[127] The House of Lords Select Committee on Adoption Legislation has observed that children in kinship care 'do as well if not better than those in unrelated foster care, in terms of their health, school attendance and performance, self-esteem and personal and social relationships'.[128]

It has been argued throughout that less restrictive alternatives to non-consensual adoption (such as kinship care) should be used if they are as effective as non-consensual adoption. This argument can be supported by reference to Bainham, who has argued that human rights 'militate against' adoption and towards less drastic means that might preserve kinship links and contacts.[129]

[120] Nandy et al (n 109) 3.

[121] ibid a114.

[122] Department for Education, *Further action on adoption: finding more loving homes* (Cm 7137, 2013).

[123] M Winokur, A Holtan, and D Valentine, *Kinship care for the safety, permanency, and well-being of children removed from the home for maltreatment* (Chichester, John Wiley & Sons, 2009).

[124] J Morris, *Children on the Edge of Care: Human Rights and the Children Act* (York, Joseph Rowntree Foundation, 2005) 21–22; Mitchell (n 117) 417; A Holtan et al, 'A comparison of mental health problems in kinship and non kinship foster care' (2014) 14 *European Child & Adolescent Psychiatry* 200; M Oosterman et al, 'Disruptions in foster care: A review and meta-analysis' (2007) 29 *Children and Youth Services Review* 53; J Selwyn and D Quinton, 'Stability, permanence, outcomes and support: Foster care and adoption compared' (2004) 28 *Adoption and Fostering* 4; J Hunt, S Waterhouse, and E Lutman, *Keeping them in the family: Outcomes for children placed in kinship care through care proceedings* (London, BAAF, 2008); Selwyn et al (n 116); T Bell, 'Permanency and Safety Among Children in Foster Family and Kinship Care: A Scoping Review' *Trauma, Violence, Abuse* (11 October 2015), doi: 10.1177/1524838015611673.

[125] Hegar and Scannapieco (n 117) 522; Mitchell (n 117) 555; D Berridge, *Foster Care: A Research Review* (Norwich, HMSO, 1997) 26.

[126] Mitchell (n 117) 508–09.

[127] M Ryburn 'In whose best interests? – post-adoption contact with the birth family' (1998) 10 *Child and Family Law Quarterly* 53.

[128] HL Select Committee on Adoption Legislation (n 12) 29.

[129] A Bainham, 'Arguments about parentage' [2008] *CLJ* 322, 350.

When adoption takes place, it is uncommon for children to maintain relationships with their birth parents or wider birth family. Kinship care does enable children to maintain relationships with birth relatives, and in some cases they may be able to develop relationships with their birth parents, even if they do not live with them. In many cases, if the contact is safe for children, it will be beneficial for them to develop and maintain relationships with their parents.

Research demonstrates that when children are cared for by relatives, contact is more frequent and more enduring than when children are placed in foster care with adults unknown to them.[130] Although parental contact may decline over time, even in kinship placements,[131] Farmer and Moyers found that after a two-year period in a kinship placement, 70 per cent of the children in the care of family and friends still had contact with their mother and 49 per cent had contact with their father.[132] Research suggests that kinship carers tend to have a high degree of commitment to maintaining contact between children and their birth parents, even when the circumstances may be challenging.[133] Hunt et al conducted a study on kinship care and examined measures such as placement stability, placement quality, relationship quality (between children and kinship carers) and child well-being. They found that 58 per cent of kinship placements scored positively across all measures, and 76 per cent of the children had positive relationships with their kinship carers even when placements ended. They state that kinship care provides a 'safe, effective and permanent'[134] care option for children, and is a viable method of permanence that ought to be promoted since, unlike closed adoption, it enables children to maintain relationships with birth relatives.

The fact that children in care often have 'serious physical, mental health, developmental and psychosocial problems',[135] however, means that once kinship carers take these children into their homes, they often have difficulties with them because they lack the support to deal with such challenging behaviour. As O'Brien has pointed out, the effort and resources invested in ensuring family continuity is not always sufficient to mitigate the effects of multiple care placements prior to kinship care. Thus, while kinship care placements are associated with fewer breakdowns when compared with foster care placements, she has suggested that the rate of breakdown in kinship care increases after the first year that the child

[130] E Farmer and S Moyers, *Kinship Care: Fostering Effective Family and Friends Placements* (London, Jessica Kingsley Publishers, 2008).

[131] J Wade, I Sinclair and L Stuttard, *Investigating Special Guardianship: experiences, challenges and outcomes* (London, BAAF, 2014) 176.

[132] Farmer and Moyers (n 130).

[133] See, eg, J Hunt, *Family and friends carers: Scoping paper prepared for the Department of Health* (London, Department of Health, 2003); Hunt, Waterhouse and Lutman (n 124).

[134] J Hunt, S Waterhouse and E Lutman, 'Parental Contact for Children Placed in Kinship Care through Care Proceedings' (2010) 22 Child *and Family Law Quarterly* 71.

[135] M Szilagyi et al, 'Health Care Issues for Children and Adolescents in Foster Care and Kinship Care' (2015) 136 *American Academy of Pediatrics* 1131. Also see A Gautier, S Wellard and S Cardy, *Forgotten Children: children growing up in kinship care* (London, Grandparents Plus, 2013).

is in that placement.[136] This is because the kinship carers' parenting skills may be insufficient to address the children's challenging behaviour.[137] Furthermore, research suggests that kinship carers have reported experiencing difficulties such as isolation, stigma, pain and depression,[138] and in some circumstances stress from managing contact with children's birth parents.[139]

Despite the benefits of kinship care, carers may face challenges without the same level of support provided by local authorities to foster carers and prospective adoptive parents. In some circumstances, then, kinship care may not necessarily serve children's best interests even if it protects various relationship rights (in particular, Article 7 UNCRC), and kinship care may be less effective than non-consensual adoption for which substantial local authority support is available before, during and after the adoption process. However, O'Brien has argued that this problem could be addressed by providing financial support and appropriate support with children's emotional issues, for example 'attachment, loss, challenging behaviour, life-cycle transitions/changes'.[140] An important question to ask, but to which there is not a clear answer, is the extent to which local authorities have a positive obligation under Article 8 ECHR to provide state assistance to kinship carers. This issue has not been directly addressed in the ECtHR, even though it has been argued that the scope of this type of positive obligation towards parents is widening (see chapter 3).

It can be argued that with appropriate investment, kinship care may, in some circumstances, strike a better balance than non-consensual adoption in protecting children's rights under Articles 2, 3 and 6 ECHR on the one hand, and the Article 8 ECHR rights of the children and parents on the other. Greater investment may lead to the greater availability of less restrictive alternatives that are just as effective as non-consensual adoption.[141] This option has the benefit of protecting children from neglect or abuse, while allowing for the possibility of maintaining or developing relationships between children and their birth parents. It may also protect the child's right to contact with his or her parents and the child's right to know his or her own identity under Article 8 UNCRC. Due to its benefits for families, as described, kinship care is potentially an equally effective method in protecting children's welfare when compared with non-consensual adoption. However, based on the jurisprudence considered in chapters 3 and 4, while the state must provide assistance to birth parents, the precise scope of this positive obligation (and whether or not it applies to other birth relatives, for example) is unclear.

[136] V O'Brien, *Kinship Care: Stability, Disruption and the Place of Support Services* (University College Dublin, 2013) 1–3; for similar conclusions on differences in variables between foster care and kinship care diminishing over time, see Bell (n 124).

[137] O'Brien (n 136) 4.

[138] Selwyn et al (n 116).

[139] Gautier, Wellard and Cardy (n 135).

[140] O'Brien (n 136) 3.

[141] For further consideration of the limitations on and importance of financial support for birth parents, kinship carers and other carers, see section IV.C.

In the light of the benefits of kinship care, it is surprising that there is still variation in local authorities' use of it. Although some local authorities in England and Wales are increasing the use of kinship care,[142] and statistically the use of formal kinship arrangements is increasing,[143] many local authorities still do not make enquiries within a child's wider family before deciding that adoption is in a child's best interests.[144] Luckock and Broadhurst conducted a case study examining 12 adoptions without parental consent. They found that some local authorities had reactive approaches[145] to the assessment of suitability of kinship carers. They stated that the local authorities in the study could have been more proactive in searching for relatives of children in care, and that when searches were initiated, the local authorities could have made more concerted efforts to place children with relatives.[146] It has been noted by Hunt et al that identifying potential kinship carers prior to care proceedings might speed up the process of securing permanence for children who cannot be raised by their parents.[147] However, even where social workers are aware of alternative carers, they are reluctant to inform them that the child is in care against the wishes of the parent.[148]

Munby LJ has stated that some parents are reluctant to reveal, even to family members, that their child is in care because parents are in a 'bubble of deniability'.[149] He suggested that, in some cases, parents hope to have their children returned to them. They may also feel ashamed that their children have been taken into care, and may seek to hide this from their families.[150] Munby LJ has argued that the difficulty in identifying potential kinship carers could be avoided by less pointed questioning, and by making general enquiries of birth parents about their family in order to build a genogram,[151] rather than telling them that their child is going to be adopted unless other potential carers can be found.[152] It is clear, though, that these problems may lead to a delay in identifying kinship carers, which means that children may spend longer in care and may be adopted without

[142] M Colton and M Williams, *Global perspectives on foster family care* (Lyme Regis, Russell House Publishing, 2006) 83.

[143] Between 31 March 1996 and 31 March 2000, the number of children in formal kinship care increased by 32%. Nandy et al (n 109) 114.

[144] Mitchell (n 117) 417.

[145] B Luckock and K Broadhurst, *Adoption cases reviewed: an indicative study of process and practice* (London, Department for Education, 2013).

[146] ibid.

[147] Hunt, Waterhouse and Lutman (n 134).

[148] NAGALRO, *Nagalro Response to the Government Consultation on Special Guardianship 15 September 2015* (NAGALRO, 2015).

[149] Munby LJ, *Between a Rock and a Hard Place. 26 weeks and Re B-S: conflicting pressures for family courts*, NAGALRO Conference (16 March 2015).

[150] B Lindley, *Between a Rock and a Hard Place. 26 weeks and Re B-S: conflicting pressures for family courts*, NAGALRO Conference (16 March 2015).

[151] A document that is like a family tree, stating who the child's parents, grandparents, aunts and uncles, and siblings are, but which may also include reference to other significant relationships in the child's life, such as step-parents or friends of the family.

[152] Munby LJ (n 149).

parental consent when a less restrictive and potentially equally effective alternative to non-consensual adoption might have been available. Furthermore, even if local authorities assess birth family members as potential carers for children in care, local authorities do not always provide documentation of their concerns prior to the assessments,[153] and where the outcome of the assessment is negative because the birth family members are not necessarily parties to proceedings concerning the children, local authorities may make other arrangements for the children, including fostering for adoption arrangements.

The duty to consider fostering for adoption (ie where children are placed with foster carers with the intention that they may be adopted by them) under the CFA 2014, section 2(3), may mean that local authorities do not look for kinship carers, and this may result in fewer children being placed with family members. This provision not only has the potential to violate the Article 8 ECHR rights of children and their birth relatives, but may violate several provisions under the UNCRC that are, according to Sloan, 'designed to protect children's kinship links'.[154] Lindley has argued in favour of a statutory duty to assess birth relatives before children are placed for adoption with non-related carers.[155] She has also suggested that kinship carers ought to be identified early on, pre-proceedings, at Family Group Conferences via a standardised viability tool.[156] This would strike a balance between avoiding undue delay in the adoption process where there are no suitable kinship carers for the child, while ensuring that, where possible, children are raised within their birth families and that de facto and legal ties are maintained.

One difficulty in the context of kinship care is that birth relatives, such as grandparents, may face obstacles in becoming kinship carers. Thus Lindley has suggested that children may lose the opportunity to be raised within their birth families because their relatives may not have access to enough information and advice on how to proceed.[157] This is particularly relevant in terms of children whose families have origins elsewhere in Europe. For example, there has been an increase in families from former Soviet bloc countries, such as Slovakia and Lithuania, coming to England and Wales; and concern has been expressed about increased care proceedings in relation to children from Eastern Europe.[158] In these cases, special guardianship orders (considered in section V) might be a less restrictive but equally effective alternative to non-consensual adoption.

Even though there is little doubt in most cases that kinship carers will protect children from harm, they are often ruled out as carers due to a refusal on their part

[153] Lindley (n 150).

[154] B Sloan, 'Fostering and Adoption as a Means of Securing Article 6 Rights in England' (2015) 26 *Stellenbosch Law Review* 363, 375.

[155] Lindley (n 150).

[156] ibid. Also see HL Select Committee on Adoption Legislation (n 12) 73.

[157] Lindley (n 150).

[158] J Porter, 'Families from Eastern Europe and care proceedings' [2014] *Family Law* 183.

to accept that their kin could have neglected or abused a child.[159] This is because, in some cases, kinship carers may fail to adhere to contact restrictions (ie preventing birth parents from seeing their children at all, or allowing only supervised contact), which may result in harm to the child.[160] Another issue in this context is the wide variability in assessments for kinship care, which means that relatives may be assessed via a 20-minute phone call or a more thorough face-to-face meeting or meetings. It is essential that social services across England and Wales develop an efficient and effective standardised approach towards identifying suitable kinship carers, since where children are adopted instead of being cared for by viable kinship carers, this may give rise to a successful claim under Article 8 ECHR. Overall, it is apparent from the discussion in this section that, in some cases, children remain in the care of the state or are placed for non-consensual adoption when it might have been possible for them to have remained with their parents with the help of state assistance, or have been placed with other relatives, including grandparents (see section IV.B).

B. Grandparents as Kinship Carers – A Pivotal Role?

Grandparents play an important role in the provision of care for children whose parents are unwilling or unable to care for them. Mitchell, for example, has observed that it is common for grandparents to seek to care for grandchildren who are being looked after by a local authority.[161] It has been suggested by Gautier et al that the majority of kinship carers are in fact grandparents,[162] which means it is important to consider the various issues that arise in relation to grandparents in the context of kinship care and adoption. In practice, grandparents and other relatives (as already considered) may face difficulties in participating in the court process, because they are not automatic parties to care proceedings. Instead, they must obtain permission from the court before they can make an application.

An important case to consider in this context is *C (A Child)*.[163] In this case, the grandparents appealed against an order placing their grandchild for adoption. They believed insufficient consideration had been given to their successful parenting of two of their children in the ultimate decision to place the grandchild for adoption instead of placing him with them. They argued that the judge was

[159] ibid. See, for example a case where the grandparents were ruled out as possible carers due to the fact that they would not accept that the children had been abused by their parents. In this case, it turned out that the parents had not abused the children: *Webster and another v Norfolk County Council and others* [2009] EWCA Civ 59.

[160] See, eg, *EH v London Borough of Greenwich* (n 46).

[161] Mitchell (117) 415.

[162] Gautier, Wellard and Cardy (n 135); Selwyn et al (n 116).

[163] *C (A Child)* [2012] EWCA Civ 1787.

plainly wrong and sought another assessment. Thorpe LJ dismissed the grandparents' appeal on the basis that it would need to be an exceptional case for the Court to conclude that the judge was plainly wrong, especially as the basis of the grandparents' argument had been that the judge had placed too much weight on one relevant factor and too little emphasis on another. However, Thorpe LJ acknowledged that the family must have felt that M (the child in this case) was deprived of his right and all the benefits or advantages that being placed with his grandparents would have offered. Although Thorpe LJ considered that M's own rights might have been affected by the non-consensual adoption, he did not provide detail on the specific rights and benefits of which M had been deprived (such as, for example, under the ECHR and the UNCRC); neither did he consider whether the difficulties in placing M with his grandparents could have been overcome with assistance by the local authority. It can be argued that M's Article 8 ECHR right to a family life (as well as the same rights of the grandparents) may have been violated by the adoption. Although ordering another assessment of M's grandparents had the potential to violate M's rights under Article 6(1) due to the potential delay, his Article 8 right may have been violated as, if his grandparents' assessment had been found to be positive, he could have been raised by his birth family, which would have been a less restrictive measure and equally effective when compared with non-consensual adoption.

Placing children in the care of their grandparents may, in many cases, provide a less restrictive but equally effective alternative to non-consensual adoption. However, there appears to be prejudice against recognising grandparents' viability as potential carers. Tingle has observed that, in some cases, grandparents are regarded as unsuitable to care for their grandchildren for reasons such as being too old.[164] Pryor has emphasised that grandparents may be viable carers, and has suggested that grandparents may often be a good choice to care for children where they are relatively young, healthy and have good energy levels.[165] By implication, then, grandparents who are older or have health problems, including disabilities, could still be ruled out as carers for their grandchildren. Such perceptions fail to consider other relevant factors, such as the practical and financial resources that may be available to grandparents or the possibility of state assistance that could help them.

[164] N Tingle, 'A view of wider family perspectives in contested adoptions' in M Ryburn, *Contested Adoptions: Research, law, policy and practice* (Aldershot, Ashgate Publishing, 1994) 1766. For example, see *P, C and S v UK* App no 56547/00 (ECHR, 16 July 2002). Also see A Levy and R Taylor, 'Grandparents aged 58 and 70 who were told they were too OLD to adopt their granddaughter, three, hit out at "wicked" treatment' *Daily Mail* (21 July 2005) at http://www.dailymail.co.uk/news/article-3170134/Grandparents-blocked-adopting-three-year-old-granddaughter-hit-wicked-treatment-shouldn-t-happen-civilised-society.html.

[165] J Pryor, 'Children's Contact with Relatives' in A Bainham et al (eds), *Children and Their Families* (Portland, OR, Hart Publishing, 2003) 47, 53.

It may be argued that age and poor health are not sufficient reasons to rule out grandparents as carers, and that more research must be conducted in this context. NAGALRO has pointed out that social workers may be 'prejudiced'[166] against some relatives, particularly grandmothers, perceiving them as the cause of the birth parent's inability to raise his or her child. Another obstacle to placement with grandparents and other members of the birth family is that they might find it difficult to accept that the children have been neglected and abused. While this might be a relevant factor to be considered by social services and the courts, it should not be a determinative factor when deciding where to place a child. Arguably, a placement with appropriate supervision by social workers would provide sufficient protection to children in these circumstances. More research needs to be undertaken to identify the extent of the difficulties that grandparents may face in becoming kinship carers, since grandparent care might in some cases be a more proportionate measure than non-consensual adoption.

C. Financial Support for Kinship Carers – Burdens and Benefits

The status of kinship carers is important, because it may have an impact on how much financial help such carers will receive from the state. It has been made clear, however, that related and unrelated foster carers must receive the same allowance.[167] Nevertheless, local authorities can award different levels of financial assistance based on foster carers' qualifications and attendance at suitable training events.[168] Carers who raise children with a special guardianship, residence or adoption order in place are typically dependent on means-tested allowances, which tend to be lower than the allowances received by foster carers.[169] Research shows that allowances paid under the CA 1989, section 17 are especially low.[170]

The availability and awareness of financial support available to relatives who have children placed with them is important, as research suggests the children's relatives are likely to receive less support from social workers than unrelated carers,[171] and are more likely to experience greater economic difficulties[172] and

[166] NAGALRO, *Nagalro Response* (n 148) 4.

[167] Department for Education, *Family and Friends Care: Statutory Guidance for Local Authorities 2011* (London, Department for Education, 2011).

[168] *R (On the application of X) v London Borough of Tower Hamlets* [2013] EWHC 480 (Admin).

[169] Nandy et al (n 109) 5.

[170] Farmer and Moyers (n 130).

[171] H Argent, 'What's the Problem with Kinship Care?' (2009) 33 *Adoption and Fostering* 6; Wade, Sinclair and Stuttard (n 131) 170.

[172] Nandy et al (n 109); Wade, Sinclair and Stuttard (n 131) 170; Gautier, Wellard and Cardy (n 135).

problems with accommodation.[173] The Local Government Ombudsman Report, *Family Values: council services to family and friends who care for others' children*, states that 145,000 children are cared for by adults who are not their parents,[174] and is critical of how families and foster carers are treated by local authorities. The Report cites an example of a case where a grandmother, who filed for bankruptcy because she had to give up work to care for her grandchild, ended up being paid £45,000 by the local authority to cover the years she had not been paid.[175]

It can be argued that the CFA 2014 includes provisions that further encourage non-consensual adoption instead of the use of less restrictive alternatives. It was suggested by the Local Ombudsman Report that the CFA 2014 could have been used as an opportunity to provide a national financial allowance, so that children could be raised by family (or friends) rather than be forced into the care system because their relatives are unable to afford to look after them. It also suggested that local authorities should have new duties to provide support services for children raised by family or friends who are unable to live with their birth parents, regardless of legal status.[176]

Furthermore, the Report proposed that these carers should have the right to paid leave when they take on children, in the same way as adopters,[177] so that they do not have to give up work and become financially dependent on the state. The extent to which relatives should have financial support from local authorities has been controversial, although the High Court has ruled that family and friends should not be precluded from receiving fostering allowance.[178] It is unclear, though, whether local authorities are under a duty to provide birth relatives with information about the support they are entitled to receive. If there was such a duty to inform relatives, this might encourage more of them to become kinship carers, thereby decreasing the need for a restrictive form of intervention such as non-consensual adoption.

Although case law under Article 8 ECHR has traditionally focused on protecting relationships between children and their birth parents, it could be argued that children have wider rights under Article 8. If the state does not proactively initiate and sustain a search for or provide financial and practical support to kinship carers, it could be argued that the child's Article 7 UNCRC right (to know and be raised by one's parents) and Article 8 UNCRC right (to know one's identity) are also engaged. Furthermore, Article 8 ECHR has relevance in the context of kinship care. It has been shown through the discussion of ECtHR case law (see chapter 3) that the state is required to be more proactive in keeping families

[173] Morris (n 124) 21–22.

[174] Local Government Ombudsman, *Family Values: council services to family and friends who care for others' children* (Coventry, Local Government Ombudsman, 2013) 1.

[175] ibid 11.

[176] ibid. Also, more generally, see Argent (n 171).

[177] See at https://www.gov.uk/adoption-pay-leave/eligibility.

[178] *R (On the application of X) v London Borough of Tower Hamlets Council* (n 168).

together, and must take practical measures (such as housing, therapeutic intervention or ongoing support from social workers) and invest more financial resources, in individual cases, so as to keep families together under its positive obligation under Article 8.[179] Although the cases considered in chapter 3 were argued by birth parents, there is also potential for kinship carers to claim that their Article 8 right is engaged and may be violated in cases where they do not receive sufficient state assistance.

It may be argued that it is very important for local authorities to be proactive not only in finding kinship carers for children in care, but also in providing efficient and thorough viability assessments; and that they should ensure that relatives are aware of the financial and practical support they are entitled to receive. Children in such kinship care arrangements may be regarded as 'in need' and receive short-term or long-term support from Children's Services under the CA 1989, section 17, for example. Thus, where birth relatives are unable to care for children because of a lack of financial support, despite the powers available to local authorities, it could be argued that such relatives could present a case that the state has violated the Article 8 ECHR rights of the child, as the state has a positive obligation to keep a family together where possible. In such circumstances, if non-consensual adoption did take place when a less restrictive but equally effective alternative might have been available, it is argued that this might amount to a disproportionate interference with the children's and parents' Article 8 rights. The difficulty is that the state's ability to fulfil its positive obligation under Article 8 may be limited by its lack of financial resources. This is why, it is argued, further research is required to determine the relative cost of different options for children in care, because in practice financial limitations may have an impact on the permanence measure chosen for a child (for further discussion, see section VII).

V. Special Guardianship Orders

A. Special Guardianship Orders: Valuable Legal Protection

Special guardianship is another alternative to non-consensual adoption in cases where children cannot live with their parents.[180] A special guardianship order (SGO) has been described by Ward LJ as 'a half-way house between a residence order and an adoption order'.[181] An SGO is an alternative to an adoption order that enables children to retain their legal tie with their birth parents while under the care of another (eg relative, friend of the family or foster carer). Special

[179] *SH v Italy* (n 50).

[180] For example, see Department for Education, *Special guardianship review: report on findings, Government consultation response* (London, Department for Education, 2015).

[181] *Re L (Special Guardianship: Surname)* [2007] EWCA Civ 196 [31], *per* Ward LJ.

guardianship was inserted into the CA 1989 (sections 14A–14G). This order primarily protects older children in care for whom adoption is not an option.[182]

An SGO is different from adoption in a number of ways: it is not irrevocable; it can suspend parental responsibility but will not extinguish it; an SGO will not alter the relationship with the child's natural family; the birth parents can still have contact under the control of the court; children can retain their own names; and there is no right, as there is with adoption, to inherit. Special guardianship thus offers both the security and permanence previously only found with adoption.[183] It envisages continuance in the connection between children and their birth families.[184] It is quite common for kinship care (considered above) to lead to a later application for an SGO.[185] This is because adoption by birth family members (eg aunts and uncles, siblings, grandparents) is often seen as inappropriate, because it may distort family relationships.[186]

In *Re S (A Child)*,[187] the Court of Appeal reviewed three separate cases and provided key guidance on the use of SGOs. The Court stated that courts considering whether to make an SGO or an adoption order must provide full reasons for choosing one order over another. In *Re S*, the Court stressed that there were differences in the status of the two types of orders, which should be borne in mind when applying the welfare checklist under both the CA 1989, section 1(3) and the ACA 2002, section 1(4). It was observed that there was no specific guidance from legislation dictating the circumstances in which either an adoption or an SGO should apply. Therefore, the courts must ask which order would better serve the welfare of the child.

The Court reflected on the human rights considerations that arise when considering whether to make an adoption or SGO. Wall LJ observed that an SGO is 'less intrusive' than adoption and amounts to a 'less fundamental interference with existing legal relationships'.[188] When Article 8 ECHR (right to respect for private and family life) is at stake, courts must decide whether the interference with family life is proportionate in the light of the harm the child faces. Wall LJ observed that when choosing whether to make an adoption order or SGO, Article 8

> is unlikely to add anything to the considerations contained in the respective welfare checklists … However, in some cases, the fact that the welfare objective can be achieved with less disruption of existing family relationships can properly be regarded as helping tip the balance.[189]

[182] Bridge and Swindells (n 63) 147.
[183] I Dey, 'Adapting Adoption: A Case of Closet Politics?' (2005) 19 *International Journal of Law, Policy and Family* 289.
[184] Wade, Sinclair and Stuttard (n 131) 175.
[185] ibid 121.
[186] ibid 115.
[187] *Re S (A Child)* [2007] EWCA Civ 54.
[188] ibid [49], *per* Wall LJ.
[189] ibid.

However, he has stressed that an SGO 'did not always provide the same permanency of protection as adoption … which in a finely balanced case, could well tip the scales in favour of adoption.'[190]

There are cases where an SGO might provide safety and stability for children while allowing them to maintain relationships with family members. Sloan has suggested that a SGO in favour of prospective adopters may be appropriate where adoption is not in the child's best interests, or if it would be incompatible with the child's rights under the UNCRC (eg Articles 7, 8 and 9) or the ECHR (eg Article 8).[191] This could apply, for example, when children are older and/or have established bonds with their birth parents, siblings or other family members, or if they express a desire not to be adopted. The orders are commonly made in favour of family members,[192] but may also be suitable for long-term foster carers, who may or may not also be kinship carers.

An examination of paragraph 18 of the Explanatory Notes to the ACA 2002 reveals that a purpose behind special guardianship is to accommodate the needs of families from cultures where adoption is rejected. It has been suggested, though, that this purpose is not readily apparent from the legislation, and the exception is 'almost hidden.'[193] Other cultures use methods other than adoption to meet children's long-term needs and regard them to be as effective at meeting a child's need for stability, without severing the legal tie between the child and his or her birth parents. Thus SGOs may be regarded as an equivalent arrangement (to '*kafalah*' under Islamic Law, for example).[194]

While in some cases an SGO may not offer the permanence of an adoption, it is argued that it may be equally effective at protecting children's best interests and rights when compared with non-consensual adoption. An SGO may be regarded as a less restrictive alternative to the making of an adoption order without parental consent,[195] which also potentially protects children's rights under the UNCRC (such as Articles 7 and 8). In *Harroudj v France*,[196] the ECtHR asserted that *kafalah* struck the appropriate balance between acknowledging the de facto relationship between a child and his or her carers, and preserving the child's tie to his or her country of origin.

It can be argued that an SGO can be an appropriate measure even in circumstances where the child's country of origin does not prohibit adoption but where

[190] ibid [65]–[68].

[191] Sloan (n 42).

[192] See, eg, *Surrey County Council v Al-Hilli & Others* [2013] EWHC 3404 (Fam); *B (Children)* [2014] EWCA Civ 814; Department for Education (n 180).

[193] M Bhamra, *The Challenges of Justice in Diverse Societies: Constitutionalism and Pluralism* (Farnham, Ashgate, 2011) 103.

[194] O'Halloran (n 42) 5.

[195] A Bainham and S Gilmore, 'The English Children and Families Act 2014' (2015) 46 *Victoria University of Wellington Law Review* 627.

[196] *Harroudj v France* App no 43631/09 (ECHR, 4 October 2010).

generally, for several reasons, adoption may not be in a child's best interests. In *A (Children)*,[197] it was argued, albeit unsuccessfully by the parents, that adoption was not a proportionate measure, nor in the best interests of the child, but that an SGO ought to have been made instead. Munby LJ has suggested that adoption should only take place if special guardianship would fail to meet the needs of the child. He stated that '[o]ne should consider special guardianship first, and address adoption only if satisfied that special guardianship will not suffice'.[198] This emphasis on SGOs is powerful support for the argument that for a non-consensual adoption to be a proportionate measure, less restrictive alternatives must be considered first.

In 2006, only 372 SGOs were made compared to 2,746 adoption orders.[199] The use of SGOs has steadily increased since then.[200] Figures from March 2013 show that 9.6 per cent of children left care through special guardianship compared to 14 per cent by means of adoption orders and 5.8 per cent through residence orders.[201] In 2014, 3,330 children left care via an SGO, accounting for 11 per cent of children ceasing to be looked after in care, compared to just 1,290 leaving care via an SGO in 2010.[202] This demonstrates that the number of SGOs made in 2014 is more than double the number made in 2010. The most recent statistics from 2017–18 indicate that 3,430 children left care via SGOs, a slight decrease from the previous year when 3,720 SGOs were made.[203] Nonetheless, courts increasingly seem to be more willing to make SGOs.

The overall trend may be attributed to the decision of *Re B-S (Children)* and can be regarded as desirable, as special guardianship is undoubtedly a less restrictive alternative to non-consensual adoption. Furthermore, it has the potential to be an equally effective measure in protecting children's best interests and rights in cases involving children raised within different cultures, or older children who have strong ties with their birth parents.[204] There are many benefits to SGOs, such as the fact that children do not have to face the stigma of being in the care system and have an increased sense of security.[205] Furthermore, as stated above, an SGO is more likely to be compliant with Article 8 ECHR because it enables children to

[197] *A (Children)* [2015] EWCA Civ 1254.

[198] J Munby, 'Special Guardianship: A Judicial Perspective' in L Jordan and B Lindley (eds), *Special Guardianship: What Does it Offer Children who Cannot Live with their Parents?* (London, Family Rights Group, 2006) 25.

[199] Department for Education, *Children Looked After in England (including care leavers) year ending 31 March 2014* (London, Department for Education, 2014).

[200] Wade, Sinclair and Stuttard (n 131) 69.

[201] ibid 20.

[202] Department for Education (n 199) 12.

[203] Department for Education, *Children Looked After in England (including care leavers) year ending 31 March 2018* (London, Department for Education, 2018) 13.

[204] See *Down Lisburn Health and Social Services Trust and another (AP) v H (AP) and another (AP)* [2006] UKHL 36 [6].

[205] A Hall, 'Special Guardianship: A Missed Opportunity – Findings from Research' [2008] *Family Law* 148, 151.

retain legal ties with their parents. Special guardianship also has the benefit that it may be a possible alternative for children from cultures that reject adoption. As noted, this can be seen in Islamic law, which has the practice of *kafalah* instead of adoption, which allows for others to be the primary carer of a child and to be a substitute family.[206] England and Wales are becoming increasingly culturally diverse, which means it is helpful to consider how adoption orders might be viewed by other cultures. In some cases, special guardianship may be a better way of respecting a child's and the child's birth family's rights to freedom of thought, conscience and religion under Article 9 ECHR.

Special guardianship orders have many advantages and, as Gilmore and Bainham have argued, there ought to be more 'proactive promotion'[207] of them. There are, however, issues affecting the success of these orders. Thus, SGOs tend to work best when they are made in favour of carers whom children know. It has been argued that where children are placed with carers with whom they do not have a prior relationship, there is a higher risk of breakdown in the placement.[208] Further research needs to be undertaken to establish whether, in such cases, SGOs were less effective for those children than adoption placements would have been. Another concern with respect to the effectiveness of SGOs when compared with non-consensual adoption, is the thoroughness of the assessment process. NAGALRO has argued that viability assessments for potential carers are variable in quality, and may be 'inappropriately influenced by the preconceptions of the assessor' and the time constraints of the child's social worker.[209]

NAGALRO has suggested that this issue could be resolved by applying a higher standard when considering whether relatives or non-relatives of the child ought to be special guardians.[210] It has argued that the assessment process for kinship carers should be as rigorous as the assessment process for other unrelated carers such as adopters. It has suggested that there ought to be DBS checks,[211] for example. Whilst this may provide increased protection for children's best interests and rights (under Article 2 ECHR and to protect them from physical harm under Article 3 ECHR), it is arguable that if alternatives to non-consensual adoption become just as lengthy to arrange as is non-consensual adoption, this would lead to further delays in achieving permanence for children,[212] which is not in their best interests.

Concern has also been expressed that the motive behind the increase in the making of SGOs may not be to protect children's welfare. It has been argued by

[206] See D Pearl and W Menski, *Muslim Family Law*, 3rd edn (London, Sweet & Maxwell, 1998) 410.
[207] Bainham and Gilmore (n 195) 646.
[208] NAGALRO (n 148) 2.
[209] ibid.
[210] ibid 4. Also see Department for Education (n 183).
[211] These are background checks that search for existing criminal convictions and other factors pertaining to potential carers that may impact on a child's welfare.
[212] ibid 3.

the charity TACT, for example, that in some cases local authorities are aggressively pursuing SGOs, often encouraging foster carers to become special guardians so that they can pay these carers less money.[213] However, as considered in section IV.C, kinship carers are now entitled to claim as much money for a child's care as foster carers. It is unclear, though, whether a kinship carer who is also a special guardian is entitled to claim the same amount of funding. This issue is not within the scope of this research and will not be explored further. Nonetheless, it can be argued that the legal provisions relating to financial provision for kinship carers, foster carers and special guardians need to be clarified.

B. Summary

The preceding discussion in this chapter has shown that state assistance, kinship care, special guardianship or a combination of these alternatives comprise less restrictive measures when compared with non-consensual adoption. It has also been argued that these measures may be just as effective at protecting children's best interests, whilst also protecting parental rights under Article 8 ECHR and children's rights under Articles 2, 3 and 8 ECHR. It is argued that these alternatives may be ruled out too quickly or might not be considered at all. Also, resource implications should not prevent the use of less detrimental alternatives – especially as there is a strong possibility, based on the evidence considered so far, that these alternatives are not necessarily more expensive than non-consensual adoption.

Having outlined various alternatives to non-consensual adoption that enable children to retain legal ties with their parents, it is important to acknowledge that there may be cases where non-consensual adoption is a necessary and proportionate measure. In some non-consensual adoption cases, however, opportunities for continuing contact may not be considered sufficiently as a viable option. This issue is discussed in section VI.

VI. Non-Consensual Adoption with Direct Contact

Non-consensual adoption with direct contact is another option that could strike the balance between protecting children's best interests, on the one hand, and children and parents' Article 8 ECHR right to respect for private and family life, on the other. Case law has long emphasised the importance of contact[214] between

[213] 'TACT express concerns over further sharp rises in Special Guardianship Orders' at http://tactcare.org.uk/news/tact-expresses-concerns-over-further-sharp-rises-in-special-guardianship-orders/.

[214] Contact orders are made under the CA 1989, s 8. This has been amended by the CFA 2014, and these orders are now (along with residence orders) referred to as 'child arrangement' orders.

children and parents in the context of family breakdown, but in the adoption context the judiciary has been reluctant to order post-adoption contact.[215] When an adoption order is made, it is common practice for contact between children and parents to be decreased or even stopped prior to an adoption,[216] and contact is thus either indirect (via letters sent from the birth parent to the adoptive parents) or non-existent post-adoption.[217]

One reason why post-adoption contact is not regularly ordered is that judges fear that post-adoption contact will destabilise the adoptive placements and threaten the security of adopters in their role as new parents.[218] However, there is no concrete evidence to support this contention.[219] In fact, there are many reasons suggesting that post-adoption contact may be beneficial.[220] Contact with the birth family assists in the development of personal identity (especially for children from ethnic minorities[221]) and enables continuance of family relationships.[222]

Research suggests that adopted children may experience a sense of loss and rejection by their birth parents, even where the adoption is successful and the children have a good relationship with their adoptive parents.[223] It has been found that adopted children place importance on knowledge of their origins,[224] as well as on social and genetic identity.[225] According to Ryburn, post-adoption contact has the benefit of replacing 'speculation' and 'fantasy' with facts,[226] and provides children with information and certainty about their identity. Moe suggests that there are benefits from open adoption with direct contact, such as lack of secrecy, a

[215] See, eg, *Re R (Adoption: Contact)* [2005] EWCA Civ 1128. For further discussion, see R Dogan, 'Wishful Thinking or Solution? The Concept of Open Adoption and its Future' (2011) 8 *Ankara Law Review* 239; C Smith, 'Trust v Law: Promoting and Safeguarding Post-Adoption Contact' (2005) *27 Journal of Social Welfare and Family Law* 315.

[216] B Lindley, 'Open Adoption – Is the Door Ajar?' (1997) 9 Child *and Family Law Quarterly* 115; Sloan (n 42); B Sloan, 'Post-Adoption Contact Reform: Compounding the State-Ordered Termination of Parenthood?' (2014) 73 *CLJ* 378.

[217] C Smith and J Logan, 'Adoptive Parenthood as a "Legal Fiction" – its Consequences for Direct Post Adoption Contact' (2002) 14 *Child and Family Law Quarterly* 281.

[218] See, eg, *Seddon v Oldham MBC (Adoption Human Rights)* [2015] EWHC 2609 (Fam). For further discussion, see Lindley (n 216).

[219] S Harris-Short, 'Adoption and Children Bill – A Fast Track to Failure?' (2001) 13 *Child and Family Law Quarterly* 405, 410.

[220] See, eg, S Jolly, 'Cutting the ties – the termination of contact in care' (1994) 16 *Journal of Social Welfare and Family Law* 299; J Triseliotis, 'Contact between looked after children and their parents: a level playing field?' (2010) 34 *Adoption and Fostering* 59; S Ryan et al, 'Open Adoptions in Child Welfare: Social Worker and Foster/Adoptive Parent Attitudes' (2011) 5 *Journal of Public Child Welfare* 445.

[221] Dey (n 183).

[222] *Re G (Adoption: Contact)* [2003] 1 FLR 270, 274, *per* Ward LJ; E Neil, 'Adoption and Contact: A Research Review' in Bainham et al (eds) (n 165) 275, 278–81.

[223] D Casey and A Gibberd, 'Adoption and Contact' [2001] *Family Law* 39, 73.

[224] J Triseliotis, *In Search of Origins* (London, Routledge & Kegan Paul, 1973).

[225] S Wells, *Within Me, Without Me, Adoption: an open and shut case?* (London, Scarlett Press, 1994) 39; J Triseliotis, 'Adoption with contact' (1985) 9 *Adoption and Fostering* 19.

[226] M Ryburn, 'In whose best interests? – post-adoption contact with the birth family' (1998) 10 *Child and Family Law Quarterly* 53.

knowledge of identity and family medical history, and a reduced need for the child to construct a fantasy of what his or her birth parents were like.[227] Furthermore, it has been suggested that contact with birth parents can sometimes enhance children's relationships with their adoptive parents.[228]

There is a perception that the courts have not fully come to terms with post-adoption contact. Hughes and Sloan have argued that the courts need to 'get to grips with the human rights implications of [adoption] cases' and 'to consider the relationship between each of these competing rights, and the relationship between these rights and the welfare provisions of the Children Act 1989 and Children and Adoption Act 2002'.[229] Hughes and Sloan have argued that the UNCRC conceptualises contact as a human right. This can be seen in UNCRC General Comment No 14, for example, which in relation to Article 9 UNCRC states that:

> When separation becomes necessary, the decision-makers shall ensure that the child maintains the linkages and relations with his or her parents and family (siblings, relatives and persons with whom the child has had strong personal relationships) unless this is contrary to the child's best interests. The quality of the relationships and the need to retain them must be taken into consideration in decisions on the frequency and length of visits and other contact when a child is placed outside the family.

Furthermore, the European jurisprudence has referred to the importance of contact between children and their parents (see chapter 3 for further discussion). As public authorities have a positive obligation to act compatibly with Convention rights under section 6 of the Human Rights Act 1998, the courts ought to protect the right to contact under Article 8 ECHR.[230] Sloan has pointed to the decision in *R and H v UK*[231] (see chapter 6), where, he has argued, the ECtHR has attached great significance to the issue of post-adoption contact in the context of Article 8.[232]

In contrast to the position taken by the ECtHR, which emphasises the importance of contact, the CFA 2014 has the objective of reducing the scope for post-adoption contact (see chapter 4 for further discussion),[233] which adds further uncertainty to the issue of contact and adoption in England and Wales. Regardless, it is clear that the courts in England and Wales have been cautious, in that they regard contact as one of the factors that may be considered under the welfare

[227] B Moe, *Adoption: A Reference Handbook* (Santa Barbara, CA, ABC-CLIO, 2007) 41.

[228] Dogan (n 215); Ryburn (n 226); *Re G (Adoption: Contact)* [2002] EWCA Civ 761 [14], *per* Ward LJ. *Note*: in *SB v A County Council; Re P* [2008] EWCA Civ 535, Wall LJ urged the courts to utilise their powers arising from the ACA 2002 to provide for post-adoption contact. For further discussion of the *Re P* decision, see Langsdale and Weston (n 74).

[229] K Hughes and B Sloan, 'Post-Adoption Photographs: Welfare, Rights and Judicial Reasoning' (2011) 23 Child *and Family Law Quarterly* 393.

[230] ibid; Smith (n 215).

[231] *R and H v UK* App no 35348/06 [2011] ECHR 844.

[232] Sloan, 'Post-Adoption Contact Reform' (n 216).

[233] ibid; Bainham and Gilmore (n 195).

checklist rather than a specific right the state has a positive obligation to protect.[234] In the High Court decision of *Seddon v Oldham MBC (Adoption Human Rights)*,[235] Jackson J made it clear that the making of an adoption order brought to an end pre-existing Article 8 ECHR rights to family life between children and their birth parents. He stated that

> the making of an order for contact at the same time as an adoption order would create a new right to contact, though not necessarily an Art 8 right. The right is not the preservation or extension of a previous right held by virtue of being a birth parent.[236]

The only right parents have, according to the English courts, in the context of post-adoption contact, is the right to correspondence under Article 8 ECHR (ie the exchange of letters).[237]

Re W (A Child – No 4)[238] was an unusual case where the father sought to have an adoption order set aside on the basis of fraud and dishonesty of the adopters. The adopters had agreed to post-adoption contact between the birth father and child, but they sought to leave the country with the child and did not wish to facilitate contact. Even though experts agreed that direct contact would have been in the child's best interests, Munby LJ refused to set the adoption order aside because of fraud, or to make a contact order in favour of the birth father. This case highlights the weight that is placed on the interests of adoptive parents.

However, while the courts' existing approach serves to protect the stability of the child's adoptive placement, there may be disadvantages to such a rigid approach. According to Neil et al, the disadvantages a child may face if he or she loses contact with his or her parents as a consequence of adoption, have yet to be explored fully by the courts in England and Wales.[239] Diver has argued that removing the presumption that children are best raised by their natural parents (see chapter 2) would do away with delays within the child protection process, and that the absence of such a presumption would necessitate greater protection of parental rights post-adoption. She has suggested that a consequence of removing this presumption might be that open adoption and indirect contact would become more 'widely accepted'.[240]

The approach taken by the judiciary and by the adoption legislation in England and Wales has been contrary to the growing body of research in favour of open

[234] *Re L, Re V, Re M, Re H (Contact: Domestic Violence)* [2000] 1 FLR 334, 364, *per* Thorpe LJ.

[235] *Seddon v Oldham MBC (Adoption Human Rights)* [2015] EWHC 2609 (Fam).

[236] ibid [53], *per* Jackson J.

[237] ibid.

[238] *Re W (A Child – No 4)* [2017] EWHC 1760 (Fam).

[239] E Neil et al, *Contact arrangements for adopted children: what can be learned from research?* (Centre for Research on the Child and Family, University of East Anglia, 2012).

[240] A Diver, 'Child Paramountcy v Family Privacy – Judicial Balancing of Human Rights Principles in Family Law' (Draft paper presented at J Reuben Clark Law School, 19 July 2005) 1.

adoption.[241] Despite the existence of this research, Harris-Short has observed that judges face 'difficulty in reconciling a move toward openness with the traditional legal understanding of the nature of an adoption order'.[242] It can be argued that regardless of whether or not the courts in England and Wales have conceptualised contact as a right, in cases concerning post-adoption contact, jurisprudence from the ECtHR (considered in chapter 3) can be used to support the notion that such a right may exist, even though this right may be limited by the children's best interests. Non-consensual adoption with direct contact would in some cases be a less restrictive alternative to non-consensual adoption. Thus, in cases which children have positive relationships with their birth parents, this approach may not only protect parental rights under Article 8 ECHR, but also serve to protect children's best interests and rights under Article 8 ECHR and Articles 7 and 8 UNCRC. Therefore, post-adoption contact should take place, where possible,[243] and children and birth parents have a right to contact with one another.

VII. Government Targets, Financial Savings and Proportionality

As has been considered throughout this book, while there may be many cases where non-consensual adoption is a necessary and proportionate measure, there have been others (considered in this chapter and in chapters 3 and 4) where less restrictive and potentially equally effective alternatives might have been used. The question, then, is why, in the light of the benefits of state assistance, kinship care and non-consensual adoption with direct contact, successive governments have not placed more emphasis on less restrictive alternatives to non-consensual adoption. It has been argued that one of the reasons is due to the perception, on the part of those governments, that non-consensual adoption is the most cost-effective measure for children in care, and that this is part of the rationale for endeavouring to increase the number of adoptions and to reduce delay in the adoption process, even though non-consensual adoption has the potential to violate children's and parents' right to respect for their family life under Article 8 ECHR. While it is true that placing a child for adoption is less expensive than looking after children in care (eg in a residential home or foster care), which has been estimated to cost £23,470 a year,[244] it is not necessarily true that non-consensual adoption is the

[241] S Harris-Short, 'Making and Breaking Family Life: Adoption, the State and Human Rights' (2008) 35 *Journal of Law and Society* 28, 41. See J Selwyn, D Quinton and W Sturgess, *Costs and Outcomes of Non-Infant Adoption* (Hadley Centre for Adoption and Foster Care Studies, April 2006).
[242] S Harris-Short and J Miles, *Family Law: Text, Cases and Materials* (Oxford, OUP, 2015) 971.
[243] See, eg, Fenton-Glynn (n 69) 47.
[244] D McNeish and S Scott, *What Works in Achieving Adoption for Looked After Children: An Overview of Evidence for the Coram/Barnados Partnership* (London, Coram, 2013) 12–13.

most cost-effective measure available, or that the emphasis on adoption for children in care is justified.

Barton has argued that there is no explanation behind the former Labour Government's aim to increase the number of adoptions by 50 per cent, how these figures were calculated or how the target was 'reconcilable with the need for a case-by-case assessment'.[245] After the enactment of the ACA 2002, local authorities were instructed to increase the percentage of adoptions of looked-after children by at least 40 per cent. Public Service Agreements about adoption figures were sometimes created between the Government and local authorities, which set specific targets for local authority performance, with the understanding that a reward grant would be paid to local authorities that met national targets for adoption.[246]

Many local authorities who reached their targets received significant financial rewards. For example, Hammersmith and Fulham Council publicly acknowledged that it had received £500,000 for placing over 100 children for adoption in three years, most of whom were adopted without parental consent.[247] Although the Government denied giving bonuses to councils for meeting adoption targets, this remains a controversial issue, with political figures such as John Hemming maintaining that there is documentary evidence that councils have been offered financial incentives to increase the number of adoptions.[248] This means, then, that there may be cases where non-consensual adoption has been or is being used in cases where less restrictive alternatives (such as state assistance, kinship care and special guardianship orders) might have been available and might have been equally effective.

In the Government's *An Action Plan for Adoption: Tackling Delay*,[249] it was advocated that local authorities ought to use 'score cards' to record how quickly adoptions take place, and that performance tables ought to exist to make local authorities accountable for delay. The scorecards, published on the Department for Education website, show how long it takes local authorities to place children in care for adoption. It can be argued that these scorecards may have a naming and shaming effect, which may encourage local authorities to speed up the adoption process instead of focusing on the welfare of the individual child. In other words, councils may again be encouraging non-consensual adoption in cases where equally effective but less restrictive alternatives to non-consensual adoption may be available.[250]

[245] C Barton, 'Adoption and Children Bill 2001 – Don't let them out of your sight' [2001] *Family Law* 431.

[246] 'Baby removed to meet targets' (26 January, 2007) at http://news.bbc.co.uk/1/hi/6297573.stm; and also see Local Authority Circular LAC (2001)33 (2007).

[247] B Leapman, 'Cash prize for council that hits adoption targets' *The Telegraph* (13 April 2008).

[248] Fenton-Glynn (n 69); See A Lusher, 'Anger as minister denies adoption bonus policy' *The Telegraph* (3 February 2008) at http://www.telegraph.co.uk/news/uknews/1577386/Anger-as-minister-denies-adoption-bonus-policy.html. See also F Moss, 'Authorised abuse?' (2007) 157 *NLJ* 1310; Moss (n 83).

[249] See n 72.

[250] 'Adoption score cards are a gamble' at http://www.local.gov.uk/media-releases/-/journal_content/56/10180/3375265/NEWS.

Academics and social workers have expressed concern about the target-driven nature of the adoption process.[251] Allen, for example, has argued that government targets may have led to social workers prematurely deciding that children ought to be adopted when after time they could have been reunited with their birth parents.[252] It has also been suggested by Dale that there should be caution in treating adoption as a 'panacea'.[253] In fact, the policy of more adoptions more quickly may result in a failure to consider alternatives to adoption, and may marginalise the rights and interests of birth parents and ultimately minimise the importance of substantive and procedural safeguards in court.[254]

Adoption policy is potentially a way of fulfilling a political agenda (especially in world of cuts in funding), which does not promote either the welfare and rights of children or the rights of their parents.[255] This pro-adoption policy may not strike the correct balance in protecting the best interests and the rights of children and the rights of their birth parents.[256] In fact, encouraging adoption means that adoption orders may be made when there may be other options available (such as special guardianship orders or kinship care) that are less intrusive in family life and thus less likely to violate the rights of children and parents under Article 8 ECHR. It is possible that the Government's pro-adoption policy is a misguided way of furthering state interests[257] rather than protecting children's best interests or their rights under Article 8. It is argued that the Labour Government, which enacted the ACA 2002, may have been influenced by the fact that adoption is regarded as a cheaper alternative to other types of placement.[258]

The current Conservative Government has continued to support the pro-adoption policy, even though it can be criticised as being influenced by the fact that it is regarded as cheaper and easier to place children for adoption than it is to undertake complex assessments and manage programmes aimed at reuniting children and their parents.[259] Figures reported during the passage of the ACA 2002

[251] See, eg, T Sagar and E Hitchings, '"More Adoptions, more Quickly": A study of Social Workers' Responses to the Adoption and Children Act 2002' (2008) 29 *Journal of Social Welfare and Family Law* 199.

[252] N Allen, *Making Sense of the New Adoption Law* (Lyme Regis, Russell House, 2003) 62.

[253] Dr Peter Dale, 'The Department of Education Contact Arrangements for Children: A Call for Views' (2012) 3 at http://www.peterdale.co.uk/downloads/.

[254] 'Holding on to the Past? Adoption, Birth Parents and the Law in the Twenty-First Century' in J Herring (ed), *Family Law: Issues, Debates, Policy* (Cullompton, Willan Publishing, 2001) 151.

[255] ibid 159.

[256] ibid.

[257] As discussed in ch 3, Guggenheim has argued that the rights of children can sometimes be used as a way of furthering the interests of another, including the state. It can be argued that a pro-adoption policy justified as in the child's best interests will not necessarily be in the best interests of every child in care.

[258] E-M Bonin et al, *Supporting adoption and supporting families that adopt: value for money*, Working Paper No 21 (London, Childhood Wellbeing Research Centre, 2013).

[259] Dale (n 253) 13.

suggested that adoption was in fact a less expensive alternative to long-term foster care. Allowances provided to adoptive parents are, in practice, significantly less than those provided to foster parents. The figures quoted were that the adoption allowance available for a child aged between 4 and 7 years was £54.89 a week, which was means-tested, and adopters receive less child benefit. However, for a child of the equivalent age who is fostered, the care allowance offered to foster parents was £153.58 a week.[260] As of 2019, the weekly allowance for foster carers can range from £129 to £226, depending on the age and location of the child.[261] Private fostering agencies pay foster parents a minimum of £450 per week.[262] These figures show that local authorities can make significant savings when children are placed for adoption rather than being kept in long-term foster care.

Between 2013 and 2014, the Government allocated £150 million of funding to local authorities to enable them to boost adopter recruitment and support, and to fund the creation of a National Gateway enabling adopters to find potential children quickly.[263] In other words, a significant amount of money has been invested in adoption. However, more recent research has suggested that it may be more cost-effective to invest in reuniting children with their parents or wider birth families. Thomas, for example, considered the findings of several studies on the costs of supporting birth families versus supporting adoptive families, and found that although the allowance provided to adoptive parents was less than that provided to foster parents, the average cost of an adoptive placement by local authorities and voluntary adoption agencies was £36,000 in the financial year 2007–08.[264] In practice, there is a range of different expenses associated with the adoption process. The Helping Birth Families study found that the mean cost of supporting birth families was £511 per year over the year-long study. The cost ranged from £0 to £4,563.[265] Similarly, Cox et al found that the use of programmes to assist parents delivered potential savings of between £450,000 and £810,000 over an 18-month period.[266]

The Family Findings study found that the costs of finding a suitable family to adopt a child could be expensive. In a swift case this would cost £4,430, but it could cost as much as £5,835 if a wider search proved necessary.[267] The Family Finding

[260] Special Standing Committee Discussion on the Adoption and Children Bill, 11 December 2001 (afternoon session).

[261] 'Foster carers' 'Simply Fostering' at https://simplyfostering.co.uk/how-to-be-a-foster-carer/fostering-allowance/.

[262] ibid.

[263] Department for Education, *Further action on adoption: finding more loving homes* (London, Department for Education, 2013). Also see at https://www.gov.uk/government/news/adoption-scorecards-and-thresholds-published.

[264] C Thomas, *Adoption for looked after children: messages from research – An overview of the adoption research initiative* (London. BAAF, 2013) 30. Also, for further information on the cost of adoptions, see Selwyn et al (n 83) 23.

[265] Thomas (n 264) 61.

[266] Cox et al, *Reducing Recurrent Care Proceedings Service Evaluation* (n 26); Cox et al 'Reducing recurrent care proceedings' (n 26).

[267] Thomas (n 264) 47.

study demonstrated that adoption support services for each child varied widely, the cost ranging from £980 to £6,270. The mean cost of this was £2,842.[268] The mean cost of support services for contact for adoptive families was £999, but could be anything between £0–£4,052 over a 12-month period. For birth families the mean figure for support was £757, costing somewhere between £0–1,984 over a 12-month period.[269] This study seems to suggest that supporting birth families may be less expensive than searching for suitable prospective adopters and supporting adopters before, during and after the making of the adoption order.

At the time of writing, the Government has acknowledged the impact of early intervention programmes, aimed at keeping children and parents together. It has pledged £84 million to projects of this nature, affirming the key principle of the CA 1989, to keep families together. Three projects are being launched with this aim in mind: Leeds Family Values; Hertfordshire Family Safeguarding; and North Yorkshire No Wrong Door. It will be interesting to monitor the success of these projects.

However, even if policies aimed at returning children to their birth parents would be more cost-effective than placing them for adoption, returning children to their parents is unlikely to be appropriate in the most serious cases of neglect and/or abuse. In fact, returning children in such circumstances would have the potential to violate the child's rights under Article 2 ECHR (the right to life) and Article 3 ECHR (the right to freedom from torture or inhuman or degrading treatment). Thus in some cases, non-consensual adoption may well be necessary and proportionate, but in others there may be less restrictive alternatives available, such as kinship care, which may be just as effective in terms of the outcomes for children. It is argued here that regardless of whether a child is placed for adoption, placed with birth relatives, returned to birth parents or remains in foster care, although financial considerations might be a relevant factor, a financial motive should not be the overriding factor influencing adoption policy. In such cases, if equally effective alternatives to non-consensual adoption were in fact available, the adoption would amount to a disproportionate measure.

VIII. Conclusion

This chapter has examined the alternatives to non-consensual adoption and has considered the extent to which each option complies with the ECHR. The alternatives considered in this chapter may, in some cases, protect children's best interests and rights, and the rights of their birth parents under Article 8 ECHR. Alternative measures, such as state assistance, special guardianship and kinship care, may also

[268] ibid 57.
[269] ibid 77.

have the benefit of protecting children's rights under Articles 7, 8 and 9 UNCRC. An important consideration underpinning the discussion in this chapter is the need to balance the state's positive obligation under Article 8 ECHR to reunite children with their birth parents (where possible) against the its positive obligation to children under Article 2 and Article 3 of the Convention.[270]

This chapter has considered that state assistance primarily consists of financial support and/or practical assistance, such as provision of parenting classes, therapy, etc. The provision of state assistance increases the likelihood that the state has satisfied its positive obligation under Article 8 ECHR to undertake reasonable efforts to reunite children with their parents, even if the state then subsequently determines that non-consensual adoption is in the child's best interests. It also makes it more probable that where an adoption takes place subsequently, it will be a proportionate measure.

It has been suggested that one way for the state to satisfy its obligation under Article 8 ECHR, to reunite children and their birth parents and to protect children's best interests (and rights under Articles 2 and 3), may be via the use of concurrent planning. However, it has been emphasised that there must be thorough scrutiny of this measure to ensure that it amounts to an equally effective alternative to non-consensual adoption and not merely a token way of acknowledging children's and parents' rights.

This chapter has argued in favour of the increased use of and potential value of kinship care as a less restrictive alternative to non-consensual adoption. It has been observed that the psychological, social and educational outcomes associated with kinship care are on a par with the outcomes for non-consensual adoption. Thus, it has been argued that efforts ought to be made to overcome potential barriers to kinship care (such as the lack of financial resources for carers and the need for assistance with parenting skills, enabling birth relatives to care for children with challenging behaviours). It has further been argued that kinship care is, in many cases, a measure of intervention that protects children from harm and also protects children's rights to develop and maintain relationships with their birth family under Article 8 ECHR (which are further reinforced by UNCRC rights such as Article 8, for example).

Special guardianship has the benefit of ensuring that children retain legal ties with their parents and wider birth family. Research suggests that the use of special guardianship orders is on the increase and, in some cases, SGOs may be made in respect of kinship carers. This chapter has shown that special guardianship orders have many uses and are potentially beneficial for older children or children from different cultures. In such circumstances, special guardianship may be a more proportionate interference with children's and parents' rights under Article 8 ECHR (and children's rights under Article 20 UNCRC).

[270] In particular, to ensure that no undue delay exists in the adoption process.

This chapter has also considered the fact that, in some cases, non-consensual adoption may be a justified, necessary and proportionate measure. However, it has been argued that non-consensual adoption with direct post-adoption contact would sometimes be a less restrictive (and potentially equally effective) measure of intervention to protect children's best interests and rights under Article 8 ECHR, on the one hand, and parents' Article 8 ECHR rights, on the other. It has been observed that the courts have, in many cases, been reluctant to order that direct post-adoption contact should take place. However, while direct contact may not be appropriate in cases of very severe neglect and abuse, there may be instances where it offers real benefits to children and their parents, since it offers them the opportunity to maintain and continue to develop relationships with one another, thereby protecting parents' rights under Article 8 ECHR and children's rights under Article 8 ECHR and the UNCRC.

The overall conclusion of this chapter is that there are cases where non-consensual adoption is a proportionate measure and offers much needed protection, security and permanence for children. Adoption is an appropriate measure for protecting children's best interests in many instances. However, there may be other cases where alternatives to non-consensual adoption may be available that are less likely to amount to an interference with children's and parents' human rights. It is clear from the discussion in chapters 4 and 5 that placing an emphasis on encouraging and investing financial resources in non-consensual adoption may mean that less restrictive alternatives are not being pursued that may enable children to retain relationships with their birth families, or which may prevent them from being taken into care in the first place.

6

Conclusion

I. An Overview of the Proportionality of Non-Consensual Adoptions

This author has examined the proportionality of the law on non-consensual adoption in England and Wales via an analysis of the Adoption and Children Act 2002 and relevant case law on adoption. The book has explored the circumstances in which a non-consensual adoption may (or may not) be regarded as a proportionate measure. In doing so, it has referred to relevant provisions of the European Convention on Human Rights (ECHR)[1] and the United Nations Convention on the Rights of the Child (UNCRC),[2] and has considered the importance of the child's best interests. The discussion has considered how ECHR and UNCRC rights, as well as European Court of Human Rights (ECtHR) jurisprudence, could assist in determining when non-consensual adoption would be the least restrictive measure available, and the circumstances in which alternatives might be more proportionate.

This book has assessed the approach taken by the High Court and the Court of Appeal in England and Wales, by the UK Supreme Court and by the ECtHR in cases where children have been adopted without parental consent. In doing so, this author has examined whether non-consensual adoption was the least restrictive measure that could have been chosen. The alternatives to non-consensual adoption have been discussed, which may have been just as effective as non-consensual adoption and which may also have amounted to less of an interference with children's and parents' rights, not only under Article 8 ECHR but also under the UNCRC (eg Articles 5, 7, 8, 9, 18, 19, 20 and 21).

It has been argued that the approach towards less restrictive alternatives to non-consensual adoption is underdeveloped and that greater clarity and a consistent use of the proportionality principle are needed to provide optimal protection for children's and parents' rights. This book has considered how the proportionality

[1] European Convention for the Protection of Human Rights and Fundamental Freedoms, as amended by Protocols nos 11 and 14, 4 November 1950 (European Convention on Human Rights (ECHR)), ETS 5, available at https://www.refworld.org/docid/3ae6b3b04.html.

[2] United Nations Convention on the Rights of the Child, 20 November 1989, 1577 UNTS 3, available at https://www.refworld.org/docid/3ae6b38f0.html.

principle can be applied in cases where alternatives to adoption may be available, and has distinguished between cases where children can be returned to their parents safely and cases where children cannot be returned to their parents.

II. The State and Less Restrictive Alternatives

The main findings are based on an analysis of the relevant legislation and case law relating to the issue of non-consensual adoption. In particular, the case law of the ECtHR has been of crucial importance when assessing the circumstances in which non-consensual adoption might, or might not be, a proportionate measure. In non-consensual adoption cases such as *RMS v Spain*,[3] *Zhou v Italy*[4] and *Pontes v Portugal*,[5] the ECtHR observed that less restrictive alternatives were available to the state, but that despite the existence of these alternatives, the national authorities in these cases nonetheless chose to place the children for adoption without parental consent (see chapter 3). An important conclusion reached by the Court in these cases was the importance of providing state assistance (such as financial or practical assistance, including housing and support from social workers) to ensure that the states in question satisfied their positive obligations under Article 8 ECHR to reunite the children with their parents.

These decisions make it clear that the state is required to use financial and practical resources to attempt to reunite children and parents, where this is possible. The difficulty is that, due to the loosely defined nature of Member States' positive obligation under Article 8 ECHR, it is unclear if and when national authorities must actively support families to stay together before determining that it is in a child's best interests for him or her to be taken into care and placed for adoption without parental consent. However, factors such as the existence of any form of state intervention, the length of time for which assistance was offered and the potential effectiveness of the type of assistance offered ought to be important considerations that affect whether or not the state has satisfied its positive obligations under Article 8 ECHR.

In other words, in this book, it has been argued that if the state does not provide practical or financial assistance to families before removing children from their parents and placing them for adoption, this may in some cases amount to a failure of the state's positive obligation to provide assistance under Article 8 ECHR. In contrast, where the state has intervened to protect children from harm, and has provided birth parents with assistance which has proved to be ineffective, then in the absence of other less restrictive alternatives (such as kinship care), non-consensual adoption is likely to be the least restrictive measure available

[3] *RMS v Spain* App no 28775/12 (ECHR, 18 June 2013).
[4] *Zhou v Italy* App no 33773/11 (ECHR, 21 January 2014).
[5] *Pontes v Portugal* App no 19554/09 (ECHR, 10 April 2012).

that will effectively protect the children's welfare (see chapter 3, section V and chapter 5).

This author has argued that in some cases, both kinship care and special guardianship may be as effective as adoption (see chapter 5). Kinship care may be appropriate to enable children to maintain relationships with their birth relatives. It also has the potential to protect children's ECHR and UNCRC rights (eg a child's right to know his or her identity under Article 8 UNCRC). This discussion has shown that social, psychological and educational outcomes for children in kinship care are comparable to the outcomes for children who have been adopted (see chapter 5, section IV). This is a strong argument in favour of increasing the use of kinship care, since not only is it a potentially less restrictive alternative to non-consensual adoption, but it may also protect children's rights. This book has, however, drawn attention to the potential barriers that kinship carers may face in becoming carers, and it has argued that these problems should be addressed at policy level by the Government. It is suggested that the UK Government needs to invest in kinship care so as to ensure that information is available to potential kinship carers, and so that they can readily access the practical and financial support which they are entitled to receive (see chapter 5, section II).

It has been acknowledged that special guardianship orders (SGOs) are also an important potential alternative to non-consensual adoption (see chapter 5, section V). Such orders are often made in favour of birth relatives, who may provide care for children who cannot be raised by their birth parents. As with kinship care, the outcomes of SGOs are comparable to the outcomes for non-consensual adoption. Thus it could be argued that SGOs made in favour of birth relatives may offer similar positive social, educational and psychological outcomes for children. They are also ideal for older children or children from different cultures, including cultures that may not recognise the validity of an adoption arrangement. However, although the use of SGOs has been supported by Munby LJ, they are used less often than non-consensual adoption. This is despite the potential effectiveness of these orders in protecting children from harm, on the one hand, and protecting their rights under the ECHR and the UNCRC rights, on the other.

This book has also shown that there has been a growth in the use of concurrent planning. It has discussed the pros and cons of concurrent planning by reference to the Coram Concurrent Planning Project (see chapter 5, section II.C). In doing so, this discussion has shown that concurrent planning has the potential to protect children's and parents' rights under Article 8 ECHR and also under the UNCRC, provided the parenting skills classes and mechanisms for attempting to reunite children with their birth parents, or to place them with other relatives, are effective.

Another matter that has been addressed is whether contact between parents and their children should be promoted more in non-consensual adoption cases (see chapter 5). It has been argued that post-adoption contact might be appropriate in some cases, thereby rendering some non-consensual adoptions more proportionate. In other words, non-consensual adoption with direct contact might protect children's best interests and protect their rights under Article 8 UNCRC (the right to know one's identity), and prevent violations of parents' and children's rights under Article 8 ECHR. This discussion has acknowledged, however, that in some cases of non-consensual adoption, it might be contrary to children's best interests for post-adoption contact to take place.

In some circumstances, facilitating such contact could be traumatic, not in children's best interests and could violate their rights under the ECHR (eg Article 3) and under the UNCRC (eg Article 6, which protects the child's inherent right to life, and Article 19 on the child's right to be protected from abuse). In cases where children tell state officials that they do not wish to live with their parents or maintain contact with them, to pursue contact might violate those children's rights (eg under Article 12 UNCRC, which protects the child's right to be heard). In cases where children are likely to be harmed by contact with their birth parents, less restrictive measures, such as non-consensual adoption with direct contact or even special guardianship, would clearly not be appropriate.

Even though there are circumstances in which non-consensual adoption is a necessary and proportionate interference with children's and parents' rights, there are other instances where it might be regarded as a disproportionate measure. Such situations could include cases where parents' circumstances have changed so dramatically that they have become able to parent their children, or may be able to do so with appropriate state assistance (see chapter 5, section II). In circumstances where children cannot be returned to their family home without harming their best interests (and potentially violating their rights under Article 3 ECHR and Articles 6 and 19 of the UNCRC), this book has shown that it may still be possible for children to be placed in kinship care (see chapter 5, section IV).

Another argument put forward is that there is insufficient discussion and analysis of children's rights in non-consensual adoption cases. Thus it has been shown that although children's best interests (and in some cases children's rights) have been analysed by the courts in England and Wales and by the ECtHR, these courts have proved somewhat reluctant to refer expressly to children's rights. Although the courts in England and Wales, and on appeal before the UK Supreme Court, refer to children's rights in general terms, in some cases (eg *In the Matter of B (A Child)*[6]) they do not always explain or analyse what these rights may be, or what state action might be required to afford protection to these rights (see chapter 4).

It has therefore been argued that interpreting children's best interests in the light of children's rights (including their UNCRC rights) would have a significant impact in non-consensual adoption proceedings. It would mean that children's relationships with their parents, siblings and other relatives would be better protected, in that the state (whether it be the courts and/or local authorities)

[6] *In the Matter of B (A Child)* [2013] UKSC 33.

might be more willing to consider the use of less restrictive alternatives to non-consensual adoption (such as state assistance, kinship care or special guardianship). Children's rights under the ECHR (eg Articles 2, 3 and 8) and under the UNCRC ought to be important considerations when the courts and local authorities are determining whether or not a non-consensual adoption is proportionate. Thus, instead of focusing on whether violations of parental rights can be justified based on children's best interests, the rights of children themselves should be taken into consideration when determining whether a non-consensual adoption is a proportionate measure. If the ECtHR was more willing to expressly consider children's rights, the courts in the UK and elsewhere in Europe might be more willing to do so too.

Using the language of rights of children rather than children's best interests would arguably 'sharpen' the courts' consideration of the different parties' interests.[7] Referring to both the ECHR rights of parents and children and the UNCRC rights of children would afford greater recognition to the interests of birth parents and children. It would also allow for a more thorough consideration of children's own rights to know and be cared for by their birth parents (under Article 7 UNCRC). The UNCRC ought to be considered by the ECtHR and the domestic courts, as it forms part of international law. An important aspect of the UNCRC is that it can be implied from various UNCRC provisions that less restrictive alternatives to non-consensual adoption ought to be chosen, where possible.

This author has argued, in particular, that Article 21 UNCRC is an important right in adoption cases and requires a more detailed analysis beyond a bare welfare test, when domestic authorities are deciding whether or not a non-consensual adoption ought to take place.[8] Thus a welfare analysis should include a consideration of UNCRC rights such as Article 7 (the right to know and be cared for by one's parents) and Article 9 (the right not to be separated from one's parents). Furthermore, in the light of the indivisibility of the provisions of the UNCRC, it can be argued that the collective family rights protected by Article 5 UNCRC are relevant when determining whether an adoption ought to take place.[9] In other words, key provisions in the UNCRC (including Articles 5, 7, 8, 9, 18, 20 and 21), as well as the UN Guidelines for the Alternative Care of Children,[10] all

[7] D Nelken 'Choosing rights for Children' in G Douglas and L Sebba, *Children's Rights and Traditional Values*, (Aldershot, Dartmouth Publishing, 1998) 325.

[8] B Sloan, 'Fostering and Adoption as a Means of Securing Article 6 Rights in England' (2015) 26 *Stellenbosch Law Review* 363, 370–71.

[9] Art 5 UNCRC provides that 'States Parties shall respect the responsibilities, rights and duties of parents or, where applicable, the members of the extended family or community as provided for by local custom, legal guardians or other persons legally responsible for the child, to provide, in a manner consistent with the evolving capacities of the child, appropriate direction and guidance in the exercise by the child of the rights recognized in the present Convention'.

[10] UN General Assembly, Resolution 64/142 of 24 February 2010 (reissued 13 April 2010), Guidelines for the Alternative Care of Children 2010.

support the argument that both parents' and children's rights should be considered in non-consensual adoption cases, and less restrictive alternatives to non-consensual adoption ought to be explored and, where appropriate, implemented (see chapter 2).

It has been concluded that in cases of severe neglect and abuse, where Articles 2 and/or 3 ECHR would be engaged, non-consensual adoption may be a proportionate measure (see chapter 3). Nevertheless, it has been shown that there are cases where non-consensual adoption might not have been a proportionate measure. In some of these cases it can be argued that the children could have remained in the care of their parents with appropriate state assistance in place, or that kinship care or non-consensual adoption with direct contact might have been less restrictive alternatives that might have been equally effective. If such alternatives had been thoroughly explored but found to be unsuitable, as not being in the best interests of the child, then a non-consensual adoption would be shown to have been both necessary and proportionate. In other words, such an adoption would not be a violation of the human rights of children and their families.

It is difficult to assess the true number of unnecessary non-consensual adoptions, and whether or not the claims, like that of John Hemming (that over 1,000 unjustified non-consensual adoptions take place every year), are true.[11] Although a small-scale case study has been undertaken by Luckock and Broadhurst, examining the procedural approaches taken by the lower courts in non-consensual adoption cases,[12] more work needs to be done to establish whether the concerns highlighted by high-profile figures such as John Hemming and the media[13] can be proved, via a quantitative and qualitative analysis of inferior court judgments. Such analysis could involve examination of the courts' references to the ECHR and the UNCRC, and an assessment of the quality of the 'best interests' analysis. Further research would be welcome, particularly because of concerns that the lower courts are not following Court of Appeal and Supreme Court decisions that highlight that non-consensual adoption is to be regarded as a last resort.[14] Although emphasis has been placed on transparency in Family Court proceedings, very few lower court decisions on adoption are made freely available to the public.

An important question raised here is whether or not non-consensual adoptions are more cost-effective than less restrictive alternatives such as kinship care, or

[11] 'MP claims 1,000 children 'wrongly' adopted every year' (13 December, 2011) at http://www.bbc.co.uk/news/uk-politics-16157124.

[12] B Luckock, and K Broadhurst, *Adoption cases reviewed: an indicative study of process and practice* (London, Department for Education, 2013).

[13] 'MP claims 1,000 children "wrongfully" adopted every year' (n 11); 'Rape victims children face "barbaric" adoption' (27 March 2014) at http://www.bbc.co.uk/news/uk-26768256; 'Families flee UK to avoid forced adoption' (6 October 2001) at http://www.bbc.co.uk/news/uk-29502832; 'Adoption: Thousands of children forcibly taken into care' (2 February 2015) at http://www.bbc.co.uk/news/uk-31089412.

[14] L Sprinz, 'Adoption in 2014' [2014] *Family Law* 335.

the provision of practical or financial state assistance. Although this book has not explored all the possible alternatives to non-consensual adoption and compared the cost-effectiveness of these alternatives, it has shown that research findings on the cost-effectiveness of non-consensual adoption appear to have been contradictory (see chapter 5, section VII).

Less restrictive alternatives, which are as equally effective as non-consensual adoption, may in some cases afford better protection to children's and parents' rights (including those under Article 8 ECHR, for example). If these alternatives are less expensive, and in some cases are less likely to violate children's and parents' rights, it is difficult to justify not using these alternatives. This author has argued that the fact that insufficient state resources are available to provide assistance to birth parents or kinship carers, is in part due to the Government's decision to redirect funding from state assistance towards the promotion and provision of a non-consensual adoption policy for children in care.[15] The continued existence of the Government's pro-adoption policy fails to recognise that non-consensual adoption may not be in the best interests of all children in care, and that such a measure may have the potential to violate children's ECHR and UNCRC rights as well as parents' ECHR rights (see chapter 4).

This book has referred to the growth in the use of concurrent planning, and in particular it has emphasised the need for further scrutiny of concurrent planning to determine whether it is as equally effective as non-consensual adoption (see chapter 5, section II.C). In the light of the potential growth in the use of concurrent planning, and the lack of independent research that has been undertaken to assess its effectiveness, further research needs to be conducted to ensure the effectiveness of concurrent planning schemes and to establish whether such schemes are human-rights compliant under the ECHR and the UNCRC.

III. A Final Word on the Importance of Proportionality

This author has discussed *Webster and others v Norfolk County Council*[16] in depth (see chapter 4), and has highlighted the injustice and potential lack of proportionality of the non-consensual adoption of the Websters' three children. The analysis in this book of *Webster*, and of other non-consensual adoption cases heard in the courts in England and Wales and in the ECtHR, has revealed the complexity involved in determining the circumstances in which non-consensual adoptions might or might not be a proportionate interference with children's and parents' rights under Article 8 ECHR (the right to respect for private and family life).

[15] See, eg, the Education and Adoption Bill 2015–2016.
[16] *Webster and others v Norfolk County Council* [2009] EWCA Civ 59.

A conundrum that has been highlighted is that if the state does not put sufficient effort into reuniting children with their parents, this might constitute a violation of the children's and parents' rights under Article 8 ECHR. However, if children are returned to an abusive family situation, this might constitute a violation of children's rights under Article 3 ECHR (the right to freedom from torture or inhuman or degrading treatment),[17] or even those under Article 2 ECHR (the right to life). Local authorities and the courts therefore have a difficult balancing act to undertake when considering how best to protect children from significant harm, while at the same time ensuring that the rights of those children and their parents are not violated. When a child has been severely neglected and/or abused by his or her parents, removal from the family home is likely to be a necessary measure to protect the child's rights under Article 3 ECHR and also under Article 2 ECHR. Thus, in such cases, where it can be shown that the parents are unwilling or are unable to change the behaviour(s) that has (have) caused significant harm to the child, a more serious intrusion into family life, such as a non-consensual adoption, may be a necessary and proportionate measure.

It has been argued in this book, however, that the existence of good reasons for removing children from the family home and for deciding that they should not be returned into the care of their parents, does not mean that a non-consensual adoption can necessarily be regarded as a proportionate measure. This author has argued throughout that, in certain cases, less restrictive measures of intervention may strike the appropriate balance between protecting children's and parents' rights, on the one hand, and children's best interests, on the other. The issues raised in this book have necessitated the untangling of complex matters, and have showed the impact of such a draconian measure on children, parents and other birth relatives. However, despite the serious injustices that have occurred in the context of non-consensual adoption, as highlighted by Mr and Mrs Webster's case, and the need for consideration of less restrictive alternatives, adoption still has an important role to play, so as to protect children in care from significant harm and to provide these children with lifelong security and stability.

[17] *In the Matter of J (Children)* [2013] UKSC 9 [1], *per* Lady Hale.

INDEX

www.ingramcontent.com/pod-product-compliance
Ingram Content Group UK Ltd.
Pitfield, Milton Keynes, MK11 3LW, UK
UKHW020814290926
15470UKWH00003B/1153

9 781509 929139